A Brief History of Egypt

Arthur Goldschmidt Jr.

Pennsylvania State University

Checkmark Books®
An imprint of Infobase Publishing

A Brief History of Egypt

Copyright © 2008 by Arthur Goldschmidt Jr.

Checkmark Books
An imprint of Infobase Publishing
132 West 31st Street
New York NY 10001

Library of Congress Cataloging-in-Publication Data

Goldschmidt, Arthur, 1938–
    A brief history of Egypt / Arthur Goldschmidt Jr.
        p. cm. — (Brief history)
    Includes bibliographical references and index.
    ISBN-13: 978-0-8160-7333-7 (pbk : alk. paper)
    ISBN-10: 0-8160-7333-3 (pbk : alk. paper)
    ISBN-13: 978-0-8160-6672-8 (hardcover : alk. paper)
    ISBN-10: 0-8160-6672-8 (hardcover : alk. paper)
    1. Egypt—History. I. Title.
    DT77.G65 2007
    962—dc22   2007007374

Text design by Joan M. McEvoy
Cover design by Semadar Megged/Jooyoung An
Maps by Pat Meschino and Dale Williams

Printed in the United States of America

MP Hermitage 10 9 8 7 6 5 4 3 2 1

This book is printed on acid-free paper.

CONTENTS

LIST OF ILLUSTRATIONS

LIST OF MAPS

NOTE ON ARABIC TRANSLITERATION AND SPELLING

Spelling in Roman letters the names of people and places that were originally written in the Arabic alphabet can be a challenge. The Arabic alphabet includes consonants that do not exist in English, such as the *'ayn*, which is pronounced deep in the throat, and the *ghayn*, which sounds almost like gargling. Some sounds, such as those represented by the letters *p* and *v*, in English, do not exist in Arabic, and short vowels, which do exist in Arabic, are not actually written and may be pronounced differently by speakers from various parts of the Arab world. The Arabic *j*, which is usually pronounced like the second letter in the English word *azure*, becomes a *g* in the dialect used in Cairo and the Nile Delta. This book uses the transliteration system established by the *International Journal of Middle East Studies;* exceptions are words found in *Merriam Webster's Collegiate Dictionary*, personal names in *Merriam Webster's Biographical Dictionary*, and place-names in *Merriam Webster's Geographical Dictionary.*

ACKNOWLEDGMENTS

It is one of the pleasures of authorship to thank those people who have helped to turn the writer's vision into a reality. My thanks go, first and foremost, to Claudia Schaab, who first approached me in the spring of 2005 about writing this volume on Egypt for the Brief History series and who has goaded me and guided the editorial process, patiently and persistently, ever since, sometimes working in her office late into the night. I would also like to thank Kate O'Halloran, who edited my manuscript. Melissa Cullen-DuPont helped me with the photo research. Melissa Ericksen and Dale Williams designed the maps, hardly an easy task, given the long span of Egypt's history and the place-names mentioned in the text. Dr. Jason Thompson, a historian and author of the definitive biographies of Edward William Lane and Sir Gardner Wilkinson, has supported me during many telephone conversations, rummaged through his extensive collection of Egyptian photographs and scanned some of the best ones (aided by his son, Julian), taught me how to access the ones he sent me on the Internet, and discussed historical and current issues. He has done all this while writing his own general history of Egypt for another publisher. Walker Yeatman, a student in the Schreyer Honors College of Penn State University, helped me to proofread the galleys and made many historical and literary corrections, as he moves toward becoming a historian in his own right.

INTRODUCTION

"Egypt is the most important country in the world," Napoléon Bonaparte said in his first interview with the governor of St. Helena, where he was imprisoned after his final defeat in 1815. This sounds grandiose, but Egypt does rank high among the countries of the world for its longevity as a civilization, the roles it has played in history, and its strategic location. Most people in the world have heard of it. No doubt Egypt owes its fame in part to its historic influence over other civilizations and countries. We may include the influence of pharaonic Egypt on the ancient Hebrews, Mesopotamians, and Syrians, and on classical Greece and Rome. It appears often in both the Bible and the Quran. Egypt has been a leading player in the history of Islam, at times as its political leader, usually as a trading entrepot, and almost always as a religious and cultural center. Modern Egypt is the most populous Arab state, and it has led the Arabs in education, literature, music, architecture, cinema, radio, and television. Its capital, Cairo, is the largest city in Africa and in the Arab world, and it hosts the headquarters of the Arab League. Hardly any Middle Eastern political issue, from the War on Terror to the Arab-Israeli Conflict, can be addressed without considering Egypt.

Egypt is important and indeed interesting to study because of the Egyptian people. Although it is hard to generalize, most Egyptians are friendly, hospitable, patient in a crowded and hence challenging environment, and fond of cracking jokes. Devoted to their families, they believe that nothing is as important as loving one's spouse, rearing one's children wisely, caring for one's aging parents, and standing up for one's brothers, sisters, and cousins. Although Egyptians are rightly proud of their nation's history, they worry about its present and future condition. They also want to be liked and respected by foreigners, and some are sensitive to critical remarks about Egypt, Arabs, or Islam.

The people of Egypt possess at least three identities: Egyptian, Arab, and Muslim. They carry Egyptian identity cards or passports and usually introduce themselves to new acquaintances as Egyptians. They speak a dialect of Arabic, either the colloquial Arabic of Cairo and the Nile Delta or that of Upper Egypt, or what they call *al-lahga al-masriya*. If educated, they read and write classical Arabic, or *al-lugha al-'arabiyya al-fusha.* Command of Arabic grammar and calligraphy has tradition-ally been the mark of a cultivated person. Egyptians identify with other Arabs because of their culture, values, and shared historical experience. Having lived through more than a century of European colonialism, followed by several decades of American political influence, Egyptians as well as other Arabs bear some psychological scars. Because of their history, Egyptians tend to side with the Palestinians in the West Bank and Gaza against Israel. They support the Iraqis who have resisted the U.S. invasion and occupation of their country.

Finally, although Egypt has an important Christian minority, the Copts, more than 90 percent of the Egyptian people are Sunni Muslims. They are committed to the Islamic community and are proud of Egypt's historic leadership in Muslim education and architecture. Many hope for a revival of the caliphate, which provided leadership for Sunni Muslims from the death of the prophet Muhammad in 632 until the rise of Atatürk in 1924. Some are involved in al-Qaeda, the network of organizations that claim to fight for the independence of Muslims worldwide from the rule of non-Muslims.

As later chapters will show, these three identities matter: They shape the political attitudes of the Egyptian people. However, they do not supersede loyalty to one's family (possibly including a clan or tribe), city, town, village, or favorite soccer team.

A Brief History of Egypt is meant to introduce the country and the civilization, in both words and images, for readers who wish to know more about Egypt. It barely scratches the surface of this broad and complex subject. The chronology and the glossary supplement the text, the pictures, and the maps, but some readers may feel they need more information than these aids provide. For this reason, a list of books appears at the end as suggested reading. Many museums have strong collections of Egyptian artifacts, which would be well worth a visit, either in person or by going to the museum's Web site.

For a really ambitious reader with the time and the means, a visit to Egypt is the best way to get to know the country, its people, its monuments, and its culture. This brief history is one small step toward understanding this important and fascinating land. As an Egyptian would say, *"Ahlan wa-sahlan"* (You have come as folk to a level plain).

1

THE LAND AND ITS PEOPLE

Egypt is one of the oldest countries in the world. It has at least 5,000 years of recorded history, and many Egyptians claim for it even more. Egypt is centrally located in relation to other concentrated population centers in Europe, Asia, and Africa. For most of its recorded past, at present, and probably well into the future we may view Egypt as being set in the middle of commercial, migration, and invasion routes that matter to Egyptians and foreigners.

Depending on how you look at the map, you can say that Egypt occupies the northeast corner of Africa or the land between the Red Sea and the Mediterranean Sea. It takes up a 30th of Africa's total land area and is 665 miles long (1,073 km) from north to south and 720 miles wide (1,226 km) from east to west. Its existence is bound up with the River Nile; without the river, almost all the land would be desert, and only a few people would live there. Because of the Nile, Egypt is a vibrant country with 80 million inhabitants. In the words of the ancient Greek historian Herodotus, "Egypt is the gift of the Nile."

Geography

The country can be divided into five regions: the Nile River Valley, the Nile Delta, the Western Desert, the Eastern Desert, and the Sinai Peninsula. Let us look at each in turn.

The Nile River Valley

The river Nile enters Egypt from Sudan, to the south, but its headwaters lie in the lakes of Rwanda, Burundi, Uganda, and Tanzania and in the Ethiopian Highlands. It is the longest river in the world and it drains about one-tenth of the African continent, yet its volume of fresh water is far less than that of the Amazon or the Mississippi. It has long eased the transport of people and goods in Egypt and parts of Sudan,

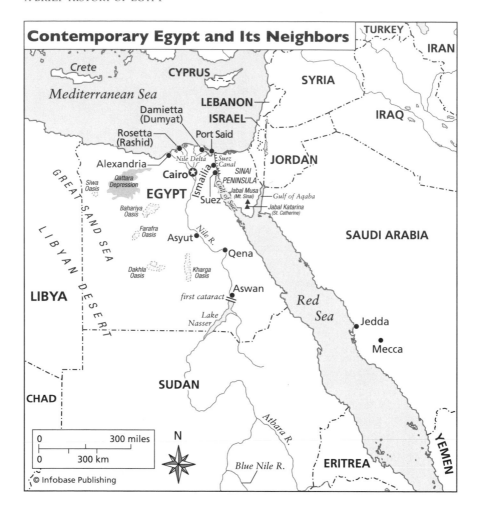

Contemporary Egypt and Its Neighbors

but no boat has ever gone the whole distance from any of its sources to its current mouths at Rosetta and Damietta. For the ancients, Egypt included only the lands along the last 500 miles of the Nile, from the First Cataract (narrow rapids) at Aswan to the Mediterranean. The upper Nile Valley is relatively narrow and flat-floored; it widens after the bend at Qena, reaching a width of 11 miles (18 km) at Cairo. After that point the river fans out, forming the Nile Delta as it reaches the Mediterranean Sea.

In Upper Egypt, the Nile Valley is never more than six miles across. The area where crops were grown traditionally formed a narrow band of green hugging the river shores and contrasting with the desert waste-

2

land beyond, a no-man's-land to the valley farmers. The Nile Valley itself was for centuries distinguished—and made habitable—by the annual Nile flood, which carries water and rich silt from the Ethiopian Highlands. Moisture-laden trade winds blow into Africa from the south Atlantic and meet dry winds from the north, producing heavy spring rains that swell the Sobat, Blue Nile, and Atbara Rivers in Ethiopia and cause the flood. Before the Aswan High Dam was built in the 1960s, dwellers in the valley would see the Nile starting to rise between mid-May and early July, with the peak flood in September. Agricultural land was inundated, not only in the valley and Delta but also in the Fayyum Oasis connected to the Nile. The receding waters left behind a layer of sedimentary mud that fertilized the next year's crops.

To take advantage of this beneficence, the Egyptian people learned how to build dams, weirs, embankments, and basins, channeling and storing the river waters to facilitate raising their crops. The river flood occurred annually, with slight variations in the dates of its rising and falling, but the amount of water could differ greatly from one year to the next. Too much water could sweep away houses, food stores, animals, and people; too little might leave the land hard and cracked, unable to support crops. Other Middle Eastern rivers flood in springtime, damaging crops and settlements; only the Nile rises at a time when it would otherwise be too

Nile River Valley. In Upper Egypt only a narrow stretch of cultivable land separates the Nile from the desert. (Shutterstock)

Delta field. North of Cairo the Nile expands, creating a widening, almost totally flat delta that contains some of the world's finest agricultural land. (Torben Larsen/Saudi Aramco World/PADIA)

hot for agriculture. In ancient times, the Egyptians thought that their king controlled these variations in the annual Nile flood. Only in the last two centuries have people come to understand how and why the flood occurs when it does.

The Nile Delta

The Nile Delta lies along Egypt's northern coast, where the river empties into the Mediterranean Sea. This region includes more than half of contemporary Egypt's farmland. A widening flat area, totaling some 8,500 square miles (22 thousand sq. km), it has been built up over time as the Nile deposited sediment near the river's mouth. The Delta is mostly level, though it contains low mounds, or tells, that mark the sites of ancient settlements. One of the most intensely cultivated areas in the world, it is dotted by thousands of agricultural villages as well as cities such as Alexandria at its northwest corner and Mahalla and Tanta in its center. Population density is as high as 4,000 people per square mile (1,545 per sq. km).

The Nile Valley and Delta regions are home to nearly all of Egypt's population. Both ancient and modern Egyptians have differentiated between dwellers in the Nile Valley south of Cairo (Upper Egypt), or

4

"Saidis," and those living in the Delta north of Cairo, or "Bahrawis." Depictions of Egypt's ancient kings contain symbols indicating a double kingship, as ancient Egypt was thought to represent the unification of the valley and Delta.

The Western Desert

The Western Desert constitutes more than two-thirds of Egypt's total land area, but is home to a tiny percent of the population; the population density of Egypt's deserts is about 1 person per 2.5 square miles (6 sq. km). The Western Desert is an extension of the Libyan Desert and hence the easternmost part of the Sahara. The land is basically a low plateau, mainly sandstone in the south, some limestone in the north, and covered by the Great Sand Sea in its western half. Some underground strata contain large quantities of water that have not yet been fully exploited. Five oases lie in depressions watered by springs: Siwa, Bahriya, Farafra, Dakhla, and Kharga. The northwest contains the very low-lying, uninhabited Qattara Depression. The sandy white beaches and coastal towns along the Mediterranean were developed during the 1990s as an area of resorts and vacation homes. Some oil and natural gas deposits have been discovered and are being exploited, as exploration in the Western Desert continues.

Dakhla Oasis. Egypt's Western Desert contains five oases large enough to support agriculture and some settled inhabitants. (Jason Thompson)

5

Eastern Desert. Between the Nile and the Red Sea, high mountains often contain deposits, such as the porphyry mined by the Romans and other minerals used by ancient and modern Egyptians. (Lorraine Chittock/Saudi Aramco World/PADIA)

The Eastern Desert

The Eastern Desert does not resemble its western counterpart. It consists mainly of elevated and mostly rugged mountains paralleling the Red Sea coast. The western and northern hills contain a lower, limestone plateau. The loftiest of the southern mountains is more than 7,000 feet (2,000 m) above sea level. Some of the mountains near the Red Sea contain mineral deposits that are not commercially exploitable. The Red Sea coastal beaches are being developed as a resort area for swimmers, scuba divers, and seashell collectors.

The Sinai Peninsula

Many people think of the triangular Sinai Peninsula as belonging more to Asia than to Africa, but its mountainous south is closely related to the Red Sea hills, from which it was separated by the geological faults that form the Gulf of Suez and have provided Egypt's largest petroleum deposits. Southern Sinai is especially renowned for Jabal Katarina (Mount Saint Catherine, the site of the famous Greek Orthodox monastery of that name) and Jabal Musa, popularly called Mount

Suez Canal. This waterway, connecting the Mediterranean and the Red Seas, became a vital link between Europe and Asia as soon as it was opened in 1869. (Library of Congress)

Sinai. (However, scholars differ on just where Moses received the Ten Commandments.) Sinai has developed rapidly since Israel returned it to Egypt between 1975 and 1982. It is now a center for oil production, mineral mining, and international tourism. The northern Sinai is a limestone plateau, relatively flat, and extremely accessible to invading armies and migrating peoples throughout history. The Isthmus of Suez was pierced in 1869 by the Suez Canal, a major maritime waterway connecting Europe with Asia and East Africa and also a barrier to migrating Bedouin.

Climate
Egypt is a hot, dry country. Summer temperatures go up as high as 104°F (40°C), and seldom do winter temperatures drop to freezing (32°F, 0°C). In Cairo, the average temperature ranges from 57°F (14°C) in January to 85°F (29°C) in July. The temperature range in Alexandria is 57°F (14°C) in January and 80°F (26°C) in August. Upper Egypt and the deserts have hotter days and colder nights throughout the

year. A prevailing north wind has a cooling effect on the country, but in spring the infamous *khamsin* winds may blow from the southwest, spewing sand, dust, and hot air through the Nile Valley and Delta, making people and animals miserable until the winds subside. Only a thin band of land along the Mediterranean coast can count on rainfall, averaging about four inches per year. Frosts are rare and snow is unknown. Egyptians and foreign residents traditionally praise the Egyptian climate as healthful. However, air and water quality have both deteriorated in recent years owing to the increased crowding of the population, especially in the cities. These trends have been exacerbated by industrialization, the spread of motor vehicles, and climatic changes caused by the Aswan High Dam, completed in 1970.

Natural Resources

Although ancient Egyptians made copious use of copper, silver, and gold, the country today has few mineral resources that can be easily developed. Limestone and sand are abundant and vital to construction throughout Egypt's history. Some iron deposits are found near Aswan, and a large coal deposit has been found in northern Sinai. Phosphates, salt, and gypsum exist. The main natural resources, as in many other Middle Eastern countries, are petroleum and natural gas. Egypt's main oil fields are in the Western Desert and lands surrounding the Gulf of Suez. Egypt is currently a net exporter of oil, but it is likely to become a net importer by 2010 unless new fields are discovered. Natural gas, found near Suez, has become Egypt's major earner of foreign exchange. Egyptians hope further exploration will uncover other sources of mineral wealth.

Economy

For most of Egypt's history the mainstay of the economy was agriculture, especially growing and exporting cereal grains around the Mediterranean basin. Egypt made the transition from a subsistence-based economy to a cash crop economy long before most other Middle Eastern countries. By the late 19th century long-staple (Egyptian) cotton had become its leading export, followed by tobacco, indigo, and sugar. Due to the rising use of synthetic fibers worldwide, cotton exports dwindled in the late 20th century. As Egypt's arable land has decreased in relation to its total population, other crops have overtaken cotton, notably maize, rice, vegetables, and fruit.

More recently, the Egyptian economy has shifted away from agriculture toward industry and services. The Egyptian government has tried to promote manufacturing. However, industries such as construction, transportation, and extraction of oil, natural gas, and minerals currently add more to the gross domestic product. International tourism is a service industry that employs millions of Egyptians, as is fitting in a culture that places great value on hospitality. But it is often disrupted by political instability and terrorism. The country remains a leader in education, finance, and culture in the Arab world.

The People

Because of its central location on routes of trade, conquest, and migration, through the centuries of its recorded history, Egypt has become home to many temporary residents and permanent immigrants. With the passage of time, each wave of new immigrants has assimilated into the local mix of peoples, making modern Egypt a combination of Libyans, Nubians, Syrians, Persians, Macedonians, Romans, Arabs, Turks, Circassians, Greeks, Italians, and Armenians, along with the descendants of the people of ancient Egypt. Upper Egyptians in antiquity were largely small and fine boned, with narrow skulls and dark wavy hair. Those of the Nile Delta, who had more contact with southwest Asian peoples, were heavier and taller and their skulls were broader. Although the artistic conventions of ancient Egypt were highly stylized, paintings and statues show men with reddish-brown skin, while women are shown with much fairer skin, perhaps because they spent more time indoors. Their facial features resemble those of sub-Saharan Africans. Assumptions about appearance must, however, be cautious.

Limestone statues, found at Maidum and now in the Egyptian Museum, depicting Prince Re-Hotep and his wife Nofret, c. 2620 B.C.E. Ancient Egyptian portraiture tends to be highly stylized, but these statues give an idea of what men and women actually looked like. (Jason Thompson)

Language and Religion

The ancient Egyptian language is considered by linguists to belong to the Afro-Asiatic language group, which includes many other languages spoken by ancient peoples. It survives in Coptic, which was a spoken language from ancient times until about 1500, but now is used by Egyptian Christians only in religious services.

Modern Egyptians speak Arabic, with a few words and phrases that may be derived from the language of ancient Egypt. Written Arabic is the same from Morocco to Kuwait, and is also the language of religious law and ritual for the world's 1.5 billion Muslims. The spoken language of Egypt is not quite the same as written Arabic, which has elaborate rules about grammar and syntax. Many Egyptians believe that having Arabic as their native tongue makes them Arabs; in popular usage, though, settled Egyptians call the Bedouins "Arabs," but not themselves. The vernacular dialects of Cairo and of Upper Egypt differ from the colloquial Arabic of the Bedouins and from that of other Arab countries, but Egyptians (like other Arabs) tend to view their spoken dialects as "slang" and written Arabic as their "true" language, even though it must be learned in school.

Egypt's pharaonic religious beliefs gave way to Coptic Christianity, but many ancient practices survived, especially among farmers. For example, the months of modern Egypt's agricultural calendar are the same as those of ancient and Coptic Egypt. From the seventh-century Arab conquest until modern times, Christianity has slowly given way to Islam, but conversion to Islam was gradual and rarely forced. Although Christians and Muslims celebrate holidays limited to their own religions, in Egypt they share a spring holiday, Shamm al-Nasim (smelling the breeze), observed on Easter Monday of the Coptic calendar, when families go out from their houses to enjoy a picnic. In addition, as long as the Nile flooded its banks each year, all Egyptians, whether Jewish, Christian, or Muslim, joined in seasonal festivities marking the onset, the progress, and the climax of the inundation that gave life and prosperity to their country (Lane 1836, chapter 26).

2

ANCIENT EGYPT
(C. 10,000 B.C.E.–525 B.C.E.)

Ancient Egypt was one of the world's great civilizations. It was blessed by a moderately warm climate, a river that flooded regularly and fertilized the land with soil carried by the floodwaters from the highlands of Ethiopia, and relative isolation from foreign invaders for the first 10 centuries of its existence. The people were industrious, obedient to a government that ensured cooperation and justice, and faithful to a pantheon of gods and goddesses who they believed ensured their well-being in this life and after death.

The accomplishments of the ancient Egyptians are many and varied. They pioneered in architecture, building comfortable homes as well as monumental temples and tombs. Their builders devised every method of joining wood (scarce even in ancient Egypt) known to carpentry, as well as methods of air-cooling houses and even building latrines. Their scribes developed one of the world's first writing systems, which they used to keep records and to create stories, poems, and religious texts. They also developed an early system of numbers, which they used to survey land, calculate taxes, and measure weight, distance, and time. Their artisans developed techniques and tools for working with copper, tin, bronze, and precious metals such as silver and gold. Their scientists explored astronomy, engineering, and medicine, and their artists created sculptures ranging from miniature figures found in tombs to the Great Sphinx of Giza, which rises 65 feet (20 m) above the bedrock out of which it was carved.

Since ancient times historians have customarily divided Egypt's past by dynasties (ruling families), usually numbering 30. Egypt's history is generally divided into the following periods: the Predynastic Period (to 3100 B.C.E.), the Early Dynastic Period (First–Second Dynasties, 3100–2686 B.C.E), the Old Kingdom (Third–Sixth Dynasties, 2686–2181 B.C.E) the First Intermediate Period (Seventh–Tenth Dynasties, 2181–2040 B.C.E), the Middle Kingdom (Eleventh–Thirteenth Dynasties, 2040–1750 B.C.E), the Second Intermediate Period (Fourteenth–Seventeenth Dynasties, 1750–1550 B.C.E), New Kingdom (Eighteenth–Twentieth Dynasties, 1550–1069 B.C.E), the Third Intermediate Period (Twenty-first–Twenty-fourth Dynasties, 1069–715 B.C.E), and the Late Period (Twenty-fifth–Thirtieth Dynasties, 747–332).

Predynastic Egypt (to 3100 B.C.E.)

The environment was the single most influential factor on the people of early Egypt. As the wet climatic phase at the end of the last Ice Age receded, North Africa began to dry up, and peoples near the Nile, accustomed to grassy plains and ample wild animals to hunt, had to adjust to increasing scarcity. Probably organized into tribes, these early peoples had begun to grow barley and emmer wheat and to domesticate the wild cattle that abounded in their area, as well as sheep and goats. In addition to the probability that these ancient tribes migrated on land, there is some evidence that they were already building boats and navigating both the Nile and the Red Sea before they settled there.

It was not easy to adapt to living along a large river that flooded annually, and people had to learn how to grow crops on shifting soil and to channel and store the floodwaters to ensure an adequate harvest to feed their families. Developing these skills by trial and error must have taken centuries. For a long period Egyptians migrated between the increasingly desiccated Western and Eastern Deserts and the Nile Valley, following seasonal patterns of vegetation and animal life.

The earliest human remains in Egypt have been found in a desert region called Nabta Playa (west of Abu Simbel). Ten thousand years ago this area was covered with trees and grass. It supported such game animals as elephant, rhinoceros, giraffe, ibex, deer, antelope, wild ass, and ostrich. Nabta contains tombs not only for humans but also for wild cattle, foreshadowing the cow cult that would prevail in ancient Egypt. By about 7000 B.C.E. these early peoples had erected stone structures aligned to the movement pattern of stars and constellations. The oldest village site, dating to about 5000 B.C.E., is in the Eastern Desert, near a modern village called al-Badari. Its people farmed, baked bread, brewed beer, herded cattle, caught fish from the Red Sea, sailed boats, fired pots, and carved religious objects from bone and wood. They traded with peoples of Southwest Asia and may have been the earliest

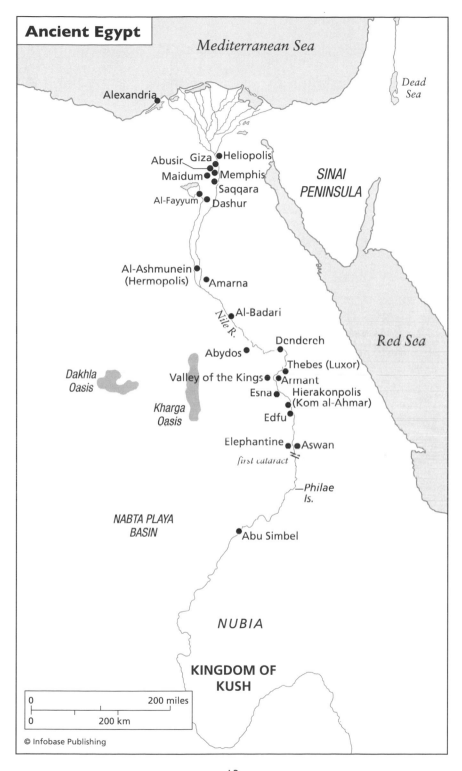

Ancient Egypt

Mediterranean Sea

Dead Sea

Alexandria

Abusir ● Giza ● ● Heliopolis

Maidum ● ● Memphis

Saqqara

Al-Fayyum ● ● Dashur

SINAI PENINSULA

Al-Ashmunein ●
(Hermopolis) ● Amarna

Nile R.

● Al-Badari

Denderah ●

Abydos ● *Red Sea*

Thebes (Luxor)

Valley of the Kings ● ● Armant

Esna ● Hierakonpolis
(Kom al-Ahmar)

Dakhla Oasis

Kharga Oasis

Edfu ●

Elephantine ● ● Aswan
first cataract

— Philae Is.

NABTA PLAYA BASIN

● Abu Simbel

NUBIA

KINGDOM OF KUSH

0			200 miles
0		200 km	

© Infobase Publishing

13

Narmer Palette. Both sides of this sheet of siltsone, incised in about 3000 B.C.E., show Narmer (sometimes called Menes) as the king of Upper Egypt (wearing a white crown) and Lower Egypt (wearing a red crown). Most scholars think that the palette shows the conquest of Lower by Upper Egypt. (Werner Forman/Art Resource, NY)

link between the peoples of Egypt and Sumer. Probably this trade connection went via the Red Sea and the Arabian Peninsula.

Recent archaeological discoveries are uncovering many such settlements, pushing back the dates for ancient Egyptian civilization well before the dynastic era, which began around 3100 B.C.E. The predynastic Egyptians had already learned to harness the Nile to irrigate their crops and to transport their goods. They had domesticated dogs, donkeys, cattle, sheep, and goats. They had created religious cults, built small temples, founded a city known as Hierakonpolis that had a surrounding wall and a ceremonial gateway, and set up a social hierarchy and political system. Tribal organization gave way to city-states along the Nile.

By the fourth millennium B.C.E. the cities were becoming united into two kingdoms, one for the Delta or Lower Egypt, called the Red Land; the other for Upper Egypt, called the White Land. The earliest Egyptians did all this while their country changed from a fertile savanna and hunting ground into a desert punctuated only by oases and the mighty river Nile. For ancient Egypt to emerge in all its glory, though, someone had to unite the kingdoms of Upper and Lower Egypt under a single crown.

The Early Dynastic Period (3100–2686 B.C.E)

Narmer (also sometimes known as Menes, but this was a title applied to several archaic kings), the first pharaoh to rule a united kingdom of the Upper Nile and Delta, is said to have ruled for 67 years. He is memorialized by a stone tablet called the Narmer Palette, which was excavated in the temple at Hierakonpolis, that depicts him wearing a conical crown that may stand for Upper Egypt and grasping a kneeling man (possibly representing Lower Egypt) by the hair. The palette's exact date is disputed by scholars, but is estimated to be about 3000 B.C.E. It is conceivable that the Upper and Lower Kingdoms had already united and broken up and that Narmer reunited them. Whatever might have happened, every one of Narmer's successors is represented as wearing the crowns of both Upper and Lower Egypt, and the pattern of dynastic rule was established.

Narmer is responsible for founding the first capital of ancient Egypt, Men Nefer, which the Greeks called Memphis, located some 12 miles (19 kilometers) south of Cairo on the west bank of the Nile. It remained the principal city of Egypt's rulers until it was eclipsed by Thebes around 1300 B.C.E. South of Memphis is the vast cemetery of Saqqara, which includes the earliest mastabas (free-standing tombs). In use for royalty and nobility, some of them were decorated with reliefs depicting the lives the deceased hoped to find in the next world. Ancient Egyptians believed that, if a dead body decomposed, its owner would not be able to enjoy the afterlife. The priests of the early dynasties discovered how to preserve the bodies of their deceased kings, commonly called "mummies," so that they might enjoy the afterlife. Since Egypt's climate is hot and dry, some bodies might have been preserved naturally, but the processes of mummification ensured their continued existence. These essential features of the Archaic Period would set a pattern for the culture of all subsequent Egyptian dynasties.

Key Features of Dynastic Egypt

By the time of the Third Dynasty and the beginning of the Old Kingdom, Egypt had become a centralized theocracy with a complex religious and political system, whose basic features are outlined below.

The Religious and Political System

The religious system developed by the Egyptians included a multitude of gods who controlled every aspect of this life and a detailed vision of the afterlife. Tied in with the religious beliefs was the ruling system, which included the idea of divine kingship. This concept turned an otherwise human pharaoh into a god on earth, a living connection between what was mortal and what was eternal. The pharaoh alone could worship the gods and maintain cosmic harmony. His crown, scepter, other visible symbols of his authority, and titles connected him to various gods, especially to Horus. His death and ritual rebirth served to reconfirm him.

Divine kingship was one solution to a problem faced by every society: how to ensure that people will work together to survive and prosper, and to defend themselves if need be. The ancient tribes in the area had been hunter-gatherers as long as their climate could support woods and plains. As the region dried up, people settled in oases or on the banks of rivers, where they adapted to farming and trade. In hard times one tribe might prey on its neighbors to take its food or other goods. The leaders of the strongest tribes evolved into warlords. Usually they were male and aggressive, gaining control by fighting their challengers. They stayed in power by attracting other men to their side and granting them special privileges. Over time each leader extended control over a wider area, but the need to support retainers was costly. Claiming divinity was a way of ensuring obedience without needing to pay so much or take so many men away from their fields, flocks, and families.

In Egypt the institution of divine kingship was reinforced by the Nile flood. Managing its waters required the organized labor of most able-bodied adults. A flood that inundated and fertilized fields that would later be sown with grain was a blessing. A high one that swept away houses, animals, and children was not. Needless to say, a low Nile that left much of the ground hard and parched was just as bad. A powerful king who commanded a corps of officials and engineers could usually make the flood benefit the people. It was natural for Egyptians to believe that the king could control how much the Nile flooded each year. Together, they called upon the gods who controlled the forces of nature to bring a beneficent flood and a bountiful harvest. By the same logic, the people thanked the gods for a good harvest, hoping that the next annual flood would serve them as well.

Life and Death

The ancient Egyptians built temples and pyramids and sought to prolong the existence of their deceased rulers by embalming, wrapping, and thus preserving their bodies. The pyramids—or, later, the tombs—that they erected were intended to guard the bodies of their kings, along with their possessions, forever. People often assert that the ancient Egyptians were preoccupied with death. In reality, they were obsessed with life. The ancient Egyptians, protected by seas and deserts, did not fear invasion by alien armies, navies, or nomadic tribes. Their religion celebrated the good life and sought to prolong it for the king and his nobles, assuming that life after death would resemble the life they already knew. A divine king, well cared for during and after his life, would ensure his subjects' prosperity, for he was the emissary of the gods.

Rulers and Their Duties

The King

The king was charged with maintaining the balance of *maat*, the rule of order that protected the world from the constant threat of chaos. It is hard to translate or to define *maat*, the principle of truth, order, balance, and justice. Ancient Egyptians believed that unless the king and his people preserved *maat*, forces outside creation would move in and destroy it. The many gods of ancient Egypt were aspects of the Creator. All people and all gods belonged to the created world, which encompassed all

17

GODS AND GODDESSES OF ANCIENT EGYPT

The ancient Egyptians believed that many gods and goddesses influenced their lives in this world and the next. As time passed the importance and function of each deity changed, but here are some commonly seen in Egyptian art:

Amun: Principal god during the New Kingdom, closely associated with Re

Anubis: God of burial and the afterlife, usually depicted with a jackal's head

Apis: The sacred bull of Memphis, closely associated with kingly authority

Aten: The sun disk; the sole deity during Akhnaten's reign

Bastet: Goddess of motherhood, usually depicted as a cat

Hapy: God of the flood, depicted as a pot-bellied man

Hathor: Goddess of kingship, music, joyfulness, and fertility, depicted as a cow

Horus: God of kingship and the sunrise, often depicted with a falcon's head

Imhotep: Deified architect of the Step Pyramid, god of learning and medicine

Isis: Goddess of motherhood and healing, wife of Osiris and mother of Horus

levels of existence. Egyptians saw every act in life as part of a divine will, mediated for them by the king.

In practical terms the king was expected to protect his people from outside enemies and natural misfortunes, maintain justice, and above all perform the religious rituals that would ensure the people's continued prosperity.

The rulers of ancient Egypt are customarily known as pharaohs. The ancients did not use the term in the Old and Middle Kingdoms; only around 1500 B.C.E. did the term *pharaoh*, originally applied to the palace in which the king lived, come to be used as a royal title.

Khonsu: God of the moon, associated with healing

Maat: Goddess of truth, justice, and harmony, the daughter of Re, depicted as a woman with a feather on her head

Min: God of male fertility, dating from the Predynastic Period, depicted as a man with an erect penis

Mut: Goddess of motherhood, wife of Amun

Nun: God of water or primeval chaos, from which order was created, depicted as a man carrying a boat

Nut: Goddess of the sky overarching the earth; important in funerary rites

Osiris: God of death, resurrection, and fertility

Ptah: God of craftsmen and creation, associated with the city of Memphis

Re: The sun god during the Old Kingdom, later the god of the underworld

Sekhmet: Goddess of pestilence, usually depicted as a lioness

Seth: God of confusion, storms, and desert, depicted as an animal

Tawaret: Hippo-headed protectress of women during pregnancy and childbirth

Thoth: God of knowledge and writing, patron of scribes, guardian of the deceased during their time in the underworld, depicted with the head of an ibis

The Vizier and Other Officials

The king was aided by a vizier, or chief minister, or often by one vizier for Upper Egypt and one for the Nile Delta. They headed a large and increasingly elaborate class of scribes who collected dues and taxes, supervised the construction of temples and other public works, and kept government records. A separate hierarchy of priests helped the rulers to carry out the religious rituals, especially those concerned with ensuring their immortality. A class of judges settled disputes, especially over land ownership, although some priests also served as judges. In addition, there were local administrators for the 42 nomes (provinces) of ancient Egypt. Egypt during the Middle and New Kingdoms also had a large army that conquered some of the lands of the Upper Nile, mainly Nubia, and also ancient Syria and Palestine.

The Old Kingdom (2686–2181 B.C.E)

It is worth noting how many of the features we ascribe to ancient Egypt generally developed during the Early Dynastic Period (First–Second Dynasties) or the Old Kingdom (Third–Sixth Dynasties): monumental stone architecture, wall paintings, elaborate burial customs, hieroglyphic writing, gold and copper jewelry, and a structured bureaucracy. The step pyramid at Saqqara, the great pyramids of Giza, indeed almost all of Egypt's pyramids were built for the Third and Fourth Dynasties. It is impressive that these early Egyptians, who lacked iron tools or draft animals, could cut, move, fit together, arrange with both geometrical and astronomical exactitude, and lift such massive granite blocks to shelter and protect the bodies of their pharaohs. They hoped that by preserving, wrapping, and hiding the

Giza pyramids. These great structures, erected during the Fourth Dynasty, were the burial sites of Kings Khufu (Cheops), Khafre (Chephron), and Menkaure (Mycerinus). The Pyramid of Khufu, who reigned from 2551 to 2528 B.C.E., is 756 feet square at its base and 480 feet high. It was higher with its original limestone facing, all of which was taken away by later builders. Of the Seven Wonders of the ancient world, the pyramids alone remain. (Jason Thompson)

Sample of Hieroglyphic, Hieratic, and Demotic Writing Systems

© Infobase Publishing

Egyptian writing systems. These are samples of the hieroglyphic, hieratic, and demotic scripts used by ancient Egyptian scribes.

pharaohs' corpses, these divine kings might live happily in the next world and assure the people's prosperity in this one. Solar boats and the Great Sphinx complemented some of the pyramids. Later Egyptians built many temples to honor their pharaohs, but none was as massive as the Great Pyramid of Cheops (Khufu), which remained the world's tallest building until 1889, when the Eiffel Tower was erected in Paris. However, the massive pyramids built during this period became an economic drain on Egypt's resources and ultimately contributed to the decline of the Old Kingdom.

Egypt was both a priestly and a bureaucratic kingdom. The state was preoccupied with managing the Nile flood, dividing the land, ensuring an adequate harvest, and storing grain and beer as a precaution against years when the flood was unsatisfactory, endangering the harvest. The early development of writing (the earliest Egyptian script was in use before 3100 B.C.E.) served both to uphold religious beliefs and rituals and to record governmental decrees and imposts. Written symbols might have a magical function, propitiating the gods, or they could convey commands from the pharaoh to his provincial governors, or reports from the provinces to the capital. The writing system evolved from pictures of objects to representations of concepts and, in later centuries, from hieroglyphic (pictures) and hieratic (symbols) to simplified, or demotic, letters.

The Old Kingdom had a central bureaucracy and provincial governors but only a rudimentary defense force. At that time Egypt was not invaded by outsiders, but it did go through periods of relative political disunity, when a ruler or the dynasty was weak. During the Sixth Dynasty, the pharaoh's power was challenged by small kingdoms in Egypt's provinces. As the government became less centralized, the pharaohs ceased to be absolute monarchs, funerary customs were broadened, and the pharaoh was no longer viewed as exceptional. The idea of an afterlife was extended beyond the pharaoh to his wives, officials, provincial governors, and other fortunate Egyptians.

The First Intermediate Period and the Middle Kingdom (2181–1750 B.C.E)

During the First Intermediate Period (Seventh–Tenth Dynasties), a term used by historians for any era when ancient Egypt was divided, the provinces assumed powers that had formerly been exercised by the central government. Egypt did not necessarily grow weaker; it dispatched more traders and explorers to adjacent parts of Africa and Southwest Asia. Some Semitic peoples did enter northeastern Egypt from Palestine, seeking refuge or trading opportunities more than conquest. After a time of power struggles, the kings of Upper Egypt triumphed over those of the Delta, and Egypt was reunited.

The Middle Kingdom (Eleventh–Thirteenth Dynasties), especially the very vigorous Twelfth Dynasty, was a high period for ancient Egypt. The pharaohs gradually regained the powers that had been usurped during the Intermediate Period by the provincial governors. The arts, including temple building, sculpture, tomb decoration, and literary and moralistic works, flourished. The Egyptian written language grew more flexible and precise, setting high standards for literary production and bureaucratic efficiency. One surviving literary work is the "Tale of Senuhe," which purports to be the autobiography of a scribe who fled to Syria to escape the tumult of Egypt during the First Intermediate Period. It became a classic copied by generations of scribes, attesting to its popularity.

During this period improved irrigation works, especially in the Middle Nile region near Al Fayyum, enriched Egypt. This led to the

ANCIENT EGYPT'S NEIGHBORS

Assyrians: Semitic people in northern Mesopotamia who around 935 B.C.E. established an empire that included Egypt, Syria, Mesopotamia, and western Iran, lasting until 612 B.C.E.

Babylonians: Semitic people in southern Mesopotamia who established several empires of which the one most relevant to Egypt is also called *Chaldean* and lasted from 626 to 539 B.C.E.

Hittites: Indo-European people, among the first to use iron tools and weapons, who ruled an empire in western Antaolia from about 1600 to 1200 B.C.E.

Hyksos: Semitic nomadic migrants into the Nile Delta from Palestine during the Second Intermediate Period whose chiefs became Egypt's Fifteenth Dynasty (1678–1570 B.C.E.)

Israelites: Semitic nomads, ancestors of the Jews, who lived in Egypt at the time of Ramses II (1304–1237 B.C.E.), and later formed the Kingdoms of Israel and Judah in Palestine.

Kush: Ancient African kingdom in Nubia that flourished 1700–1500 B.C.E., revived after 1000 B.C.E., and provided Egypt's Twenty-fifth Dynasty (715–656 B.C.E.)

Libyans: Term applied to a number of nomadic tribal peoples who traded with Egypt or occasionally invaded it from the west

Mesopotamia: The valleys of the Euphrates and Tigris Rivers and the lands situated between them, roughly corresponding to modern Iraq

Nubia: The land directly south of Egypt, from the confluence of the Blue and White Niles to the first cataract, and the site of several kingdoms similar to Egypt, notably Kush

Persians: Indo-European people, originally from Central Asia, who established a large Middle Eastern empire and ruled over Egypt from 525 to 404 and from 343 to 332 B.C.E.

Sea Peoples: An obscure group, possibly related to the Philistines, who invaded Egypt and other lands of the eastern Mediterranean in the 13th century B.C.E.

Sumerians: Earliest people in Mesopotamia to form a civilization, probably around 3000 B.C.E. and trading partners with predynastic and Old Kingdom Egypt influx of growing numbers of migratory tribes from southwest Asia and Nubia. Egypt bought or took as tribute gold, ivory, ebony, incense, and slaves from the Nubians. The Middle Kingdom began sending expeditionary forces up the Nile and even built a series of fortresses in Nubia, but ruled over that land only occasionally.

The Second Intermediate Period (1750–1550 B.C.E)

The Second Intermediate Period (Fourteenth–Seventeenth Dynasties) is marked by the rule of a migratory tribe, the Hyksos. The Hyksos are often depicted as invaders. In fact, they were probably Semitic immigrants from Palestine whose numbers gradually grew until they managed to seize control over parts of the Delta, though Egyptian pharaohs continued to rule the Nile Valley. Egyptian daily life was enriched by Southwest Asian imports during this period: the horse and the chariot; the upright loom for weaving; such musical instruments as the lyre, long-necked lute, and tambourine; the hump-backed bull; and the olive and pomegranate trees. The Hyksos were perceived as foreign conquerors, however, and their rule was deeply resented by Egypt's chroniclers because Egyptians expected foreign chiefs to pay tribute and not to rule over them. By 1550 B.C.E. the Hyksos had been driven out of the Delta by the Seventeenth-Dynasty pharaohs. From then on Egypt would maintain a standing army, using horse-drawn chariots and composite bows introduced into Egypt by the Hyksos.

The New Kingdom (1550–1069 B.C.E)

The Egyptian pharaohs of the Nile Valley who had succeeded in driving out the Hyksos established their own dynasty (the Eighteenth), which united Egypt and founded an empire. Once it had restored control over Nubia, its armies crossed the Sinai into what we now call the Middle East. The areas of Syria and Palestine were then composed of small, competing city-states, easy for the Egyptians to subdue but hard to rule for long periods, especially once the Hittites rose to power around 1350 and challenged them. At this time the Egyptians controlled the world's first empire, stretching from Nubia to the Euphrates River in Asia.

For the next century the tides of war shifted between the Hittites and the Egyptians. At last the two parties drew up a defensive treaty sealed by a marriage in 1283 B.C.E. between Pharaoh Ramesses II

CITIES OF ANCIENT EGYPT

Abydos: Major religious site on the west bank of the Nile in Upper Egypt, containing First and Second Dynasty royal tombs, as well as New Kingdom temples of Seti I and Ramses II

Hierakonpolis: Largest and most developed urban complex of the Predynastic Period, located in the southern part of Upper Egypt, it contains a mud-brick enclosure, a painted tomb, and a temple dedicated to Horus, as well as many statues and votive offerings

Karnak: A vast religious complex on the east bank of the Nile near the modern city of Luxor, it contains an immense temple complex dedicated to Amun-Ra and a slightly smaller complex devoted to the goddess Mut

Memphis: Commercial center and administrative capital, located on the west bank of the Nile near the junction of Upper and Lower Egypt and 12 miles (19 km) south of Cairo, it contained the royal residence and administrative offices, the building for embalming the sacred bull, or Apis, the fallen colossus of Ramses II, and two temples devoted to Ptah

Thebes: Extensive site in Upper Egypt on both sides of the Nile, including the modern cities of Luxor and Gurna, it contains the tombs of the Eleventh Dynasty kings, the mortuary temples for the Eighteenth to Twentieth Dynasties, the valley of the kings, and the tombs of the nobles, and was prominent in the Middle and New Kingdoms as an administrative center.

(1290–1224 B.C.E.) and the daughter of the Hittite king. By the end of the century, however, Egypt faced invasions by Libyans from the west and by the piratical "Sea Peoples," whose identity remains a mystery, in the Mediterranean. Egypt had to withdraw from its conquered lands in Nubia and Palestine. Although Egyptians often blame foreign invaders for their misfortunes, it was rebellious viceroys and generals, however, not Libyans or Sea Peoples, who brought the New Kingdom to an end in 1069 B.C.E.

The power of the pharaohs during the New Kingdom is evident in their monumental art and their brief foray into theology. Ramesses II was especially active as a patron of poets, sculptors, and architects, who

Great Temple of Karnak. The Great Temple of Karnak is actually a complex of temples, chapels, and other buildings erected over a period of 2,000 years to honor the god Amun. The foreground shows the Sacred Lake used by the priests for their purification ritual. (Shutterstock)

wrote epics, carved colossal statues (notably the four hewn out of the side of a cliff at Abu Simbel), and erected lofty temples at his command. When sandstone replaced limestone as the main building material, it became possible to span wider spaces. The eventual result was the creation of such monuments as the mortuary temple of Queen Hatshepsut, the Great Temple of Karnak, and the Luxor Temple of Amenophis III, all of which can be seen to this day by visitors to the Upper Egyptian city of Luxor.

Akhenaton

During the Eighteenth Dynasty the pharaoh Akhenaton (1353–1335 B.C.E.) challenged ancient Egypt's polytheism by instituting a cult of sun worship centered on Aten to the exclusion of all other gods. Akhenaton closed all temples devoted to the worship of other gods, smashed their statues, and impounded their revenues. New temples were built at Karnak for the worship of Aten, followed by a whole city at Amarna. This new city became the home of a revolutionary school of Egyptian

Luxor Temple. Built during the reign of Amenhotep III (1391–1354 B.C.E.) to honor the god Amun, it was later modified by Ramesses II (1279–1213 B.C.E.). (Shutterstock)

Head of Nefertiti. A famous example of ancient Egyptian art at its best, this bust of Akhenaton's wife is illustrative of the special style developed during the Amarna era. (Shutterstock)

painting that represented men and women with rounded bodies and more natural poses than the stylized portraits typical of ancient Egypt in other periods. A noted example is the Head of Akhenaton's queen Nefertiti. Only the pharaoh's family could participate in the new rituals for Aten; other Egyptians continued worshiping Amun, Osiris, and their other gods in their homes, a practice that Akhenaton tried unsuccessfully to ban.

Tutankhamun

After the death of Akhenaton his successor, Tutankhamun (r. 1333–1323 B.C.E.), gave up this early attempt at monotheism, restored the temples, and revived the rites familiar to the priests and the people. By a quirk of fate, Tutankhamun would become the most famous pharaoh in the modern world. His tomb in the Western Desert was almost untouched by grave robbers. In 1923 the tomb, with its contents largely intact, was found by archaeologists. This discovery has added greatly to our knowledge and understanding of ancient Egypt. Aside from Tutankhamun's death mask, the tomb contained coffins within coffins, fine furniture, guardian statues, papyri containing protective spells, decorated chests, and 143 golden objects wrapped in various parts of his mummy.

The Third Intermediate Period and Late Period (1069–525 B.C.E)

By the Third Intermediate Period (Twenty-first–Twenty-fourth Dynasties), Egypt was entering a period of decline both as a culture and as a military and economic power in the region. This was a time of division, with some pharaohs ruling only in the Delta or only in Upper Egypt, and invasions by Libyans from the west and Nubians from the south. The Nubians had created a kingdom called Kush between 1700 and 1500 B.C.E. Although

Tutankhamun's Funerary Mask. The discovery of Tutankhamun's tomb was the greatest Egyptological find of the 20th century. This mask is one of hundreds of priceless objects found in that tomb. It is now in the Egyptian Museum, Cairo. (Jason Thompson)

conquered by Egypt during the New Kingdom, it regained its independence around 1000 B.C.E. The pharaohs of Kush began or perhaps expanded the trend of reviving the glories of earlier Egyptian dynasties by imitating their funerary inscriptions, paintings, costumes, and hairstyles.

In the seventh century B.C.E., in what is considered part of the Late Period, the Assyrians, who had built a great empire in what is now Iraq, invaded Egypt twice and set up a puppet Twenty-sixth Dynasty to rule. This later evolved into the Saite dynasty, a strong native dynasty that upheld ancient traditions and even managed to resume rule over Nubia and to invade Syria and Anatolia. The Babylonians invaded in 568 B.C.E. but stayed only briefly; they later made an alliance with Egypt against a rising power farther east: the Persian Empire.

3

PERSIAN, GREEK, ROMAN, AND ARAB RULE (525 B.C.E.–1250 C.E.)

In 525 B.C.E. Egypt ceased to be ruled by Egyptians. With very few exceptions, the head of the Egyptian state would always be a foreigner until the 1952 revolution. For most of this time Egyptians would still serve as administrators, scribes, judges, religious leaders, and village headmen. Egypt's subordination to the Persians, Macedonians, Greeks, Romans, and Arabs, described in this chapter, set the pattern for later colonization by other outsiders. Usually the Egyptians accepted their lot, but sometimes they rebelled openly and often they subverted or influenced their foreign masters. A modern Arabic proverb sums up the popular view: *Fi bilad Misr khayruha li-ghayriha* (In the land of Egypt, its good things belong to others).

Persian Rule

The year 525 was when Cambyses II, the Persian emperor, defeated the last Saite pharaoh, conquered Egypt, and established the Twenty-seventh Dynasty. The Persians, originally tribal nomads in what now is Iran, were united by Cyrus, a powerful king, in the middle of the sixth century B.C.E. He and his sons conquered a vast empire, the largest one known up to that time, extending from the Indus River in what is now Pakistan across the Middle East to North Africa and southeastern Europe. Cambyses was a son of Cyrus, a proud Persian, but he found it politic to honor Egyptian customs. Taking the name Mesut-i-Re ("offspring of Re," one of the gods of ancient Egypt), he ruled for three years as a pharaoh. Hoping to ensure that the Egyptians would obey their orders, the new rulers took the titles and followed the forms of their pharaonic predecessors. Maintaining the ancient rituals, they built new

30

temples and public works, reformed the legal system, and strengthened the economy. Persian rule facilitated Egyptian trade with southwest Asia. Egypt's agriculture, and hence its people, prospered.

Cambyses's successor, Darius (r. 521–486 B.C.E.), made Egypt a Persian province and appointed a satrap, or provincial governor, to govern it. The satraps' rule was challenged by three Egyptian dynasties. The Twenty-eighth and Twenty-ninth Dynasties ruled only in the Nile Delta. In 380 B.C.E. Nectanebo, an Egyptian general, overthrew the last ruler of the Twenty-ninth Dynasty, declaring himself king. He gained control of all Egypt and founded the Thirtieth Dynasty. This dynasty is remembered for its naturalistic portraiture, statuary, and new temples, most notably the Philae Temple near Aswan. The Thirtieth Dynasty marked ancient Egypt's flickering revival; it ended when the Persians reoccupied the country in 343 B.C.E. under Artaxerxes III. This Thirty-first Dynasty came to an end in 332 B.C.E. when Alexander the Great, hailed by the Egyptians as their savior from Persian domination, conquered the country.

Alexander the Great (r. 332–323 B.C.E.)

Alexander (356–323 B.C.E.) was a brave fighter and a master strategist who became king of Macedonia when he was 20. By 331, after a series of rapid military successes, his empire stretched from the Adriatic Sea to the Indus River and from the Danube to the Nile, including the entire Persian Empire. In this vast empire he laid the political basis for Hellenistic (Greek-like) civilization. The conquest of Egypt occurred in 332 B.C.E. Alexander treated Egypt's culture with respect. He offered sacrifices to Apis and other Egyptian gods and trekked across the Western Desert to Siwa to consult Amun, whom he claimed as his divine father. Some Egyptians even believed that their last native king had assumed the shape of a serpent to impregnate the wife of Alexander's earthly father, King Philip of Macedon, thus making Alexander a true pharaoh. His most lasting contribution was the creation of the port city of Alexandria, which blossomed into a cosmopolitan center of power and culture, linking Egypt economically to the Mediterranean world.

Alexander died suddenly in 323 B.C.E. His death was followed by a power struggle for control of his empire. In Egypt his childhood friend Ptolemy became satrap. By 306 B.C.E. Ptolemy had declared himself king of Egypt, founding the Ptolemaic dynasty that ruled Egypt for 300 years.

Temple of Philae. *Dedicated to the goddess Isis, this temple complex was built during the Ptolemaic period. It was flooded after the first Aswan Dam was incrementally raised in 1907–1912. After the Aswan High Dam was built, the complex was moved to another island. This painting by David Roberts shows the complex as it looked in the 19th century.* (Jason Thompson)

The Ptolemies

For Egypt the Ptolemies' rule was highly beneficial at first. Trade flourished in the Mediterranean and the Red Seas. As wheat replaced emmer and barley, Egypt became the breadbasket of the Mediterranean world. Fruit trees, grapevines, flax, and papyrus also contributed to a general prosperity. For the Egyptian people, though, life under these rulers, who were Greek-speaking Macedonians, did not improve. Even though the Ptolemies acted like pharaohs, honored the gods, maintained the temples, and built new ones at Edfu, Esna, and Dendera, the Egyptians resented them. Their main reasons were economic. Alexandria's magnificent architecture, high culture, museum, and library were justly famous, but they were supported by taxes paid mainly by toiling Egyptian peasants. Their resistance flared into periodic open revolts, both in the cities and in the countryside. A peasant uprising in 132 B.C.E. involved the whole Nile Valley.

A cultural chasm divided ruler from ruled. The Ptolemies did not intermarry with the people of Egypt; by custom kings usually married their sisters and few learned the Egyptian language. Lower Egyptian

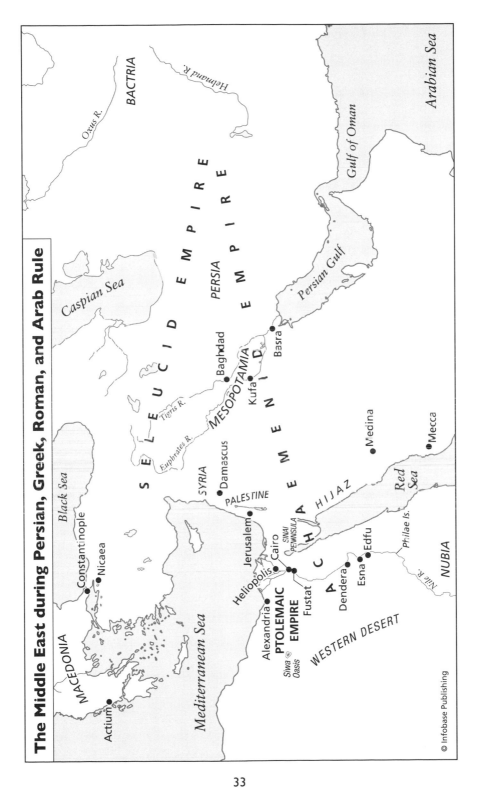

The Middle East during Persian, Greek, Roman, and Arab Rule

BACTRIA

Helmand R.

Oxus R.

Arabian Sea

Gulf of Oman

Caspian Sea

E M P I R E

S E L U C I D

PERSIA

Persian Gulf

E M P I R E

A C H A E M E N I D

Black Sea

Baghdad

Basra

Tigris R.

MESOPOTAMIA

Kufa

Euphrates R.

Medina

Mecca

Constantinople

Nicaea

Damascus

SYRIA

PALESTINE

Jerusalem

Cairo

HIJAZ

Red Sea

MACEDONIA

Heliopolis

SINAI PENINSULA

Dendera

Esna

Edfu

Philae Is.

Actium

Alexandria

PTOLEMAIC EMPIRE

Fustat

NUBIA

Siwa Oasis

WESTERN DESERT

Nile R.

Mediterranean Sea

33

officials were not expected to know Greek, yet Alexandria and parts of the Delta were being colonized and developed by Greek settlers.

The Ptolemies had rivals for control of the region. At first they competed for control of Syria and Palestine with the Seleucid Empire, founded by another of Alexander's generals in what is now Afghanistan, Iran, Iraq, and Syria. The Nubians regained parts of Upper Egypt around 200 B.C.E. But the greatest contender for control of Egypt was the Roman Republic, which was conquering most of the Mediterranean lands between the third and first centuries. During the last century B.C.E. the Ptolemies came to depend on Rome to protect them against their other enemies. The Romans long tried to avoid conquering Ptolemaic Egypt, fearing that any general who led the conquest would gain so much wealth from Egypt that he would become a dictator in Rome itself. Only under Queen Cleopatra VII (r. 47–30 B.C.E.) did Egypt become a Roman colony.

The story of Cleopatra has long fascinated people. This fascination may be due in part to her love affairs with Julius Caesar (100–44 B.C.E.), the general who became proconsul and dictator of the Roman Republic, and Mark Antony, a Roman general whose own career had been promoted by Julius Caesar; partly to her adept use of material luxury as a means of impressing other rulers; but most of all to the fact that she was a woman who had gained and shrewdly wielded immense power. After living in Rome for several years as a young woman, she ruled Egypt capably for almost two decades and was adored by the Egyptian people. She was the only Ptolemaic ruler to learn their language.

When Caesar was assassinated in 44 B.C.E., Mark Antony turned to Cleopatra and other Near Eastern leaders to consolidate his power. Cleopatra supported Mark Antony against his rival Octavian, who later became Caesar Augustus. When Octavian declared war on Mark Antony, Cleopatra raised and commanded an army to support him. They lost the war in the famous Battle of Actium in 31 B.C.E., which put an end to Ptolomaic rule and to Egypt's status as a country independent of the Roman Empire. Her suicide following that of Antony, who was to blame for the defeat, was inspired not only by love but also by fear of being paraded through the streets of Rome, which viewed winning Egypt as a triumph too long deferred.

Roman Rule (30 B.C.E.–640 C.E.)

Roman and Byzantine Egypt lasted longer than any one of ancient Egypt's dynasties. As soon as Octavian had defeated Antony and Cleopatra, he took control of Egypt's treasury and levied new and

Roman amphitheater. The Romans built theaters in many cities of their empire, including Alexandria. This theater, built in the second century C.E., was discovered in 1963 and has been excavated and restored by a Polish archaeological team. (Art Resource, NY)

higher taxes on the Egyptians. The country became his personal property, a land exploited on behalf of a ruler living elsewhere, one that no Roman senator might enter without his consent. Alexandria continued to prosper as a provincial capital and as a center of trade, manufacturing, and culture, but it no longer enjoyed the privileges it had known under the Ptolemies. The main basis of Egypt's wealth was its agriculture, and one-third of Egypt's annual grain harvest fed the empire. The senators understandably refrained from interfering in the governance of a land whose productivity benefited so many Romans.

Another important development during the Roman period was the rise of Christianity in Egypt. The Apostle Mark is said to have made his first convert among the Jews in Egypt around 40 to 60 C.E. He became the first patriarch of the National Church of Egypt, which is usually called Coptic Orthodox. As life under Roman rule was very different from life in pharaonic times, the ancient religion of Egypt seemed less relevant. Egyptians converted to the new faith of Christianity in large numbers and with great fervor, despite intermittent persecution. That of Roman Emperor Diocletian caused the death of so many Egyptian Christians that the onset of his reign in 284 marks the beginning of the

Coptic calendar. In 313, when Constantine issued his Edict of Milan, which granted freedom of worship throughout the Roman Empire, persecution ended and Christianity flourished.

The Coptic Challenge to Rome

Unfortunately, however, Egypt became the cockpit for the theological disputes and chasms that divided Christendom. The disputes began with an Alexandrian priest named Arius who taught that Jesus Christ, though divinely sired and inspired, ranked lower than God the Father. Arian views spread widely throughout North Africa and later Europe. They posed a challenge to Christianity, but were opposed by Athanasius, Alexandria's Coptic patriarch, and by the Council of Nicaea (325 C.E.), chaired by none other than the Emperor Constantine himself. There the Christian bishops agreed upon a statement that Christ is of one substance with God the Father, the basis for the doctrine of the Trinity, to which nearly all Christians still adhere, hence the so-called Nicene Creed.

Al-Muallaqa ("Hanging") church. The name comes from the suspension of this Coptic church over an entrance to the ancient fortress of Babylon (Old Cairo). Originally built in the fourth century, it was rebuilt in 977 and heavily restored in the 19th century. Damaged in the 1992 earthquake, it is now being restored again. (Shutterstock)

Other church councils met during the fourth and fifth centuries to refine Christian doctrines further. The Coptic Church, along with the Syrian Jacobites and the Armenians, came to believe that Christ was wholly divine, whereas the Orthodox view was that Jesus contained within his person both a human and a divine nature. The later Roman emperors and the patriarch of Constantinople required Egyptians to support Orthodox Christianity. As a consequence Egypt developed parallel Orthodox and Coptic hierarchies and churches during the fifth and sixth centuries, posing a severe financial burden on the people and alienating them from their Roman rulers. Perhaps as a sign of passive resistance to foreign control, one of Egypt's main contributions to Christianity was monasticism. Starting with St. Antony (252–356), devout Christians became hermits or founded monasteries in the Egyptian desert, living a communal life devoted mainly to study and prayer remote from the centers of wealth and power.

The Roman Empire depended heavily on the wheat and wine produced in the Nile Valley and Delta. However, the Egyptian people had no right to citizenship in the empire, and Egypt's Roman rulers did not respect the region's cultural heritage. Many statues and obelisks were taken from Egypt to the empire's eastern and western capitals, Rome and Constantinople. In 330 C.E. the center of the empire shifted from Rome to Constantinople, marking the transition to what is usually called the Byzantine Empire. This change was of no consequence to Egyptians. Greeks and Romans in Egypt remained a privileged and separate caste. With all these grievances against Roman rule, it is hardly a surprise that some Christian Egyptians hailed the return of Persian rule in 619 or that many welcomed the Arab conquest in 640.

Arab Conquest

In 640 an event took place that would profoundly affect Egypt. The Arab general Amr ibn al-As (d. 663) led a band of warriors across the Sinai Peninsula and into the Nile Valley, defeating the Byzantines at Heliopolis near what is now Cairo. Within two years the Arabs had conquered the Nile Valley, the Delta, and Alexandria itself, marking the beginning of Islam in Egypt.

Much controversy rages over this conquest of Egypt. Did the Egyptian Christians welcome the Arabs as liberators from the Byzantine yoke? Did they resist the Arabs and make common cause with their fellow Christians against the coming of Islam? Both sides are partly correct. Most Egyptian Christians had adopted the view that Christ was fully divine. Their Byzantine rulers tried to impose the Orthodox belief that Christ combined human and divine natures within his person. The Byzantines had imposed high taxes and discriminatory laws against the Egyptian Christians, or Copts. For these reasons, among others, many Egyptians did view the Arab conquest as liberating them from Orthodox tyranny. The Arabs did not try to convert the Egyptians to Islam, in part because their laws allowed them to tax Jews and Christians at a higher rate than Muslims, and also because the early Arabs assumed that only they could be Muslims. For the Egyptians the taxes imposed by the new rulers were lower at first than they had been under the Byzantines. Also most of the tax collectors and government accountants were Coptic Christians. Those few non-Arabs who did embrace Islam were given client status within the Arab tribes; called *mawali*, they played a major political role in those early days of Islam, notably in the rise of Shiism. The conversion of Copts to Islam was not as significant, numerically and politically, as the Islamization of the peoples of Iran and Mesopotamia. An Egyptian Christian who embraced Islam cut himself off from his family and village community, but his conversion enabled him to enter the higher ranks of the administration or the army.

Islam

Islam teaches that there is only one God, the Creator and Sustainer of this world and the next, all-knowing and all-powerful, who has made himself known to humanity through scriptures revealed to a succession of prophets, culminating in the revelation of the Quran to Muhammad, who lived in the Hejaz (western Arabia) from 570 to 632. Those who accept Muhammad as the last of the prophets and the Quran as God's revealed word are Muslims. The word *Muslim* means "one who makes peace [with God]." The word *Arab* originally meant a camel-herding nomad living in Arabia, but now is applied to people who speak Arabic as their native language and who embrace what can broadly be called Arab culture. Most Arabs are Muslim, but some are Christian. Nowadays, only a sixth of the world's Muslims are Arabs.

Muhammad's successors as leaders of the Muslim community were known as caliphs. The first four caliphs are called Rashidun, a term commonly translated as "right-guided." The third caliph, Uthman, was assassinated, and Muhammad's cousin and son-in-law, Ali, became the fourth caliph. But a dispute arose over the legitimacy of his appointment. Ali did not attempt to prosecute the men who killed his predecessor. Uthman's cousin, Muawiya, who was a member of the Umayyad family, claimed

Decorative page from a Quran. Muslims believe that the Quran is the record of God's revelations to Muhammad, the last prophet of Islam, and treat the book with great reverence. This manuscript was created between 1368 and 1388 and is now displayed in the Egyptian National Library (Dar al-Kutub), which has the world's largest collection of Quranic manuscripts. (Art Resource, NY)

THE ESSENTIALS OF ISLAM

Islam literally means "making peace [with God]." A man who practices Islam is a Muslim, a woman, a Muslima. Believing Jews and Christians, having come to know God through revealed scriptures, are also, in a generic sense, *muslim*. God's existence was revealed to a series of prophets, including Adam, Noah, Moses, David, Solomon, and Jesus. The last, Muhammad (570–632), received the Quran, or sacred text of Islam. Muslims believe that the Quran is God's perfect revelation and will never be superseded.

beliefs: The basic articles of Muslim belief are the oneness of God, the existence of angels, God's revelations through prophets, sacred scriptures (mainly the Bible and the Quran), and the Day of Judgment. Some Muslims add Predestination, the idea that God has determined all human actions, but others state that God allows free will to humanity, obliging everyone to discover and choose to follow the right path.

the Five Pillars: In popular belief the right path is equated with the universal Muslim duties summarized as the "Five Pillars of Islam." These are *shahada* (witness), *salat* (ritual prayer), *sawm* (fasting from daybreak to sunset in the month of Ramadan), *zakat* (tithing, or paying a fixed share of one's wealth or income to the needy), and *hajj* (pilgrimage to Mecca and Medina). Some Muslims add a sixth pillar, *jihad,* variously translated as "struggle" or "holy war." Muslims do recognize many prescribed and proscribed actions, ranging from injunctions about remembering God's power and treating other human beings kindly to rules about food and clothing, relations between the sexes, and the rules of war and peace.

sharia: This is the body of Islamic rules and laws, derived from the Quran during the first few centuries after Muhammad's death, the sunna ("way" of Muhammad or, in some cases, earlier prophets), analogy, consensus, and decisions by early judges. Those who know the sharia and who teach or administer it are called ulama. They have played a leading role in Muslim governments and societies, including Egypt's.

Sunni Muslims are those (including nearly all Egyptian Muslims) who believe that the caliphs had the right to rule the Muslim community after Muhammad's death.

Shiite Muslims (including the Fatimids, who ruled Egypt from 969 to 1171) believe that Ali and his descendants should have succeeded Muhammad.

Sufism is organized Islamic mysticism. A Sufi can be either Sunni or Shiite. Many Egyptians, past and present, have made Sufism a major part of their lives.

the right to seek revenge for Uthman's death. Fighting broke out between those who supported Ali and those who supported Muawiya. The conflict resulted in Ali's assassination. In 661 Muawiya claimed the caliphate for himself, moved the capital from Medina, Saudi Arabia, to Damascus, Syria, and made the post hereditary within the Umayyad family.

Most Muslims accept all four caliphs as legitimate; they are called Sunni, from the Arabic word for "tradition." Others believe that Ali was the first legitimate successor of Muhammad; they discount the first three caliphs. They are known as Shiites, from the name Shiat Ali, or the Party of Ali. In modern times most Shiites believe that this leadership was passed down by Ali to his sons and their sons, who are called imams (leaders). They claim that the 12th imam vanished in 874 but that he remains alive and in hiding until the time when God has ordained that he will return to restore righteousness on earth. But there are also Shiites who believe that Ismail, the man who should have been the seventh imam, was wrongly passed over in favor of a brother; these Shiites are known as Ismailis.

Early Arab Rule (640–868)

Given the lack of pressure by Egypt's foreign rulers, both Islamization and Arabization occurred only slowly over time. Arabic did not become the official language of Egypt until 706. Between 640 and 868 Egypt was ruled by governors appointed by the caliphs. Egypt's role as a province in an empire whose primary purpose was seen as supplying the central government with taxes and grain did not change. Egypt's Muslims, mainly soldiers living in the garrison town of Fustat, accepted Umayyad rule. Some *mawali* in Persia objected to Umayyad favoritism toward the Arabs—launching a revolt that brought the Abbasid family to power in 750 and moved Islam's capital to Baghdad. Egyptian Muslims acquiesced in these changes. Indeed, Egypt's role in the politics of early Islam was remarkably quiet.

But resistance against foreign rule increased in the early eighth century when rising taxes and other government demands inspired Coptic farmers to rebel against Arab rule, as they would do frequently between 725 and 832.

Local Dynasties Take Control (868–969)

By the ninth century internal conflict within the Abbasid Empire reduced the empire's control of outlying areas. In 868 Ahmad Ibn Tulun (r. 868–884), a Turkish officer sent to Egypt as governor, established himself as

Ibn Tulun Mosque. This mosque in southern Cairo was built for the founder of the Tulunid dynasty in the late ninth century. Its minaret, unique in Egypt, is shaped like a Mesopotamian tower, or ziggurat. (Adam Woolfitt/Saudi Aramco World/PADIA)

the independent ruler of Egypt, founding the Tulunid dynasty. Ibn Tulun kept Egypt's tax revenues in Egypt, rather than sending them to the caliph in Baghdad. This enabled him to build Egypt into an autonomous state that could compete for power against Iraq. His improvement of the Nile irrigation works increased his tax revenues, which enabled him to support a huge army. Tulunid control extended eastward into Syria (and sometimes parts of Iraq) and westward into Libya. Ibn Tulun never realized his dream of moving the Abbasid caliphate to Egypt, but he used some of his revenues to build palaces, hospitals for men and for women, and the great mosque north of Fustat that bears his name. Ibn Tulun's son succeeded him as ruler of Egypt, but he and his heirs wasted their inheritance, spending and drinking recklessly. The Abbasids regained their power as a dynasty and retook Egypt in 905.

For the next 30 years Egypt suffered riots and invasions under successive Abbasid-appointed governors. Then, in 935, Muhammad Ibn Tughj was installed as governor. He took the honorific title *ikhshid,* a Persian word meaning "prince." The Ikhshid ruled Egypt, Syria, and most of the major land and sea routes for a decade. He was succeeded by his sons, but effective power was held by an Ethiopian officer named Kafur, a former slave who was named regent for Muhammad ibn Tughj's young heirs. After both of the Ikhshid's sons died, Kafur took the surname al-Ikhshid and ruled in his own name. Between 963 and 969 a series of low Nile floods disrupted the crops and brought famine to Egypt; as a result the Egyptian people looked to the western part of the Muslim world for relief.

Fatimid Rule (969–1171)

Help came from the Fatimid dynasty in what is now Tunisia. The Fatimids adhered to the Ismaili branch of Shiite Islam and claimed to be descended from the Prophet Muhammad's daughter, Fatima, who was married to Ali. The Fatimids had built up a powerful state in North Africa. They called their leaders caliphs, thus challenging the legitimacy of the Abbasid caliphs of Baghdad. Hoping to reunite the Muslim world under their Ismaili standard, the Fatimids needed to extend their empire into Egypt and Syria. Their propagandists found willing ears among the Muslims of Egypt, distressed by quarreling troops, low Nile floods, and high taxes. Egyptian Muslims tended to be Sunni and might have been expected to support the Abbasid caliphs, but Fatimid propagandists allayed their fears and played on their hopes. In 969 the Fatimid leader Jawhar defeated Kafur's soldiers and established a

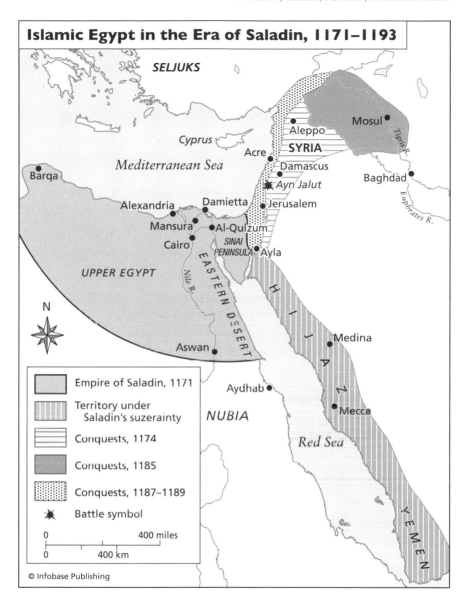

Islamic Egypt in the Era of Saladin, 1171–1193

SELJUKS

Cyprus

Mediterranean Sea

Barqa

Aleppo
SYRIA
Acre
Damascus
Mosul
Baghdad

Tigris R.

Ayn Jalut

Alexandria
Damietta
Jerusalem
Mansura
Cairo
Al-Qulzum
SINAI
PENINSULA
Ayla

Euphrates R.

UPPER EGYPT

Nile R.

EASTERN DESERT

N

Aswan

Medina

Aydhab

Mecca

NUBIA

Red Sea

HIJAZ

YEMEN

Empire of Saladin, 1171

Territory under
Saladin's suzerainty

Conquests, 1174

Conquests, 1185

Conquests, 1187–1189

Battle symbol

0   400 miles

0   400 km

© Infobase Publishing

(opposite page) Entrance to al-Azhar. This mosque, begun in 969 just after the Fatimid conquest of Egypt, contains the world's oldest continuously existing madrasa (school of Islamic law). This depiction is by the 19th-century orientalist Edward William Lane. (Jason Thompson)

45

MAJOR MUSLIM DYNASTIES

Abbasids: Sunni Muslim, Arab family of caliphs descended from Muhammad's uncle, Abbas, that ruled from Baghdad (750–1258 C.E.) and in name from Cairo (1258–1517) and Istanbul (1517–1924)

Ayyubids: Saladin and his descendants, Kurdish Sunni Muslims, who ruled in Egypt (1171–1250), Syria (1174–1260), and occasionally western Arabia

Buyids: Shiite Persian family that ruled Persia and Iraq (932–1055)

Fatimids: Ismaili Shiite, Arab family who ruled North Africa (909–972), Egypt (969–1171), and occasionally parts of Syria, Hejaz, and Yemen

Ghaznavids: Sunni Turkish family that ruled in Afghanistan, parts of Persia, Central Asia, and India (977–1186)

Hamdanids: Shiite Arab family with branches ruling in Aleppo and Mosul (890–1004), sometimes a rival to the Fatimids

Hashimites: Arab family descended from Muhammad, contenders for power in early Muslim times, and rulers in Hejaz (1916–1924), Iraq (1920–58), and Jordan (1921–   )

Ikhshids: Literally "Princes" but actually Turkish warriors sent by the Abbasid caliphs to govern Egypt (935–969)

Mamluks: Members of a Turkish or Circassian military oligarchy ruling Egypt (1250–1517), Syria (1260–1516), and occasionally the Hejaz.

new capital, Cairo, which was destined to become the largest city in the Muslim world. The Fatimids also established the mosque-school al-Azhar, originally meant to train new Ismaili propagandists, which survives today as the world's oldest Islamic university.

Fatimid rule in Egypt lasted from 969 to 1171. The area controlled by the Fatimids usually included Libya, Syria, Palestine, and the Hejaz, or western Arabia. The first century of Fatimid rule saw general prosperity. Egypt's peasants continued to produce a surplus of grain that could be sold throughout the Mediterranean world, as well as flax, which supported a thriving linen industry. Egypt was a center of long-distance trade, with thriving ports on the Mediterranean and Red Seas.

Most of the Fatimid caliphs adopted a tolerant policy toward Egypt's Copts, Jews, and Sunni Muslims. One exception was al-Hakim (r. 996–1021), who placed severe restrictions on Jews, Christians, and Sunni

During the era of Ottoman rule, some Mamluks continued to wield power in Egypt until Napoléon's invasion (1798)

Mongols: Tribal nomads from the Asian steppes north of China who conquered Central Asia, Persia, Iraq, and Syria in the 13th century but were stopped by the Mamluks in 1260 before they could enter Egypt. Pagan at first, the Mongols ruling in the Middle East gradually embraced Islam and became known as the Ilkhanid dynasty (1256–1349)

Ottomans: Sunni Turkish family, also called Osmanli, that ruled southeastern Europe, most of the Middle East, and North Africa, including Egypt, from 1517 to 1798 and nominally until 1914

Qajars: Shiite Turkish family that ruled Persia (1794–1925)

Safavids: Shiite Turkish family, originally Sufi, that ruled Persia (1501–1736)

Timurids: Sunni Turkish and Mongol family that ruled most of Persia and Central Asia in the late 14th century and briefly challenged the Mamluks for control of Syria (1400–1405). Their descendants included the Mughals (Moguls), who ruled India (1526–1858)

Tulunids: Sunni Turkish family sent by the Abbasid caliphs to govern Egypt (868–935)

Umayyads: Sunni Arab family, originally from Mecca, that ruled most of the Muslim world from Damascus (661–750) and later ruled over Muslim Spain

Muslims. Al-Hakim disappeared in 1021; it is believed he was assassinated on his sister's orders. The Fatimid caliphs gave considerable leeway to merchants to manufacture and sell goods, using the head of the merchant guilds as an agent to maintain order. A series of low Nile floods and factional struggles among the troops caused a crisis in the 1060s. In 1073, to restore order the caliph appointed a chief minister or vizier. From that time on the vizierate was a key administrative post in Egypt.

Saladin and the Ayyubids (1171–1250)

The last great dynasty to rule Egypt during this era of Arab Islamic dominance, the Ayyubids, began with a Fatimid vizier. He may well be the Muslim warrior best known in the West: Salah al-Din, commonly called Saladin (c. 1137–93). Saladin succeeded his uncle, Shirkuh, as vizier. In

Cairo Citadel. *Built for Saladin in 1176–83 to protect Cairo in case of a crusader invasion, this palace and barracks complex has been enlarged and restored frequently and served as the headquarters for various foreign armies, including the French and the British. It is depicted here by David Roberts.* (Library of Congress)

1171 he deposed the Fatimid caliph and restored Sunni Islam in Egypt. Although Saladin had to face several attempts to restore Fatimid rule, he won strong popular support in Cairo. He ordered the construction of the citadel that still overlooks the city and also strengthened Egypt's Mediterranean and Red Sea fleets. Saladin built up a Muslim state that stretched from Tunisia to northern Iraq and from northern Syria to Yemen. In 1187 Saladin's forces recaptured Jerusalem from the crusaders, European Christians who fought to take the "Holy Land" from Muslim control.

Saladin has come down in history as a heroic fighter. Yet despite his efforts to master Fatimid court and bureaucratic procedures, he failed to set up an orderly administration in Egypt. Saladin's Ayyubid successors did not surmount these difficulties. Egypt lacked an institutional structure that might have limited factional struggles and made the government more efficient. Yet the country prospered, due largely to its extensive commerce with the Italian city-states and with other Muslim countries. By the time of the Ayyubids most of the Egyptian people spoke Arabic and practiced Islam. The collapse of Ayyubid rule came from within. The Ayyubids had built up a corps of Turkish soldiers recruited from Central Asia and trained as slave-soldiers. Known as Mamluks (*mamluk* in Arabic means "owned man"), these slaves had saved Egypt from European invaders, specifically the Seventh Crusade. Now they took the country for themselves and opened a new chapter in its history.

4

MAMLUK AND OTTOMAN
RULE (1250–1798)

I n 1250 Egypt fell under rule by the Turks. Once again as so often in its past, the rulers spoke a different language from their subjects, who by now spoke mostly Arabic. This difference mattered little to most people at the time, because the Mamluks and the Ottomans, who came later, were Sunni Muslims like most Egyptians. A shared religion, common values, and the same social institutions bound the ruling Turks together with their subjects. Occasionally, though, the people grumbled about rulers who taxed too heavily or failed to defend them from invading nomads, plagues, or a low Nile flood. This chapter mentions, for example, a major revolt that broke out in 1523, soon after the Ottomans defeated and replaced the Mamluks. There was no love lost between Egyptians and Ottomans. To quote a popular street chant: *Yal-mutajalli, ihlik al-osmanli* (O God the Manifest, ruin the Ottoman).

Mamluks

Mamluk means "owned man." When the word is capitalized, it denotes a class of former slaves who ruled in Egypt and Syria. The first mamluks were slave-soldiers who served the Abbasid caliphs. These soldiers were recruited as boys, mostly from non-Muslim families in Central Asia and lands around the Black Sea. Because they came from outside the empire, they had no link to any of the warring factions within the empire. Some were kidnapped by slave traders; others were sold by their impoverished families. These boys were housed in barracks or dormitories with other mamluks the same age. They were given basic instruction in Islam and Arabic, as well as thorough training as cavalry soldiers. This rigorous education lasted eight to 10 years, during which the youths were kept under the strictest discipline. Because they lived and trained together for so long, each group of soldiers developed a feeling of fraternal loyalty that lasted the rest of their lives. When a mamluk completed his military training, he received his liberation paper, a horse, and his fighting equipment.

Even though the mamluks were technically no longer slaves after they finished their training, they were still obliged to serve the sultan or amir who trained them. Each group of trainees tended to become a faction within the army. Many mamluks rose to positions of authority within the empire. In 1250 they succeeded in seizing power in Egypt.

RECRUITMENT AND TRAINING OF MAMLUKS

Although the word *mamluk* means "owned man" or "slave," its connotation in Egyptian history is different from what Western readers may assume, because the Mamluks ruled over Egypt, and usually Syria and western Arabia as well, from 1250 to 1517, and they continued to control most of Ottoman Egypt up to Napoléon's invasion in 1798.

The Ayyubids (1171–1250) made a systematic practice of importing boys from the Turkic tribes of Central Asia, a practice that can be traced back at least to the Abbasid caliphate, which began in 750. The Ayyubids trained the boys to become their main warriors. The mamluk leaders, called *amirs* (princes), not only commanded the Ayyubid armies but seized control of the central administration in 1250. They carried on the practice of buying boy slaves, typically between the ages of 10 and 13, from the Central Asian steppes and deserts.

Temperatures in Central Asia exceed 100°F in summer and drop below 0°F in winter. Winds blow most of the year. Because food was scarce, some Turkic tribes were reluctantly willing to sell some of their children before they reached puberty to dealers who would then transport them over land and water to their new homes in Egypt and Syria. Most of the boys would become soldiers; the girls became domestic servants, concubines, or wives. By the time they arrived in Egypt, these children would have already learned to ride ponies and horses, to shoot bows and arrows while riding (thanks, in part, to the Chinese invention of the stirrup), and to hunt small game.

The Turkish (Bahri) Mamluks (1250–1382)

In 1249 European soldiers of the Seventh Crusade laid siege to the Egyptian city of Mansura. The Mamluks in the Ayyubid army defeated the crusaders. Shortly after this victory, the Ayyubid ruler of Egypt, al-Salih (r. 1240–49), died unexpectedly. His widow, Shajar al-Durr, seized power to avert a succession struggle among his relatives and ruled Egypt for six months. She then married the Mamluk commander, Aybak (r. 1250–57), who soon took power. His major accomplishment was to halt the Mongol conquest of the Middle East at the Battle of Ayn Jalut (in present-day Israel) in September 1260. Two years earlier the Mongols had taken Baghdad, destroyed what had once been the

Sultans, amirs, and indeed former mamluks all purchased boys, converted them to Islam, housed them in barracks, and subjected them to intensive training in cavalry tactics and military discipline. Conditions varied among groups of boys owned by the sultan, by the amirs, and by those who had themselves been imported as boy slaves earlier, but in general they were well fed and clothed and conditioned to feel loyalty to those who owned and trained them, as well as to the other boys in their group of trainees. They had no freedom to roam the streets of Cairo, Damascus, or Aleppo. Their excursion to the public bath on Thursdays, preparatory to obligatory Friday group prayers, was the high point in their week. Once tested and judged competent as soldiers on horseback, they were set free, but they continued to view themselves as mamluks because of the intense training they had undergone and their bonding with the others in their class.

Most became cavalry officers, among the best in the Middle East, capable of warding off attacks from both Mongols and Crusaders. Some were given tracts of agricultural land in fief; others received salaries from the government for their military service. A few rose to become sultans because of their fighting abilities, the respect that they had earned from the sultans whom they had served, or from their fellow mamluks. Rarely did a son succeed his father to the throne; if one did, he was usually incompetent to rule and quick to be replaced by an ambitious mamluk who had made his reputation on the battlefield.

It is hard to believe that the system of succession worked, yet the Mamluk sultanate lasted longer than most Islamic dynasties, and mamluks continued to be imported and to wield power within Ottoman Egypt for three additional centuries.

world center of Islamic culture and political authority, and brought down the Abbasid caliphate. In 1259 they had taken and sacked the cities of Aleppo and Damascus in Syria. The victory at the Battle of Ayn Jalut stopped the destructive advance of the Mongols. In part due to their rise to power under the shadow of the Ayyubids, the Mamluks developed a succession pattern unique in Egypt's history. Unlike the usual dynastic system, although at times a son might succeed his father as Mamluk sultan, he usually had only a brief reign during which the major factions would fight for power. As soon as one Mamluk party had defeated the others, its leader would seize the sultanate.

One reason for the success of this system was that it enabled gifted leaders to rise to the top and stay there. An excellent example is Baybars (r. 1260–77), who had served his predecessor, Qutuz (r. 1259–60), at Ayn Jalut. Soon after the victory he killed his master and convinced the other Mamluks to accept him as their new sultan. Ever mindful of the Mongol threat to the east, Baybars tried to bring much of Syria under Mamluk control. This meant absorbing a few lands still under Ayyubid princes and reducing the crusaders' territories to a coastal strip. He did not let religion or nationality stop him from making useful alliances. He courted the Byzantines and the Christian rulers of Aragon, Sicily, and several Italian city-states, all of which became Egypt's trading partners. Continuing the Ayyubid policy of promoting international trade, Baybars made Egypt the richest Muslim state. He also took in a fugitive Abbasid prince from Baghdad and proclaimed him caliph, thereby gaining some prestige, but gave him no real power. Although both Muslims and their opponents today talk of a revival of the caliphate, the institution mattered little in the 13th century. Muslims cared more that Baybars earned the title "Servant of the Two Holy Cities," when Mecca and Medina accepted Mamluk sovereignty. This title meant that, until those cities were taken by the Ottoman Empire in 1517, any Muslim making the hajj passed through Mamluk lands. Many also spent time in Egypt or Syria.

For most Egyptians, then as before or since, religion was at the center of their lives. Mamluk sultans did rule in Cairo and did appoint governors for the provinces. But for the Muslim majority, the learned elite, or ulama, led prayers in the mosques, preached the Friday sermons, adjudicated domestic or commercial disputes, and taught children the fundamentals of Islam. Some ulama also owned land, or administered properties that had been set aside as *waqfs*, lands that pious Muslims had willed to support religious or charitable endeavors. Numerous madrasas (schools), most notably in Cairo but also in the provincial towns, trained Muslim boys to become ulama. Most Egyptian Muslims also took part in devotional activities organized by Sufi (mystic) orders, some for men, others for women. These included chanting, dancing, observance of the birth or death dates of past religious leaders, exorcism of evil spirits, fasting, and vigils.

Egypt's Christians, or Copts, made up a gradually decreasing but still substantial part of the population. Their priests and bishops also taught children and judged disputes, in addition to performing their pastoral functions. Christian Egypt also had many desert monasteries, some of which have survived until now, and it was not unusual for a young Christian man or woman to become a hermit for a few years, even if he or she did not take holy orders. Although Christians were gradually abandoning the ancient Egyptian language for Arabic as their spoken and written language, they continued to use Coptic as their language for prayer and religious scholarship. Copts continued to serve as accountants for the Mamluk government and land surveyors in the countryside, because they retained an elaborate record-keeping system that went back to the scribes of pharaonic Egypt. Many skilled trades, notably in commerce and manufacturing, were still dominated by these Coptic Christians. Other skilled trades were limited to Jews, who lived mainly in Cairo, Alexandria, and some of the larger towns. Politically, Egypt's Christians and Jews were known as *dhimmis* (protected peoples), subordinate to Muslims in general and Mamluks in particular, but they could nevertheless become learned, wealthy, or powerful within their own communities. Occasionally, the *dhimmis* suffered: If a Mamluk sultan found that he was short of funds, he might increase the tax on Christians and Jews known as the *jizya*.

The Mamluks who ruled Egypt from 1250 to 1382 were called Bahri because these soldiers were initially housed in a castle on the island of Roda on the Nile, called *bahr* (sea) in Egypt. Most of the Bahri Mamluk sultans were capable rulers, promoting prosperity at home and expanding Egyptian rule from Libya to Syria, Hejaz, and Yemen. They commissioned palaces and mosques that continue to grace the city of Cairo, making it the leading center of Muslim architecture. Cairo also became the center of both overland trade between Africa and Southwest Asia and maritime commerce between the Indian Ocean and the Mediterranean world. The Mamluks maintained several Red Sea ports, from which camel caravans carried goods across the Eastern Desert to Upper Egypt to be floated down the Nile to Cairo's port village of Bulaq. Although Jewish and Coptic Egyptians, as well as Genoese and Venetians, played a role in maritime commerce, the leading group

Sultan Hasan Mosque. One of Cairo's most beautiful mosques, it was built between 1356 and 1363 near the Citadel. It serves as a congregational mosque and contains facilities for teaching all four Sunni rites of Islamic law. The depiction is by Pascal Coste, a French architect and traveler who lived in Egypt from 1817 to 1829. (Jason Thompson)

of merchants was the Karimis, Egyptian Muslims who traded spices and fine textiles and invented or refined such innovations as the letter of credit and the check to facilitate their trade. At its height, in the early 14th century, Karimi commercial activities extended from Southeast Asia to the western Mediterranean.

Despite the Bahri Mamluks' success as rulers of this prosperous state, factional fighting, a plague outbreak in 1347, a Cypriot crusader raid on Alexandria in 1365, and falling agricultural revenues gradually undercut their legitimacy and led eventually to the end of their rule.

The Circassian Mamluks (1382–1517)

The second group of Mamluk sultans, called Circassian (from the Turkish word for the Caucasus region where most originated), ruled from 1382 to 1517. Founded by Sultan Barquq (r. 1382–99), the Circassian Mamluks focused initially on rebuilding a government ravaged by the plague epidemics that beset much of Europe and the Muslim world in the late 14th century. These bubonic and pneumonic plagues recurred on 16 occasions during the Circassian period, striking hard at cities like Cairo, where a quarter of a million inhabitants crowded into a narrow area between the Nile and Saladin's citadel. Other challenges faced by the Circassian Mamluks included occasional pirate forays against Alexandria, the invasion of Syria by the Mongol ruler Timur Lenk (Tamerlane) in 1400–01, Bedouin raids in the countryside, and occasional usurpation of power in Upper Egypt by Arab or Nubian tribes.

Many a Circassian bey (roughly corresponding to "knight," bey was a title used by these later rulers) was corrupt or incompetent, but some were capable sultans. These included Barsbay (r. 1422–38), who regained control over Syria and conquered Cyprus; Qait Bey (r. 1468–96), who fended off the Ottoman Turks and built the Alexandria fortress that still bears his name; and Qansuh al-Ghuri (r. 1501–16), who revitalized the Mamluks after a long period of factional infighting. Only months after Qansuh al-Ghuri's death, however, the Ottoman army crossed the Sinai Peninsula, defeated the Mamluks, and occupied Cairo.

The Mamluks' downfall can be ascribed to several factors, some internal and some external. Internal factors included the rivalry among various Mamluk factions and their failure to defend their lands against

Qait Bey Fortress. Jutting out in Alexandria harbor, this military structure was erected in 1477–80 for Qait Bey, one of the few great Circassian Mamluk sultans. (Jason Thompson)

55

outside invaders. Another factor was Egypt's economic deterioration, caused in part by the breakdown of public order, excessive taxation of both the peasants and the merchants on whom Egypt's prosperity depended, and the recurring plagues. The final factor came from outside Egypt. In 1498 sailors from Portugal rounded the Cape of Good Hope on Africa's southern tip. This enabled Europeans to establish commercial and naval bases in East Africa and India, bypassing Mamluk taxes and tolls to purchase and transport spices from South and Southeast Asia. By the early 16th century, Muslims no longer controlled the Indian Ocean or the Arabian Sea. And Egypt had lost the spice trade.

Ottoman Rule in Egypt (1517–1798)

At the same time, a formidable opponent was developing in the area that is known as Turkey today. The Ottoman Empire, founded in the late 13th century, had been steadily expanding. From its source in northwestern Anatolia the empire extended across the Dardanelles into southeastern Europe. In the 15th century, after it had conquered most of the Balkan region, the empire turned south and east, absorbing most of the petty states of Muslim Anatolia. Soon the Ottomans came into conflict with the Mamluks in central Anatolia and northern Syria. Both empires had disciplined infantry corps that could use firearms; however, the Ottoman janissaries, or foot soldiers, were better trained and more disciplined than the Mamluks, and their cannons were more advanced. After defeating the Safavids of Persia in 1514, the army of Ottoman Sultan Selim I moved southward, taking Syria in 1516 and Egypt a year later.

Although Selim appointed a governor for Egypt, the Mamluks, the ulama, and the Egyptian people did not happily accept Ottoman rule. Selim took many artisans and scholars from Cairo and sent them to Istanbul to help build up the imperial capital. This caused distress to the wives and children of these artisans and impoverished Egypt's mosques, madrasas, and bazaars. The Ottomans imposed new and unfamiliar laws (and Turkish judges) on the Egyptians. Inevitably these sources of unrest led to uprisings against Ottoman rule. A large-scale revolt broke out in 1523, inspired by the ulama of Cairo but spearheaded by groups of Circassian Mamluks, with some involvement by Bedouin tribal soldiers. It was suppressed by Ottoman janissaries (infantry soldiers bearing firearms) in 1524. In 1525 Sultan Selim's successor, Suleyman the Magnificent (r. 1520–66), agreed to let the Mamluks collect taxes and maintain public order in Egypt as long as

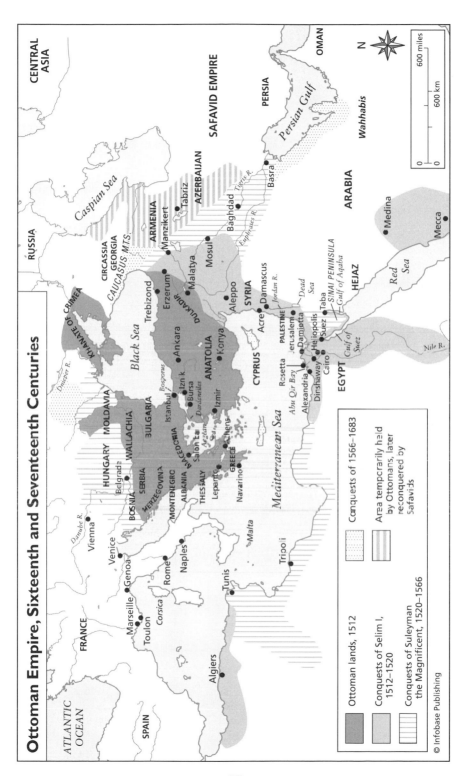

Ottoman Empire, Sixteenth and Seventeenth Centuries

Legend:

- Ottoman lands, 1512
- Conquests of Selim I, 1512–1520
- Conquests of Suleyman the Magnificent, 1520–1566
- Conquests of 1566–1683
- Area temporarily held by Ottomans, later reconquered by Safavids

N

600 miles

600 km

© Infobase Publishing

Labels on map:

CENTRAL ASIA · OMAN · SAFAVID EMPIRE · PERSIA · *Persian Gulf* · *Wahhabis* · RUSSIA · *Caspian Sea* · AZERBAIJAN · Tabriz · ARMENIA · Manzikert · *Tigris R.* · Baghdad · Basra · ARABIA · Medina · Mecca · *Red Sea* · CIRCASSIA · GEORGIA · CAUCASUS MTS. · Mosul · Malatya · *Euphrates R.* · HEJAZ · KHANATE OF CRIMEA · Trebizond · Erzerum · DIYARBAKIR · SYRIA · Damascus · Aleppo · *Dead Sea* · *Jordan R.* · SINAI PENINSULA · *Gulf of Aqaba* · *Nile R.* · *Dnieper R.* · *Black Sea* · Ankara · ANATOLIA · Konya · Acre · PALESTINE · Jerusalem · Damietta · Heliopolis · Suez · Taba · *Gulf of Suez* · Iznik · *Bosporus* · Bursa · Izmir · CYPRUS · Rosetta · Cairo · EGYPT · *Dardanelles* · Istanbul · Abu Qir Bay · Alexandria · Dinshaway · MOLDAVIA · WALLACHIA · BULGARIA · MACEDONIA · Salonika · *Aegean Sea* · GREECE · Athens · *Mediterranean Sea* · HUNGARY · Belgrade · SERBIA · MONTENEGRO · ALBANIA · THESSALY · Lepanto · Navarino · BOSNIA · HERZEGOVINA · *Danube R.* · Vienna · Venice · Genoa · Rome · Naples · *Malta* · Tripoli · FRANCE · Marseille · Toulon · *Corsica* · Tunis · Algiers · SPAIN · ATLANTIC OCEAN they paid tribute to Istanbul and recognized Ottoman authority. From that year until Napoléon Bonaparte's invasion in 1798, Egypt was ruled by the Ottomans in name only; in fact, the Mamluks continued to govern, aided by the local ulama.

Broadly speaking, the 16th century was one of prosperity for Egypt, as it was for most of the Ottoman Empire. Public order led to high agricultural production, making Egypt the main supplier of rice, sugar, and lentils to the sultan's court in Istanbul. The Circassian Mamluks continued to control the rural areas, especially in the Delta; their power was enhanced by tax farming, a system in which the state gave to designated agents (usually, in Egypt's case, Mamluks, but also ulama and even Copts and Jews) the right to collect land taxes from the peasants as long as they paid a percentage or a fixed amount to the Ottoman rulers in Istanbul. Arab tribes held power in many parts of Upper Egypt. Ulama and merchants prospered in Cairo and the port cities; al-Azhar, founded in Cairo by the Fatimids in 972, emerged as preeminent among Egypt's madrasas. Muslim mysticism, or Sufism, grew ever more central in the lives of most Egyptians. Christians and Jews suffered sporadic persecution from the governors or the troops, often in the form of demands on the religious group as a whole to come up with specified sums of money, but generally managed their own affairs and lived well.

Nevertheless, some observers have considered the Ottoman period a dark age in Egypt's history (see, for example, Young 1927, 24–28; Ghorbal 1928, 1–2; Little 1967, 25–26). Egypt did suffer as a commercial center, because some European nations were building long-distance sailing ships and expanding their power. Portuguese forays around southern Africa and across the Indian Ocean, and Columbus's successive voyages across the Atlantic to the Americas, opened up new commercial routes to the Europeans. Ottoman and Egyptian trade with Genoa, Venice, and Marseille continued, but gradually waned in importance. The growth of the coffee trade in the 17th century provided new opportunities for Yemeni and Egyptian merchants, while sugar and flax exports declined. Agricultural production could suffer during periods of low Nile floods or outbreaks of plague, but these tended to occur at random times. Any loss of world commerce meant less money for maintaining public works, schools, and mosques, as well as less revenue for the Ottoman imperial government in general and particularly for Egypt.

At the end of the 16th century a general military and financial crisis led to changes in the empire. As the Ottoman administration grew more bureaucratic and tied to Sunni Islam, Egypt became a refuge for discontented troops fleeing Anatolia. This led to street brawls in Cairo, fac-

TAX FARMING

Egypt was, up to recent times, a mainly agrarian country, and most of the government's revenues came in the form of taxes exacted on the country's agricultural produce. When the Ottomans conquered Egypt, the collection of all agricultural taxes was entrusted by Sultan Selim I to his appointed governor in Cairo. He in turn assigned the collection in Egypt's provinces to their chief administrators, most of whom were mamluks, the locally based military hierarchy.

In the early stages of Ottoman rule the central government was able to maintain control over the provincial administrators, who received salaries and were required to turn over all tax revenues to the governor, who in turn sent the lion's share to the imperial capital, Istanbul. Later, as state control weakened, the provincial governors were allowed to turn over collection of agricultural taxes to tax farmers, who would pay a fixed sum to the provincial governors, who would remit most of that sum to the governor in Cairo, who in turn would pay tribute to the Ottoman sultan's government in Istanbul.

It was in the tax farmer's interest to collect as much revenue as possible from the peasant and to pocket as many of the proceeds as he or she could. The tax farmer did not necessarily pay attention to the productivity of the land or the welfare of the peasants, as a landlord might have done. In Egypt most of the tax farmers were mamluks, but some were *ulama* or rural landowners who had acquired the right to collect the taxes from their less wealthy neighbors. Although the tax-farming system guaranteed revenues for the government, it tended to impoverish and demoralize the peasants. It should be added that taxation was usually apportioned to each village as a whole. If some peasants fled from the lands they were supposed to till, the other residents of that village could be forced to make up any loss of revenue that resulted from their flight. Some villages were totally abandoned and had to be stricken from the tax rolls. Consequently, Egypt as a whole tended to lose both agricultural output and rural population during the Ottoman period.

tional strife, and competition for power. These officer-refugees acquired tax farms, partly to make up for irregular payment of their salaries by the Ottoman government; their exactions tended to impoverish the peasants. Following an Ottoman social pattern, Egypt generally became divided into distinct households, which were patron-client networks not necessarily related to kinship, and the Mamluks increasingly split into competing factions that took money from the peasants and the merchants at a time when their factional feuds caused a breakdown in social order both in the rural areas and in the cities.

Egypt in Decline

In the first half of the 18th century Egypt prospered owing to its high agricultural output and its leading position as a seller of coffee, sugar, and rice to Europe and to other parts of the Ottoman Empire. Later, however, Egypt's economy declined as Europeans took control of seaborne trade in these commodities and increasingly imported them from the Americas. One interesting exception was the introduction of an American product, tobacco, into Egypt, where it became a significant cash crop.

Local Mamluks, notably Ali Bey (r. 1760–72) and his lieutenant, Muhammad Bey Abu al-Dhahab (r. 1772–75), tried to reform Egypt's government and economy by cutting it off from Ottoman rule. Their efforts may be seen as harbingers of the more successful reforms undertaken by Mehmet Ali in the 19th century. Nevertheless, their attempts to conquer Syria, in open rebellion against the Ottoman sultan, proved to be costly failures. Abu al-Dhahab later turned against his former mentor, Ali Bey. After Abu al-Dhahab's death in 1775, the Mamluks again fought bitterly for control of Egypt, doing great harm to the Egyptian economy.

Between 1750 and 1798 the country suffered a number of natural disasters, Mamluk revolts, factional strife, and Bedouin raids. Unable to pay the huge sums that the tax farmers demanded, many peasants left their villages and turned to a nomadic lifestyle. As food grew scarce, some city dwellers were reduced by starvation to eating dogs, cats, rats, and dead animals found in the streets, and reportedly even their own children (al-Sayyid Marsot 1984, 15). The population, estimated at 7 million in pharaonic times and possibly as high as 12–14 million at the time of the Arab conquest, had fallen to 3.8 million in 1798 (McCarthy 1976, 1).

The political and economic decline brought Egypt to its lowest point. To the French soldiers and savants who invaded Egypt in 1798, and to later generations who read their descriptions of Egyptian society, it appeared that the country had declined for centuries and its people had long wallowed in misery. But the truth is that Egypt's power, prosperity, cohesion, and intellectual glory have declined and revived many times throughout history. The late 18th century marked only a brief interlude.

5

EARLY WESTERNIZING
REFORM (1798–1879)

Conventional accounts depict 18th century Egypt as a poor, isolated, and neglected Ottoman province. It was not, however,
utterly stagnant. Even if Egypt had lost its central place in the international coffee trade, many East Asian spices and some African gold still
passed through Suez and Cairo. Egyptians went on spinning cotton,
flax, and wool into thread and weaving fine textiles, but in smaller
quantities than before. They still raised sugar, rice, and wheat for sale
to Europe. But the recurrent plague, famines caused by insufficient Nile
floods, and civil disorders resulting from Mamluk rivalries and power
struggles with Ottoman governors combined to impoverish the country. Egypt needed a comprehensive program of reform.

Even in those dark times Egypt had would-be reformers. Such
Mamluks as Ali Bey and Muhammad Bey Abu al-Dhahab proved that
a strong government could concentrate military and political power
and mobilize Egypt's resources, although these leaders failed in their
attempt to detach the country from the faltering Ottoman Empire, and
the cost of their invasion of Syria weakened Egypt's economy. Young
estimates that cost at 26 million pounds sterling. (Young 1927, 27)

At the same time, Egypt had a vibrant intellectual and cultural life. Al-
Azhar, the world's oldest Islamic university, was growing even as other
Muslim madrasas, or schools, were faltering. One of its leading scholars
was Murtada al-Zabidi (1732–91), whose *Taj al-arus* did for Arabic what
the *Oxford English Dictionary* does for the English language. Hasan al-
Attar (1766–1835) began his long career as a theologian, philosopher,
logician, and finally rector at Al-Azhar. Abd al-Rahman al-Jabarti (1754–
1825), a prolific biographer and historian, started writing his chronicle
of contemporary events, now the major source for Egypt's political and
social history in that era. So there was light amid the gloom. A French

invasion in 1798 would throw Egypt into the glare of European political rivalry, but this chapter will discuss whether the ensuing reforms occurred because of the West or whether Egypt was already developing and the reforms would have happened anyway.

The French Occupation (1798–1801)

The two major European powers, Britain and France, had long been in conflict with each other. They fought a series of bitter wars, including the Seven Years' War (known in North America as the French and Indian War), which led to France's cession of Canada and India to Britain in 1763. France avenged its loss of Canada by aiding the American colonists during their Revolutionary War, but it still hoped to regain India. The French talked about Egypt as a stepping-stone toward this goal. The French Revolution of 1789 only intensified the rivalry, as Britain joined the coalition of European monarchies seeking to restore the Bourbon kings in France.

The French pinned their hopes on a young Corsican general, Napoléon Bonaparte. By 1798 he had already led France's army on a conquering swath across northern Italy and knocked Austria out of the hostile coalition. Napoléon was clearly an asset to the French, but to the government he was also a liability. His ambition might prompt him to seize power in Paris. The government decided to have Napoléon and his troops strike at England by way of Egypt. Although England had almost no stake in Egypt at the time, the French were sure that it would fight to keep France from crossing the Middle East and retaking India.

Napoléon's armada, with some 40,000 troops, 13 large battleships, and 6 frigates, set out from Toulon, on France's Mediterranean coast, in April 1798. It swiftly captured Malta, evaded the faster British fleet commanded by Admiral Horatio Nelson, and landed near Alexandria on July 1. The sword-wielding Mamluks on horseback and irregular foot soldiers bearing scythes could not stop the advance of the well-armed French soldiers.

The main challenges for the French expeditionary force were not military but logistical. Traversing the Delta meant crossing numerous canals and desert wastes, passing deserted villages, and enduring mosquitoes and dysentery—all under a hot Egyptian sun. Napoléon's troops suffered more casualties from thirst and tropical diseases than from their enemies in battle. Lacking modern arms and discipline, the Mamluks were routed near the Pyramids. On July 21, 1798, the French entered Cairo.

Napoléon Addressing His Troops. The Battle of the Pyramids *is a grandiose but misleading name for the action in which the French troops commanded by Napoléon defeated the Mamluks and took Cairo in July 1798. The artist, Antoine-Jean Gros, took liberties in depicting a scene that glorifies France.* (Réunion des Musées Nationaux/Art Resource, NY)

Upon his arrival Napoléon assured the Egyptians: "Peoples of Egypt, you will be told that I have come to destroy your religion. This is an obvious lie; do not believe it. Answer back that I have come to restore your rights and to punish the usurpers; that I worship God more than the Mamluks do; and that I respect His prophet Muhammad and the admirable Quran" (Herold 1962, 69). Most Muslim Egyptians were not convinced.

Napoléon had managed to evade Nelson's fleet on his way to Egypt, but the British admiral did not give up his pursuit. On August 1, 1798, Nelson destroyed Napoléon's fleet in Abu Qir Bay, near Alexandria. The reputation of the French was damaged; however, the Egyptians had no means to resist Napoléon's troops on land. It would take the British and the Ottomans months to sign a defensive alliance treaty (for the text, see Hurewitz 1956, I, 65–67) and to send an expedition to drive him out.

Meanwhile, Napoléon set up a *diwan*, a provisional governing council selected by the French generals commanding in Egypt's provinces and made up of ulama and rural landowners. They were charged with organizing provincial assemblies, formulating new civil and criminal codes, systematizing the succession system, and revising the laws concerning property and taxation (Ghorbal 1928, 72–73). The Cairenes, who suspected that the *diwan* was intended to raise taxes, opposed it. Soon they started a rebellion, led by the merchant guilds and Sufi brotherhoods. Firing down on the main mosques from the Citadel, the French proved that their rule would be as repressive as that of the Mamluks. Local Muslims were also offended by the French troops' behavior, including public drinking, stealing private property, and accosting local women.

Napoléon's expedition consisted of more than soldiers, however. It also included 167 artists, scholars, and scientists. They set out to explore and describe Egypt thoroughly. Their findings were published in a remarkable 23-volume work, *Description de l'Égypte,* which gave a detailed picture of the country and awakened Europe's interest in pharaonic Egypt. While the expedition's main aim was conquest, not scholarship, such finds as the Rosetta Stone, which eventually enabled historians to decipher hieroglyphics, added greatly to the understanding of ancient Egypt.

Napoléon viewed Egypt as the first step toward his goal of building a larger empire. He wrote to a woman friend: "In Egypt, I found myself freed from the obstacles of an irksome civilization. I was full of dreams. . . . I saw myself founding a religion, marching into Asia, riding an elephant, a turban on my head and in my hand the new Quran that I would have composed to suit my needs" (Herold 1962, 5). The French Directory (government) encouraged him to proceed to India, and he even wrote to Tippoo Sahib, sultan of the Kingdom of Mysore in southern India, offering to help his revolt to free his land from "the iron yoke of England." Napoléon's vision of a new empire, patterned after that of Alexander the Great and centered in Alexandria, would drive him and his men toward India.

In pursuance of this goal, he led his troops into Palestine. His failure to take the Ottoman fortress at Acre raised Egyptian hopes for a rescue from French rule, but in July 1799 Napoléon's troops easily repulsed an Ottoman landing at Abu Qir Bay. A month later he turned over command of the Egyptian expedition to General Jean-Baptiste Kléber and sailed back to France, where he promptly seized control of the country. Kléber reached an agreement with the Ottomans, the Convention of al-Arish, that would have restored Egypt to Ottoman control and allowed the French troops to leave peacefully. The British government, however, rejected the Convention and ordered its fleet not to let the French pass until they surrendered. By the time the British reconsidered their position, fighting had resumed, the French had defeated the Ottoman army at Heliopolis, and Kléber had been assassinated.

The new French commander, General Jacques Abdallah Menou, had converted to Islam to marry an Egyptian woman. Less interested than Kléber in leaving Egypt, he restored the Egyptian *diwan* and drew up elaborate plans to promote agriculture, commerce, and industry. These reforms would clearly require higher taxes. When Menou began to survey landholdings to raise their assessments, all social classes in Egypt became alarmed. But relief was in sight. A joint Anglo-Ottoman force occupied the Delta in March 1801 and defeated the French. Both the British and the Ottomans were eager to hasten France's departure from Egypt, but they disagreed on how to achieve it. Britain and the Ottoman Empire ended up signing separate peace treaties with France in 1802. The French troops left, followed by the British. An Ottoman army of occupation remained to restore order.

Effects of the French Occupation

In spring 1998 this writer attended a meeting of Egyptian historians who decried a decision by Egypt's culture minister to take part in celebrating, with France, the bicentennial of the French occupation. Most of them argued that the occupation's direct effect on Egypt was negligible. Napoléon's innovative *diwan* vanished once his army left. A few French soldiers stayed in post-Napoleonic Egypt, just as some Mamluks and Egyptians accompanied Napoléon back to France. However, Britain's policy of restoring the Mamluk regime also failed. Napoléon had strengthened the ulama. No longer would they defer to the Mamluk factions that had contended for mastery of Egypt before 1798. The Ottomans, then carrying out their own Westernization program, hoped to use their appointed governor to rule Egypt directly. They soon found, however, that they were no longer in charge. The French occupation had accelerated changes that had begun under Ali Bey and Abu al-Dhahab. Egypt would never go back.

Mehmet Ali (1769–1849) and His Reforms

But who would rule Egypt, if not the French, the British, the Mamluks, or the Ottomans? The traditional leaders of the Egyptian people were the ulama and the heads of the Sufi orders, but they were unaccustomed to political responsibility and had split into many factions. This political void was filled by an unlikely candidate: a stocky adventurer named Mehmet Ali (Muhammad 'Ali in Arabic). He had come to Egypt in 1801 with a 300-man Albanian regiment sent to augment the Ottoman army opposing the French forces. Although his background was Albanian, he had been trained as an Ottoman officer. He spoke mainly Turkish, not Arabic. He did not learn to read until he was 45. Yet Mehmet Ali succeeded where Napoléon had failed and accomplished more for Egypt than any of his better-educated royal descendants.

To anyone coming from the Balkans, the Nile Delta and Valley seem a paradise of verdant fields and flowing waters. Though for the past quarter century Egypt had been battered by plagues, natural disasters, and incompetent rule, it still could recover its ancient prosperity. But it needed a single powerful ruler, not a rabble of competing warriors. By 1805 rivalries among the various Mamluk factions, abetted by the British, the French, and the Ottomans, had dissipated their strength and eliminated their leaders. Mehmet Ali won the support of the *ulama* and trade guilds, discredited two Ottoman governors in succession, and persuaded the sultan to appoint him viceroy in their stead. To ensure his hold on power, he had to get rid of the Mamluks. No longer were they allowed to replenish their ranks by importing new slaves from the Caucasus or Central Asia; they had either to turn into a hereditary caste or to die out altogether. In 1811, to hasten their end, Mehmet Ali invited most of the Mamluk chieftains and their supporters to a ceremony at which his men proceeded to massacre them. Seemingly, he now reigned supreme.

Mehmet Ali had not come to power with a plan to regenerate Egypt; he wanted only to consolidate his new position and to avoid being overthrown, as so many previous Ottoman governors had been. He wanted to seem, in the eyes of the sultan, indispensable to the Ottoman Empire. When the Wahhabis, puritanical Muslims who ruled in central Arabia, seized the holy cities of Mecca and Medina, it was Mehmet Ali's army that defeated the rebels and restored the land to Ottoman control in 1818.

Agricultural Reforms

Mehmet Ali was preoccupied with building an army and the means to support it. Land was his obsession. If he collected taxes from the peasants at rates as extortionate as any Mamluk tax farmer, it was because he wanted to enlarge his treasury as a means of expanding his army and bodyguard. In 1808 he established a government monopoly over the grain trade, ordered a cadastral survey, or census, of who owned what parcels of land in 1813–14, and abolished the tax-farming system throughout Egypt by 1820. His government also seized many family and religious *waqf*s (endowments, pl. *awqaf*), which had controlled much of Egypt's cultivated land.

In their place he established state control over the land, giving his government the power to decree what the peasants sowed; to supply their seed, tools, fertilizer, and irrigation water; and to set the prices it would pay for their produce. Later in his rule, when Egypt could afford to hire French engineers to supervise the construction of canals, dams, and weirs in a few favored areas of the Nile Valley and Delta, the government replaced the traditional basin irrigation system. The new system, called perennial irrigation, lengthened the time span during which Nile floodwaters were stored for irrigation. This change enabled peasants in those areas to raise three crops annually on lands where formerly they had grown only one.

Cash crops, such as wheat, had long been grown in the Delta. Now, as European markets expanded, new cash crops, such as indigo, tobacco, and long-staple cotton, were introduced. Gradually, Egypt regained its former agricultural prosperity. However, to effect this, the peasants had to work harder. The increased work also gave them an incentive to have larger families, as they needed their children's labor in the fields. The population, which had fallen in the late 18th century to 3.8 million, began to rise. By 1880 there would be 7.5 million Egyptians.

Greater agricultural yields, higher state revenues, and more Egyptians all facilitated the processes by which Mehmet Ali strengthened his rule and built up his army. As the Albanian soldiers whom he had originally brought with him to Egypt diminished, Mehmet Ali tried replacing them with European officers (especially the French following Napoléon's final defeat in 1815), Ottoman Turks, North Africans, Bedouins, and Sudanese slaves, but none of them fulfilled his military needs. Starting in 1821, his government conscripted Egyptian peasants into the army. No ruler since the Ptolemies had done this, and the peasants hated it. The villagers often held funerals for their conscripted sons, for few of them ever returned. They had to be trained, disciplined, housed, clothed, fed, and kept healthy. Local industries, together with barracks, schools, hospitals, and an expanded bureaucracy, were needed to sustain this army, which would grow to 130,000 in 1832. But arming those Egyptians made them into a disciplined force and ultimately empowered their descendants to play a role in Egypt's national life.

Early Industrialization

Expanding cash crop production called for corresponding developments in transportation and distribution. Mehmet Ali's reign saw the growth of a network of barge canals, river ports, and cart roads, together with grain weighing and storage facilities, cotton gins, sugar refineries, and other capital improvements. These improvements facilitated the rise in agricultural output and also furthered industrialization, for the government needed to get around the high cost of importing goods from Europe and the Ottoman Empire.

Egypt became the first non-Western state to attempt an industrial revolution, creating factories to make soap, paper, cloth, warships, and armaments. For this industrial revolution to succeed, factory workers were needed. Peasants were conscripted to work in the factories at low and irregularly paid wages, for the bureaucracy was inefficient and often corrupt. Workers, resenting their low pay, long hours, and the discipline of factory work, resorted to throwing sand into the imported machinery or other forms of sabotage. Most of the engineers and managers were foreign, and none of the industries would yield any profit to the Egyptian government. But as time passed the factory system, with its demands for worker discipline and fixed schedules, came to dominate the lives of some Egyptians. With the expanded army and the factories came schools of engineering, medicine, midwifery, languages, administration, and even arts and crafts.

Increased Military Power

Mehmet Ali made Egypt a military power second to none in the Middle East. Having subdued the Wahhabi rebels and restored Mecca and Medina to Ottoman control in 1818, the Egyptian army went on to capture the Upper Nile, hoping to control the slaves, ivory, and gold that Egypt had long imported from what is now Sudan. Much of that land had been ruled by the Funj sultans of Sennar since about 1607, but that sultanate was losing power to local tribes by the early 19th century. Mehmet Ali's troops easily defeated them and gradually established Egyptian rule.

In 1823, when the Greeks seemed to be winning their war for independence from the Ottoman Empire, Mehmet Ali's eldest son, Ibrahim, led an Egyptian force to support the Ottomans. The European powers sank the Turco-Egyptian fleet, however, giving victory to the Greeks, and the Ottoman sultan reneged on a promise to reward his Egyptian viceroy with Syria and Crete. Mehmet Ali, angered at the sultan's perfidy, sent a large army commanded by Ibrahim, into Syria. By the end of 1832 his rule extended from the Hejaz to central Anatolia. Had the Ottomans not won Russia's timely backing, they could have lost their whole empire to Mehmet Ali and Ibrahim.

British Opposition to Mehmet Ali

At the beginning of the 19th century Britain's main interest in Egypt was to oust the French from ruling over it and make certain that they did not return. When Mehmet Ali first became governor in 1805, Britain focused on guarding its routes to India. Passage from the Red Sea to the Mediterranean across Egypt or Sinai was dangerous and expensive, so the British were trying to establish ties with the sultan of Oman and the various Arab amirs and sheikhs along the Persian Gulf. Britain was willing to back anyone who could establish control in Egypt—including Mehmet Ali. By the 1830s, however, the British had come to distrust Mehmet Ali. They realized that an Egyptian empire that included Syria could keep them from developing a passage to India via the Euphrates River and the Persian Gulf. Another reason was that Mehmet Ali, backed by French officers and advisers, posed a threat to the Ottoman Empire. If Mehmet Ali were to overthrow the Ottoman ruler, Sultan Mahmud II (r. 1808–39), and seize the empire, he could upset the European balance of power that had been established after the defeat of Napoléon in 1815. Finally, if Mehmet Ali's fledgling industries succeeded, they could take markets from British manufactures, and the newly enfranchised British factory owners pressured the government to take resolute action to uphold their economic interests.

Ibrahim's conquest of Syria and his invasion of Anatolia prompted Sultan Mahmud to turn to Russia for help in 1833. The Ottoman Empire signed a treaty that made the Russians the guarantors of its territorial integrity. The British saw this as giving Russia the right to send warships through the Turkish straits into the Mediterranean. To forestall Russian domination of southeastern Europe, Britain signed a commercial pact with the Ottoman Empire that made Britain the Ottomans' main trading partner for the rest of the 19th century. By limiting protective tariffs on manufactured goods imported into Ottoman territories, the treaty also enabled cheap British manufactures to undercut local handicrafts, weakening and destroying industries wherever the treaty was applied. After 1840 this would include Egypt.

In 1839, after an unsuccessful Ottoman expedition to recapture the lands taken earlier by Ibrahim, Sultan Mahmud II died. His entire fleet sailed to Alexandria and defected to Egypt. To preserve the European balance of power, Britain, Russia, Prussia, and Austria supported the Ottomans against Egypt, which was aided only by France. After protracted negotiations, Mehmet Ali agreed to pull out of Syria and to reduce the size of his army to 20,000 men. In return the Ottoman sultan, backed by the European powers, issued a decree that recognized Mehmet

Mehmet Ali Negotiating with the Europeans. This painting by the 19th-century artist David Roberts shows the Egyptian viceroy (khedive) discussing his country's future with the British following their intervention against him in 1839–40. (Library of Congress)

Ali's right to pass down the governorship to his heirs. Starting in 1841 Egypt was an autonomous province within the Ottoman Empire.

Egypt was now an independent state in all but name. It had its own bureaucracy and army (although the latter was limited). Its government could pursue its policies with only limited reference to the wishes of the Ottoman sultan. One setback for Egypt was its subjection to the 1838 Anglo-Ottoman commercial treaty. No longer could Egypt protect its infant industries from competing foreign manufactures. But these businesses were neither numerous nor profitable. Chagrined at being deprived of Syria and of his large army in 1840, Mehmet Ali lost interest in his factories, schools, and estates and began turning control over to his surviving sons and his most trusted aides. Clearly, Mehmet Ali saw Egypt and its people as the means by which he could gain and keep power for himself and his family. He was the founder of the modern Egyptian state; he was not the first Egyptian nationalist. He never meant Egypt to be ruled by or for Egyptians.

Mehmet Ali's achievement lies in what survived his final years of demoralization. Egypt's new bureaucratic and military institutions, severed from those of the Ottoman Empire, gave his heirs room to maneuver and a freedom recognized by the European powers—with only vestigial restraints from Istanbul. Egyptians, Ottomans, and Westerners became accustomed to regarding Egypt as an autonomous state. Even though Mehmet Ali's schools closed down or shrank in enrollment in the last years of his reign, Egypt now had a corps of trained bureaucrats and army officers, some of whom were committed to Westernizing reform and to Egypt's autonomy. The foundations of modern Egypt were firmly laid.

Given the conditions prevalent in the 19th century, Europe's economic and cultural ascendancy over Egypt was unavoidable. But Europe's political and military control could have been delayed or lessened if the Ottoman Empire had been stronger and, more important still, if Mehmet Ali's heirs had been as wise as he. Mehmet Ali may have been uneducated, but he was shrewd. He refused to borrow money from European banks to finance his reforms. He blocked any scheme

Mehmet Ali's palace. This photograph, probably taken in the late 19th century, shows the palace occupied by Mehmet Ali and his successors. Shubra, once an elegant Cairo neighborhood, is now rather shabby and overcrowded. (Library of Congress)

to cut a canal from the Mediterranean to the Red Sea, fearing that such a strategic waterway would prove irresistible to European powers. Knowing Britain's interest in controlling access to India, Mehmet Ali expected that it would eventually seize any canal piercing the Isthmus of Suez.

Mehmet Ali's Successors

As Mehmet Ali lapsed into senility, his eldest son, Ibrahim (1789–1848), who had so successfully led the Egyptian army in a number of campaigns, acted as regent and governed on his behalf. Ibrahim was Mehmet Ali's intended heir. Ibrahim's unexpected death in November 1848 meant that a new regent was needed. According to the custom of Muslim dynasties, the eldest male member of the family succeeded, making the new regent a grandson, Abbas Hilmi I, who was 10 years older than his uncle, Said, the next in line. On Mehmet Ali's death, Abbas (1813–54) became the new viceroy. Abbas reduced taxes and continued the policy of divesting the state lands, factories, and schools that his grandfather had created but had allowed to deteriorate after 1841.

Having long been ignored by Mehmet Ali and Ibrahim, Abbas now dismissed their officials and advisers and reversed their pro-French policies. One consequence of this change was that in 1851 Abbas awarded the British a concession to build Egypt's first rail line, linking Alexandria and Cairo. More and more people and goods were moving between Europe and India, but the usual journey was by sailing ship, taking four months via the Cape of Good Hope. Egypt's first rail line shortened the journey from London to Bombay to about six weeks; travelers went from London to Alexandria by ship, with transfers to a train at Alexandria, a stagecoach in Cairo, and another ship at Suez.

Understandably, travelers and traders would have preferred a canal across the Isthmus of Suez. Canals linking the Nile River to the Gulf of Suez had been built by one of the pharaohs and by the Fatimids, and Europeans had long argued for a canal connecting the Mediterranean with the Red Sea. France had commissioned Napoléon's expedition to study the feasibility of a canal. Mehmet Ali opposed the project because he thought that a canal would create the same problem for Egypt that the Ottomans had defending the straits connecting the Mediterranean with the Russian-dominated Black Sea. In 1841 a British officer of the Peninsular and Oriental Shipping Line, which owned many of the ships

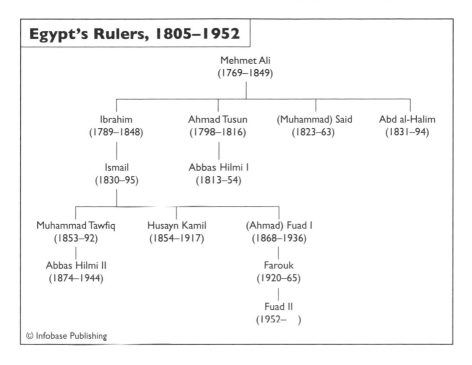

Egypt's Rulers, 1805–1952

Mehmet Ali
(1769–1849)

Ibrahim
(1789–1848)

Ahmad Tusun
(1798–1816)

(Muhammad) Said
(1823–63)

Abd al-Halim
(1831–94)

Ismail
(1830–95)

Abbas Hilmi I
(1813–54)

Muhammad Tawfiq
(1853–92)

Husayn Kamil
(1854–1917)

(Ahmad) Fuad I
(1868–1936)

Abbas Hilmi II
(1874–1944)

Farouk
(1920–65)

Fuad II
(1952–   )

© Infobase Publishing

that carried goods between England and India, drafted a detailed canal project. By the early 1850s the obstacles to a maritime canal through Egypt were more political than technical.

In 1854 Abbas was murdered by his palace guard. Mehmet Ali's eldest surviving son, Said (1823–63), became Egypt's new viceroy. Educated by European teachers, Said favored his father's policy of Westernization from above. One of his oldest friends was Ferdinand de Lesseps (1805–94), a former French diplomat. When Said came to power, De Lesseps, who had resigned from the diplomatic corps, hastened to Egypt. Soon he persuaded Said to let him set up a company, chartered in Egypt, to cut a canal across the Isthmus of Suez from the Mediterranean to the Red Sea. The company would be financed by selling shares to investors from every nation, including the Egyptian government, which would furnish the laborers needed to dig the canal. It would be managed by a board of directors, whose chairman would be named by Egypt's viceroy. De Lesseps depicted in glowing terms the benefits that the Suez Canal would bring to European business, to Egypt, to Muslim pilgrims, and, of course, to Said, whose name would be immortalized by the world for sponsoring this engineering marvel.

Hired Egyptian workers and their donkeys remove earth from the future bed of the Suez Canal in early 1869. Although dredging machines had replaced unpaid peasant laborers for most excavation work, human labor was still needed as the deadline for completing the canal drew near. (Illustrated London News, March 13, 1869)

De Lesseps was a shrewd bargainer and a persuasive advocate. Said's motives remain obscure. He probably wanted the glory of having patronized the canal and may also have sought a barrier to the passage of armies or Bedouin nomads between his lands and those of his Ottoman overlord in Syria and Palestine. As a large landowner, he may have hoped to promote the sale abroad of such cash crops as sugar, rice, and long-staple cotton. De Lesseps seems to have sincerely believed in the canal; his material reward would be slight. But the Ottoman sultan, preoccupied with the Crimean War, withheld his consent. Even though France and Britain were currently allies in that war against Russia, the British government opposed a canal built by a French national. Britain could remember when Napoléon and Mehmet Ali had threatened to seize control of the main routes to India. In addition, a British subject had built the rail link between Alexandria and Cairo, a competing venture. British investors were dissuaded from buying stock in De Lesseps's company by the opposition of the prime minister, Parliament, and the press. This prevented the Suez Canal Company from raising the 200 million francs (worth U.S. $40 million in 1860) needed to fund the construction.

The logistics of building a canal were formidable. The work would require at least 20,000 laborers each year. Egypt's government would conscript them from a population of 5 million, even though slavery and forced labor had been outlawed by an Ottoman decree in 1841. A special canal would have to be cut from the Nile to carry water to the work site. Food, equipment, and supplies would have to be transported into this bleak desert environment. De Lesseps was neither an engineer nor a manager. But he was an inspiring leader, willing to flout conventional wisdom, Egyptian interests, and Ottoman laws to build the canal. Most of the canal was dug before the company had amassed the necessary capital and before the labor supply dried up. When the company's shares failed to sell, De Lesseps persuaded Said to buy more of them. When he needed to buy or sell land along the canal site, the viceroy helped.

The use of forced Egyptian labor to build the Suez Canal was a major issue. Said had agreed to conscript peasants to work on the canal. When the Ottoman government called a halt to conscription of peasant labor, the Egyptian government paid the company a handsome indemnity that enabled the company to buy dredging machines. Egyptians maintain that the peasants had to provide their own food, water, and tools; that they were often reduced to digging the canal with their bare hands; and that 120,000 peasants may have died of malnutrition, disease, and overwork while digging the canal. In the early phases of the project, working conditions were indeed bad, for no one really foresaw how much it would cost, how many workers would be needed, or indeed how much of the work could be completed by dredging machines. During the early 1860s, with slavery already abolished in all British, French, and Ottoman dominions, with the American Civil War under way, and with the abolition of serfdom in Russia, liberal-minded Europeans questioned the conscription of Egyptian peasants. The company learned how to ensure that they were properly fed, housed, and cared for if they fell ill. They received compensation at the end of their labors, and most returned safely to their villages. As De Lesseps told one of his foremen: "Treat the natives well; they are men" (Karabell 2003, 167–179; Kinross 1969, 171–175; Marlowe 1964, 192–193).

Other changes were taking place within Egypt during Said's reign. The process of dismantling Mehmet Ali's monopolies on industry and farmland had continued under Abbas and was completed under Said. One of the dominant themes in Egypt's modern history has been the gradual movement of ethnic Egyptians toward stage center. Later chapters of this book will show how nationalist leaders such as Ahmad Urabi (1841–1911) and Saad Zaghlul (1860?–1927), Muslim reformers such as Muhammad Abduh (1849–1905), and intellectuals such as Ahmad Lutfi al-Sayyid (1872–1963) would rise to eminence from Egyptian peasant backgrounds. In 1858 a new Ottoman Land Law, applicable also to Egypt, permitted individuals to buy and own land or other property within the empire. Ethnic Egyptians bought land and created new estates. Some became state officials and army officers, for Said often took the sons of village headmen to be trained in his military and naval academies. This was his means of controlling the village headmen, but it helped some of their sons rise to powerful posts later on.

Europeans, too, became more prominent in the time of Said, who encouraged them to settle in Alexandria and Cairo. Many served Egypt as entrepreneurs, engineers, and educators, but some were swindlers and petty criminals. All were protected by a series of agreements known as the Capitulations that originated in the 15th century, when Ottoman sultans granted them to some European powers to facilitate trade. In general these agreements said that foreign residents were subject to the laws of their home countries, not the Ottoman Empire. They exempted Westerners from the obligation to pay any taxes unless their governments had agreed to them. Greeks and Italians, often fleeing poverty back home, were the most numerous abusers of the Capitulations, but every Western country exploited them to some degree to import goods, open business firms, and even defy Ottoman or Egyptian laws with impunity. Native minorities, especially Armenians and Jews, were often hired as local consuls, interpreters, or attachés by European or U.S. diplomatic missions. This gave them foreign nationality and hence legal and fiscal immunity. Although Egypt's Muslims may have benefited from the canals, railways, paved streets, piped water, gas lights, and modern schools and factories that European enterprise brought, at least to Alexandria and Cairo, they resented the economic advantages granted to foreigners, the exalted status of minorities, and the rising prices for houses and farmland. This resentment would surface later, with the rise of the Arabic periodical press in the 1870s (Ahmed 1960, 17–23; Hunter 1984, 179–201; Landes 1958, 324–326).

Said's reign was short. Near its end an ominous new trend began. Said was constantly pressured by European settlers and investors for various claims against the Egyptian government (Karabell 2003, 65–72, 179–182; Marlowe 1975, 87–99). Although Egypt's land usually yielded enough taxes to meet state expenditures, Said began borrowing money from European bankers to finance railroads, telegraph lines, and ambitious public works projects, not to mention his guarantee to De Lesseps to buy any Suez Canal Company shares that were not sold to the public. When Ismail succeeded him in 1863, Egypt had a foreign debt of about 6 million pounds sterling (U.S. $30 million).

Khedive Ismail (r. 1863–1879)

Ismail, the son of Ibrahim and grandson of Mehmet Ali, seemed to both Europeans and Egyptians a promising ruler. Educated in the West, he spoke fluent French. His private estates had become model farms. Speaking to the European consuls following his accession, he pledged not to increase the Egyptian national debt. He did not keep this promise.

The early years of Ismail's rule were a boom period in Egypt. The American Civil War was preventing Southern cotton from reaching England's textile mills. British spinners and weavers, facing financial ruin, offered to pay premium prices for cotton from other sources. Only a few countries could grow cotton on a large scale. Of these, only Egypt could produce large quantities of the long-staple cotton used in the finest textiles. By 1863 all Egyptian cotton was being sold to Europe at inflated prices. The country's economy was thriving. Bankers and other moneylenders flocked around Ismail, luring him into various public and private investments.

The wisdom of his fiscal policies was debated at the time and in retrospect. All praise Ismail's investment in public schools, bridges, canals, railroads, cotton gins, sugar refineries, telegraph lines, and harbors (Bell 1884, 3–23; Crabitès 1933; Hunter 1984, 70–79; Karabell 2003; Landes 1958, 128–134; Marlowe 1975, 104–117). Some of his funds financed the Egyptian army and navy, the exploration of the Upper Nile, and military campaigns in East Africa. Ismail's munificence helped pay for the Egyptian Museum, the National Library, and the Geographical Society. He also developed what has become downtown Cairo, from the Ezbekia Gardens to the Nile, hired France's best-known landscape gardener to beautify the shoreline and the main avenues of the city, erected the Opera House, and paid for the composition of Giuseppe Verdi's opera

Aida. He made the 1869 inauguration of the Suez Canal the occasion for a huge celebration, attended by royalty, the aristocracy, and the artistic and intellectual leaders of Europe. These latter expenditures gave Egypt the appearance—to the Europeans but possibly also to the Egyptians— of being more like the "advanced" countries of Europe.

But Ismail's other expenditures were criticized by contemporary observers and later Egyptian and foreign historians (Cromer 1908, I, 11–146; Jerrold 1879; Marlowe 1975, 119–126). To further Egypt's autonomy from the Ottoman Empire, Ismail's agents bribed Ottoman politicians and increased the tribute Egypt paid to the sultan. As a result of these payments Ismail was authorized to take the title of khedive (a Persian term meaning, roughly, "prince" and used by some earlier viceroys without Ottoman permission), to enlarge his army and to build a navy, to name his son as successor to the khedivate instead of Prince Abd al-Halim (Mehmet Ali's last surviving son), and to float foreign loans without prior Ottoman consent. Much of the borrowed money went to build palaces and yachts, to support his cronies, to buy Paris gowns for his wives, and to bribe influential journalists to write positive articles about him in the European press. Egypt's foreign debt skyrocketed. Once the American Civil War ended and Southern cotton again became available, Egypt's cotton boom ceased, tax revenues fell, and the terms demanded by foreign lenders became stricter.

By the mid-1870s Khedive Ismail had pledged all his available collateral and was desperately seeking new revenue sources. He offered to forgive Egyptian landowners half their taxes in perpetuity if they paid six years' land tax in advance. In 1875 he sold his government's shares in the Suez Canal Company to Britain for 4 million pounds (approximately $20 million), a fateful step toward British control. A British parliamentary commission investigated Egypt's finances and issued a report warning that the government was nearly bankrupt. To allay the fears of Egypt's foreign bondholders, the khedive agreed in 1876 to create a debt commission made up of representatives of Britain, France, Italy, and Austria. When a new budget crisis arose, caused by a low Nile and high military outlays for Egypt's involvement in the 1877 Russo-Turkish War, he allowed Britain and France to set up their Dual Financial Control over Egyptian state revenues (i.e., collecting taxes) and expenditures, including the salaries of officers and officials, support of the schools, and maintenance of the irrigation works, ports, telegraphs, and railways. All this control was intended to restore the credit of the Egyptian government and to ensure that its creditors, mainly Europeans, got repaid for their earlier loans.

Khedive Ismail Greets the Prince of Wales. *The future Edward VII arrived at the Cairo Railroad Station in November 1875 for an Egyptian visit on his way to India. Ismail's best days as khedive were behind him, and Egypt's government was almost bankrupt.* (Illustrated London News, November 20, 1875)

Even the Dual Control failed to solve Egypt's fiscal crisis. Ismail tried again to address it in August 1878. He added an English and a French minister to his cabinet and named an Armenian as its premier. He pledged to rule through his ministers, ending the despotism that had characterized Egyptian government since Mehmet Ali's reign. In making his pledge, he remarked: "My country is no longer in Africa; we are now a part of Europe" (Crabitès 1933, 263).

The changes that had occurred in Egypt during the preceding half-century were indeed amazing. Egypt's cities were becoming part of Europe. When Napoléon landed in Alexandria, no road in the country could accommodate wheeled vehicles. When Edward Lane, the British Orientalist, lived in Cairo in the 1830s, he felt obliged to wear Muslim clothing. Egyptians still took their meals seated cross-legged on cushions and eating with the first three fingers of their right hands. By 1878, Alexandria, Cairo, and the new Suez Canal towns—Port Said and Ismailia—had wide avenues where Europeans and Westernized Egyptians raced their horse-drawn carriages. With their railroad stations, hotels, restaurants, and department stores, these cities had come to resemble Marseille or New Orleans, if not Paris or New York. They had gaslights, piped water, and telegraph lines; the first telephones were installed in 1881, before they came to most small towns in North America. But these were superficial changes, benefiting only a small upper class. Most Egyptians still lived in abject poverty, illiterate, burdened by hard labor and high taxes, and affected only indirectly by the Westernized lifestyle of the palace and urban elite.

Early Signs of Nationalism

More profoundly, new ideas and institutions were arising among Egypt's intellectuals. Al-Azhar University remained as committed as ever to the traditional Islamic sciences, but some teachers and students were breaking away. The most famous apostle of Muslim unity, Jamal al-Din al-Afghani (1838–97), came to Cairo in 1871. When the ulama barred him from lecturing at al-Azhar, he rented rooms in a nearby bazaar where he received many young Egyptians distressed at the state of their country. He inspired such Azharites as Muhammad Abduh to seek a reformed Islam and such writers as Adib Ishaq (a Syrian Christian) and Yaacub Sanua (an Egyptian Jew) to found newspapers. Masonic lodges, which had been introduced in Cairo and Alexandria by Europeans, afforded secrecy to Egyptian malcontents as they formed the first revolutionary societies in 1878–79.

Khedive Ismail inadvertently helped create a sense that Egypt was a nation and that his subjects were citizens with political rights. He did this by financing the earliest daily newspapers, setting up state schools, convoking the first representative assembly in 1866 to raise more taxes from rural landowners, and establishing the Mixed Courts (to try civil cases involving foreign residents in Egypt) in 1876. The rudimentary journals, schools, parliaments, and law courts combined to nurture a class of educated Egyptians whose occupations called for an articulate response to events in their country. Between 1879 and 1882 some would join the army officers in forming Egypt's first nationalist party, as is explained in the next chapter.

Educated Egyptians especially resented British and French intervention in their country's government via the Dual Control. The European debt commissioners tried to trim Egyptian state expenditures. They placed the khedivial family on a tight budget and cut appropriations for public works, education, and the military. This

Al-Azhar courtyard. Schools to train ulama, experts in religious laws, are essential in Islam. Al-Azhar, founded in 972, was still Cairo's leading Islamic law school in the 19th century. Several leaders of Egypt's first nationalist movement, including Ahmad Urabi, were educated at al-Azhar. (Library of Congress)

caused long delays in paying the salaries of the officers and soldiers, many of whom were reduced to poverty as a result. An announcement in February 1879 that 1,600 of Egypt's 2,600 officers would temporarily be retired at half pay led to a noisy street demonstration during which some Egyptians seized the finance minister's carriage and manhandled several high-ranking officials. Ismail soon arrived and ordered the demonstrators back to their barracks, but he also dismissed the European ministers and appointed a caretaker cabinet headed by his son, Prince Tawfiq. Led by one of Ismail's most Westernized ministers, Sharif, a group of Egyptians started to draw up a constitution that would have given real power to an elected assembly. The khedive then rescinded the pay cuts and put Sharif in charge of a cabinet with nationalist leanings.

The European powers scrutinized these developments. Having watched Ismail's debts rise to 93 million Egyptian pounds (an astronomical sum in 1879), they doubted that an independent government

EGYPTIAN CURRENCY

In Ottoman Egypt the standard coin was the silver para, 40 of which made one piaster. The government's unit of account was the kis (purse), worth 25 thousand paras, or, in the time of Mehmet Ali and his successors, about 500 piasters. Because Ottoman coins tended to lose value, foreign merchants in Egypt used European currencies, such as the Austrian thaler and the Spanish rial. From 1836 to 1885 the main unit of currency for Egyptians was the piaster, commonly abbreviated to PT (French: *piastre tarif*); 97.5 piasters equaled one British sterling pound. The Egyptian pound (Cairene Arabic: *gineh,* from the English "guinea"), commonly abbreviated £E (French: *livre égyptienne*), consisted of a hundred piasters. Foreign coins circulated widely because of the shortage and uneven quality of Egyptian coins.

Money was backed with both gold and silver until 1885, when Egypt based its currency on gold, each pound containing 8.5 grams of gold at standard fineness. In 1887 the finance minister limited foreign currencies to the sterling pound, the French 20-franc piece, and the Turkish pound; the Egyptian government issued almost no gold pounds of its own. The sterling pound, the least undervalued of these currencies, soon became Egypt's standard. The National Bank of Egypt began issuing paper money in 1898, but its note issue stabilized at £E2.7 million until 1914. Egyptian landowners and peasants still preferred gold currency for the financing of their cotton crops.

With the outbreak of World War I in 1914, the National Bank of Egypt's notes were declared legal tender and no longer redeemable with gold. From 1916 until 1949 Egypt was on a sterling exchange system under which its currency was backed by British war loans and treasury bills. Since 1949 the Egyptian government has managed its own currency, which initially remained strong because of the large sterling balances it had accumulated during World War II. In recent years, however, the Egyptian pound has fallen in value from $4.20 in 1949 to 22 cents in 2002. The pound was tied to the U.S. dollar until January 2003; when it was allowed to float, its value soon fell to 16 cents.

Source: Based on entry in Arthur Goldschmidt Jr. and Robert Johnston, *Historical Dictionary of Egypt,* 3d ed. (Lanham, Md., and Oxford: Scarecrow Press, 2003), 119–120.

could raise the tax revenues needed to repay its European creditors. France, which had done the most to Westernize Egypt under Mehmet Ali and Ismail, claimed the right to send in troops and take over the Egyptian government. But Britain opposed a unilateral French occupation and control over Egypt, the stepping-stone to India. Britain also viewed France as having been weakened politically when it lost the Franco-Prussian War to Germany in 1871. Germany, acting on behalf of all the European powers, formally protested against Ismail's efforts to change Egypt's financial agreements and pressured the Ottoman sultan to depose him and appoint Prince Tawfiq in his place.

This crisis discredited khedivial claims to absolute rule over Egypt. The system begun by Mehmet Ali and developed by Said and Ismail had centralized state power and created a fairly competent bureaucracy and army. It started to involve ethnic Egyptians in addition to the foreign Muslims who had traditionally run the central administration. It gave Egypt a modest degree of autonomy and westernization. But it also made the economy far too dependent on Western investors, causing social and political unrest in the country.

Later on, Egyptian nationalists would regret that some form of parliamentary democracy did not replace khedivial absolutism, but indigenous political leadership was still scarce and weak, whereas the power and ambitions of the Europeans were strong. The British and French governments were willing to bully the khedive on behalf of their own (mainly capitalist) constituents. The hopes and fears of the Europeans who had settled in Egypt, or who had purchased its government's bonds, or who feared for the security of the Suez Canal, all combined to influence the Egyptian policies of Britain and France. The national interests and desires of Egypt's popular leaders did not. In summer 1882 Britain would act on its own.

6

THE BRITISH OCCUPATION AND NATIONALIST RESISTANCE (1879–1918)

On June 25, 1879, two telegrams reached the khedive's palace in Alexandria. One was addressed to "Ismail, ex-khedive of Egypt"; the other was for "His Highness Khedive Tawfiq." In this way the Ottoman government made it known that it had deposed Ismail in favor of his son. Two days later Ismail sailed off on his yacht to a gilded exile in Naples. He never saw Egypt again. The European envoys in Constantinople, mindful of their bondholders' claims against Egypt, had intervened. However, these actions would have unintended consequences. Soon, Egypt's most politically articulate army officers, ulama, teachers, and journalists would start a revolutionary nationalist movement. This would lead to British military intervention and a protracted occupation of the country.

Khedive Tawfiq (r. 1879–1892)

Egyptians look back on Tawfiq with disdain. Historian Afaf Lutfi al-Sayyid writes, for example, that he was noted for his "pusillanimity and vindictiveness" (Sayyid 1968, 68). Before his accession Egyptians who favored constitutional government had hailed him as a nationalist, less flamboyant than his father, sympathetic to Sharif's liberal ideas, and a member of Jamal al-Din al-Afghani's secret society. Once he had taken over, he realized that he stood between two fires: European military might and rising Egyptian nationalist resistance to foreign financial control. Both could encroach on his powers. Khedive Tawfiq chose the Europeans as the safer side. He named a new cabinet, headed by the autocratic Riyad, and restored the powers of the Dual Control; however, he did not readmit British or French ministers to his cabinet. Riyad was an experienced cabinet minister willing to heed the demands of Egypt's foreign creditors and to restrain Egyptian nationalism. The government expelled such agitators as Jamal al-Din and Ya'qub Sanu from Egypt and closed the most radical newspapers. Khedive Tawfiq probably feared that spreading nationalism, whether military or civilian, might stir up new riots. A popular revolt could overthrow him, or draw in the Europeans to restore order. By deposing his father, the European powers had reduced the khedivate to a pawn in a larger game. Egypt's ruling family would never recover its independence.

In 1879 Egypt remained what it had been since 1840—an autonomous Ottoman province. Egypt had no colonial governor and no foreign army of occupation. But the debt commission created in 1876, which included representatives from Britain, France, Italy, and Austria, was starting to affect Egyptians of every class and economic level. In 1880 the commission took more than half the government revenues in payments on Egypt's huge foreign debts. This meant that funds were not available for other expenses. The government had to cut back expenditures for the army, schools, public works, and even essential maintenance.

The Egyptians felt that they bore an unfair share of the cuts, as evidenced by petitions sent to the government (most notably, complaints about high taxes to the finance ministry), while the Turks, Circassians, and other foreigners in Egypt went practically unscathed. European residents benefited from the Capitulations, which exempted them from obeying local laws and paying local taxes. Most people could only grumble about service cuts and high taxes. But Egyptian army officers had the power and organization to protest effectively. Essentially the officers' grievance was that they had been brought into the army by Mehmet Ali and his successors, but their advancement had been blocked by Ismail, who had appointed and promoted foreign officers, mainly Turks and Circassians. Now, under Tawfiq's austerity budget, they were being paid late, pensioned off, or assigned to undesirable posts. The enlisted ranks, overwhelmingly Egyptian and Sudanese, shared these grievances.

The Urabi Revolution (1881–1882)

In January 1881 a deputation of Egyptian officers, led by Colonel Ahmad Urabi (1841–1911), visited Prime Minister Riyad. The deputation also sent a petition to Khedive Tawfiq. The war minister, Uthman Rifqi, called them into his office, planning to have them arrested and court-martialed, but the officers arranged to have their men storm the war ministry building and rescue them. When even Tawfiq's palace guard, hitherto presumed loyal, defected to the mutinous officers, he and Riyad gave in and replaced Rifqi as war minister.

The new minister, Colonel Mahmud Sami al-Barudi (1839–1904), supported the soldiers' demands. Barudi was already revered by the

Ahmad Urabi on Horseback. *This probably fanciful portrait of the Egyptian nationalist leader was drawn by an artist just before the British bombarded Alexandria in July 1882.* (*Illustrated London News*, July 22, 1882)

Egyptian people as an officer, patriot, and poet. Once Colonel Urabi had acted to better the lot of the officers and soldiers, he felt encouraged to make new demands. The Egyptian officers still suspected that the khedive or Riyad were plotting against them with the European commissioners or the Turkish and Circassian officers. These suspicions were strengthened in September 1881 when Barudi lost his position as war minister and several regiments were transferred out of Cairo. In response Urabi organized a huge demonstration in front of Abdin Palace, the official khedivial residence. Urabi told a British supporter of the nationalists that Tawfiq, accompanied by the British controller, confronted Urabi, with his 2,500 armed Egyptian soldiers arrayed about Abdin, boasting: "I am the khedive of this country and will do as I please." To this Urabi replied, "We are not slaves and will never from this day on be inherited" (Blunt 1907, 114).

These words may never have been spoken, but they reflect the mind-set of the khedivial house and the spirit of the Egyptian officers who, one generation removed from their peasant origins, were groping toward national dignity. Tawfiq, lacking any force with which to counter Urabi's men, acceded to the officers' demands: the dismissal of Riyad's cabinet, the strengthening of the representative assembly, and the enlargement of the Egyptian army. Sharif, the minister who had pressed for a constitution under Ismail, was invited to replace Riyad. A group of legal scholars was convened to draft a new Egyptian constitution, and Sharif's government promptly called back all the retired officers and enlarged the army.

The Egyptian people—landlords and peasants, professionals and government clerks, Christians and Muslims—hailed Urabi as the nation's savior. Demonstrations were staged wherever he went. The new constitution was proclaimed in November 1881, elections were held, and the khedive opened Egypt's first representative body with legislative powers. But the European reaction was far less positive. Europeans living in Egypt feared for their safety. Those who had invested in Egypt's economy feared for their bonds. In January 1882 Britain and France issued a joint note, threatening military intervention in support of the khedive.

Far from intimidating the Egyptian nationalists, this gesture only emboldened them further. They insisted that their new parliament must have the right to vote on the 1882 Egyptian budget—a prerogative claimed by the Dual Control, which wanted to keep the confidence of Egypt's creditors. Some moderates, among them Sharif (who promptly resigned as prime minister), broke away from the nationalists.

87

However, the popular former war minister Barudi took over as premier, and Colonel Urabi took charge of the War Ministry. Both vowed to stress Egypt's interests over those of its European bondholders. They suppressed a plot by some of the Turco-Circassian officers, discussed deposing Tawfiq and declaring a republic, and stirred up popular demonstrations against British and French interference in Egypt.

But Urabi failed to gauge the determination of the Europeans, especially the British, to safeguard their interests: the security of the Suez Canal, the repayment of the Egyptian government debts, and the safety of European residents in Egypt. The French wanted a joint military occupation with the British, and both powers sent warships to the eastern Mediterranean. The British wanted the Ottoman government to intervene.

The Turks' stance was ambiguous. Publicly they appeased the Europeans; privately they urged Urabi to resist them. The Ottoman Empire had been greatly weakened by military defeat in the Russo-Turkish War. Russia had captured most of the Balkans in 1877, expelled many of its Muslim inhabitants, and kept part of eastern Anatolia in the 1878 settlement that ended the Russo-Turkish War. Under the terms of that treaty, Britain had been allowed to occupy Cyprus and Austria had taken Bosnia. Then France occupied Tunisia in 1881. By 1882 the Ottoman government—and, indeed Muslims everywhere—opposed any further European expansion at their expense.

This strident opposition shook London's confidence in an Ottoman-controlled Egypt. The British government was headed by William Gladstone (1809–98), who was loath to send troops to Egypt, for Britain's traditional policy was to protect the Ottoman Empire and promote its reform. The European powers met in Constantinople during the summer of 1882, but their deliberations were inconclusive and overtaken by events in Egypt.

In early June riots broke out in Alexandria. The Egyptian government tried to quell them and arrested the instigators. Even though 3,000 Egyptians and only 50 Europeans were killed or wounded, the riots frightened many foreigners into taking refuge on the British and French battleships anchored offshore. The commander of the British fleet sought a pretext to fire on Alexandria. When the Egyptian army refused to dismantle its coastal fortifications, British ships bombarded them. Instead of aiding the British, the French fleet sailed away. In Paris a new ministry had taken over that refused to commit itself to a military occupation of Egypt. When fire broke out in Alexandria, British forces went in alone to restore order.

Khedive Tawfiq, summering in Alexandria and fearful that Urabi's men were plotting to depose him, sided publicly with the occupiers, but in Cairo the Egyptian cabinet declared war on Britain. The British fleet entered the Suez Canal and landed at Ismailia, violating the canal's neutrality, but neither the company nor the Egyptian government had fortified the new waterway. The British expeditionary force met the Egyptian army on September 13 at Tel-el-Kebir and won decisively, occupying Cairo the next day. Egyptian nationalism seemed to fade like a mirage. Urabi surrendered and was arrested. Along with many of his fellow nationalists, he was tried for treason. Although he was convicted, his death sentence was commuted to exile in Ceylon (Sri Lanka). Tawfiq, whose behavior seems to modern Egyptians more treasonous than Urabi's, was propped back on his throne. A pro-British government took the place of the nationalist one.

The first Egyptian nationalist movement may have been popular, but it was too diffuse in its membership and too unfocused in its goals to succeed. Most nationalists agreed that Ismail had put the country too far into debt and that the measures taken by the Dual Control to reassure Egypt's creditors were intolerable. These were the only points, however, on which all were in agreement. Some nationalists were revolutionaries, prepared to depose the khedive and join with Muslims elsewhere to resist Western power. Some were landowners of Egyptian extraction, anxious to keep privileges only recently gained through Ismail's policies. They backed the Egyptian army officers, who feared losing their limited power to their Turkish and Circassian rivals. Some belonged to the new class of journalists, teachers, and civil servants, an emerging elite pursuing national rights and duties. The nationalists were weakened by their diverse backgrounds and varied agendas, but even a more united and popular movement could not have withstood the military and naval might of the British Empire in 1882.

The British in Control

Gladstone's government had earlier expressed sympathy for Urabi's aims and had opposed him mainly to prevent the French from taking over Egypt. Now it had to decide whether to remove the 20,000 British troops who occupied the country. The British did not want a long-term occupation because they recognized that it was likely to antagonize the French and inflame Muslim anger. The British army was small and might later be needed elsewhere. They promised that they would stay just long enough to restore order in Egypt. But that was the problem. If restoring order meant giving back power to the khedive and suppressing the nationalist movement, the British had achieved these aims. But if it meant solving Egypt's financial problems, which had caused the disorder, the British would need to stay for many years.

The outbreak of an anti-Egyptian rebellion in the Sudan, led by Muhammad Ahmad (1844–85), who had assumed the title of Mahdi in 1881 and vowed to overthrow the khedive and eventually every Muslim ruler whom he deemed hypocritical, put off Britain's evacuation plans. (The term *mahdi* means rightly guided one.) A British force sent to relieve the Egyptian garrison at Khartoum was ambushed in the desert, and the government put off evacuating Egypt until the Mahdist revolt could be quashed.

In November 1882 the British abolished the Dual Control and named a British financial adviser with cabinet rank. A commission headed by Lord Dufferin, former high commissioner in Syria and governor general of Canada, came to study Egypt's government and issued a report whose recommended constitutional reforms were largely adopted by the British.

Egypt's economy was now so weak that the government feared it would be unable to raise enough tax revenues to pay its creditors. More than half the revenues had to go to the Debt Commission. All other government expenditures had to be pared to the bone. The government also owed indemnities to Europeans whose property had been destroyed during the Alexandria riots and was obliged to pay the costs of the British occupation. The Egyptian army was dissolved and reorganized with fewer men and a small officer corps, mainly British. The bureaucracy, too, was cut back. Many schools were shut down or reduced in size. Although the nation's irrigation system needed critical repairs, funds could not be allocated to make them. All such measures were a necessary part of Egypt's struggle against bankruptcy.

Cromer and His Reforms

That struggle was almost lost. The government was still trying to address the spreading revolt in the Sudan. In 1883 a severe cholera epidemic broke out. Poverty had caused many peasants to leave their villages and to turn to crime. The Egyptian Debt Commission was supposed to serve as a watchdog on state expenditures. But now that British troops had occupied Egypt, the representatives of the other European powers, especially France, habitually blocked Egyptian government outlays. Jealous of Britain's position in Egypt, they hoped to

Delta Barrage. This dam was built by French engineers for Mehmet Ali to control the flow of Nile waters into the Rosetta and Damietta branches of the Nile and thus to facilitate the perennial irrigation of the Nile Delta. It soon developed leaks, which British engineers repaired during the Cromer era. (Library of Congress)

make it admit failure and withdraw its troops. The British government sent a new diplomatic representative who had earlier served as one of Egypt's debt commissioners and could overcome their obstructionism, Sir Evelyn Baring, later Lord Cromer (1841–1917). Cromer stayed for 24 years, gradually becoming the country's de facto governor.

At the outset Cromer and his home government assumed that the occupation would be brief. They had no long-term plans to modernize Egypt; they proposed to put the country's government and finances in order and then leave. Short-term measures were needed. Cromer concentrated his efforts on fiscal reform and irrigation. He believed that lowering taxes and demands for forced labor, combined with better management of the Nile waters, would make the peasants more productive. To achieve this the British financial adviser looked for ways to abolish the imposts that bore most heavily on peasants, such as the taxes on sheep and goats, grain weighing, and salt. Within five years the government managed to abolish forced labor, except for the requirement to guard the Nile during the flood season.

Although money for large-scale construction projects was not available during the first years of the military occupation, British irrigation engineers managed to repair existing dams such as the Delta Barrage, a huge dam designed to keep the water level in the Delta uniform throughout the year. Built under Mehmet Ali, it had been laid on weak foundations, had failed to channel the Nile flow, and had been abandoned by Said. British engineers stanched the leaking foundations and enabled the Barrage to back up the annual flood. By making other emergency repairs to the Nile's dams and canals, the British achieved a dramatic rise in agricultural production at little public expense. Higher output yielded more tax revenues for the government, hastening the abolition of nuisance taxes and lowering the rates of the taxes that remained. After five years, the British claimed that they had won the race against bankruptcy.

But many of Egypt's other problems remained unsolved. The Mahdi's rebellion in the Sudan continued to spread, and the British could neither defeat nor make peace with the rebels. An attempt by General Charles Gordon to effect an Egyptian withdrawal from the Sudan in 1884–85 also failed. Gordon and his troops (plus thousands of Egyptians) were killed by the rebels. As a result the Sudan, which had been won by Egyptian forces under Mehmet Ali and his successors, was lost to Egypt from 1885 to 1898. Even Upper Egypt was menaced by pro-Mahdi insurrections during the 1880s. The first Egyptian government under the British occupation, headed by Sharif, resigned in protest over Britain's decision to leave the Sudan. The next government quit because of an ill-fated British effort to reorganize the interior ministry, the department responsible for maintaining public order. The British put off police reorganization, but rural crime reached such alarming proportions that the government resorted to extrajudicial "commissions of brigandage" to arrest and punish suspected criminals. On the eve of the British occupation the Egyptian government had devised a new system of secular courts, the National Tribunals, which began operation in 1883, following laws and procedures taken mainly from France's Napoleonic Law Code. Its jurisdiction was limited to Egyptian subjects, as distinct from the Mixed Courts, which handled civil and commercial cases involving foreign nationals in Egypt. The British would rather have adapted the simpler legal structures that they had set up in India, but not expecting to remain in Egypt, they put off changing the legal system until the 1890s. By this time Egypt had a growing corps of judges and lawyers trained by the French, so the British were unable to institute the legal reforms that they wanted.

The British had actually drafted a withdrawal plan, one that would have allowed their forces to reenter Egypt for a three-year period in case a new revolution occurred. They thought that they had gained the consent of the Ottoman government to the plan. However, French and Russian diplomats convinced the sultan that the British would use the right of reentry to make their occupation permanent and to cut Egypt off from Ottoman control. As a result this plan was never carried out.

Khedive Tawfiq knew that he owed his throne to the British. As long as he remained alive, Cromer governed Egypt from behind the scenes. A few dozen capable and dedicated British advisers quietly patched up the parts of the government in the greatest need of repair, while Egyptian ministers seemed to be in charge. The fiction was maintained that Egypt was an autonomous province of the Ottoman Empire, with the khedive serving as viceroy. He and his ministers, together with the British financial adviser, constituted the cabinet. Cromer expected to be consulted privately about the khedive's choice of ministers, and they in turn were expected to heed British advice as long as the occupation lasted, but the formal arrangements were honored. Egypt even had two representative bodies, the Legislative Council and the General Assembly, which had been formed on the Dufferin Commission's recommendation. Neither one, however, could initiate legislation or block actions taken by the British-dominated ministers.

Khedive Abbas Challenges the British

Khedive Tawfiq died suddenly in January 1892. The ensuing crises tore the veil from Britain's protectorate. Tawfiq's son, Abbas Hilmi II (1874–1944), was a high-spirited 17 year old studying at an Austrian military academy at the time of his father's unexpected death. At the same time, the Ottoman government was strengthening control over its peripheral provinces and threatening to reassert its claim to the Sinai Peninsula. Because of this, both the Egyptian cabinet and the British wanted to avoid setting up a regency that might invite Ottoman intervention. By using the Muslim calendar (in which one year consists of 12 lunar months, or 354 days) instead of the Gregorian one, Abbas was reckoned to be 18 and hence ready to assume formal power. He and Cromer worked together to resist not only an Ottoman attempt to retake the Sinai but also French and Russian efforts to sway him in choosing the members of his staff. Before long, however, the two men clashed.

Their dispute was partly generational. In his reports to the Foreign Office Cromer expressed paternal feelings for this promising lad, whereas the young khedive naturally wanted to assert his personal independence. But their differences were also political. Abbas wanted to choose his ministers, but Cromer had to be consulted on his choices; in effect this meant that Cromer expected his suggestions to be obeyed. A crisis arose in January 1893 when the pro-British prime minister, Mustafa Fahmi, offered his resignation. Without asking Cromer the khedive appointed a nationalist in his place. Cromer reacted strongly. He called on the British government to send additional troops and to issue a letter expressing the expectation that his advice would be followed as long as the occupation lasted. Abbas and Cromer compromised by appointing a veteran politician, Riyad.

Neither the khedive nor the consul was satisfied. A year later the khedive, while inspecting Egypt's southern border defenses at Aswan, publicly criticized some British-led units of the Egyptian army. Sir Herbert Kitchener (1850–1916), newly appointed as commander of the army, took umbrage at Abbas's criticism and offered to resign. The khedive tried to stop the quarrel before it spread, but word of the incident reached Cromer, who blamed it on a nationalist deputy war minister. If Egypt's army became infected with anti-British sentiment, a new Urabist movement might threaten the peace. Cromer told Riyad that the khedive must issue a statement expressing his complete satisfaction with all units of the army. Abbas obeyed but remained embittered. After that, all Egyptians knew that their ministers, and above all the khedive, had to obey the orders of the British, especially Lord Cromer. The Egyptians found that they had acquired yet another foreign master.

Nationalist Resistance

Britain's military occupation of Egypt in 1882, purportedly temporary, had no standing in international law, no formal recognition from the other European powers, and no formal acknowledgment from Egypt's internationally recognized overlord, the Ottoman Empire. The British government promised many times after 1882 to withdraw all its troops. It never pulled them out, though, for their presence supported not only the restoration and maintenance of order but also the strategic needs of the British Empire. Britain pared its troops from 20,000 to 5,000, and the people of Egypt—from Khedive Tawfiq down to the peasants—acquiesced in their presence. Although Tawfiq admitted to his intimates that he resented the occupying army, he knew better than to resist openly. He realized that he would probably have been deposed—or worse—by Urabi's supporters. Although the French and the Ottoman governments opposed the British, only after Abbas succeeded Tawfiq in 1892 did nationalist resistance reappear.

The Egyptian nationalist movement that began in the 1890s saw Egypt as a nation-state that deserved the loyalty of its citizens. The founders of this movement belonged to an elite that had been educated abroad, in local schools set up by Europeans, or in Egyptian government schools, many of whose teachers were European. Most of them were lawyers, journalists, or teachers. They viewed Egypt as a nation, the world's oldest, waking up after centuries of sleep. They acknowledged the benefits of Westernization to themselves and to their country. They wanted it to become a parliamentary democracy with a constitutional monarch. The rights of citizenship should be enjoyed by all people who lived in Egypt, whether they were Muslim, Christian, or Jewish, or whether they were descended from ethnic Egyptians, from immigrants from other parts of the Muslim world, or from Europeans. These nationalists refuted all foreign charges of xenophobia or religious fanaticism. Their first and main demand was for the British troops to leave Egypt.

This nationalist movement was not purely spontaneous, nor was it free from governmental influence. It began as a secret society headed by young Khedive Abbas and influenced by Europeans in his palace staff. Their common bond was not so much love of Egypt as hatred of Lord Cromer. The man now hailed as the founder of the movement, Mustafa Kamil (1874–1908), was initially a spokesman for Abbas. Both men were 18 years old in 1892 and resented Cromer's interference, buttressed by a growing number of British advisers in Egyptian government ministries as well as by the army of occupation. They sought support from the Ottoman sultan, the French in Egypt, and European factions that opposed the British occupation.

Mustafa Kamil

In 1892 Mustafa Kamil, a student at the Khedivial Law School, was a leader among his peers. He was already editing Egypt's first student journal, *al-Madrasa* (The School). In January 1893 he led a protest march to the office of *al-Muqattam,* a pro-British daily newspaper, to support Khedive Abbas during his contest with Cromer. Mustafa then transferred to the French Law School, which taught the Napoleonic Code (the main basis of Egypt's Native Penal Code) to would-be Egyptian lawyers. That summer he went to Paris, ostensibly to pass his first-year finals there, but also to make contacts for the khedive and

Mustafa Kamil. This charismatic lawyer revived the Egyptian nationalist movement between 1895 and 1908, when he died tragically before his 34th birthday. (J. Alexander, *The Truth About Egypt*, p. 38)

MUSTAFA KAMIL

Mustafa Kamil was a highly articulate advocate for Egypt's independence from Britain. The son of an Egyptian army officer, he was born in Cairo and educated in government schools, the French Law School in Cairo, and the University of Toulouse in France, where he earned a law degree in 1894. He formed early ties with an influential member of the French Chamber of Deputies and with the editor of *La nouvelle revue,* Juliette Adam, who published some of his early writings. An ardent opponent of the British occupation, Mustafa took both material and moral support from Khedive Abbas Hilmi II and Ottoman Sultan Abdulhamid II. He organized a secret society, the Society for the Revival of the Nation, initially headed by the khedive. This society soon became known as the National Party, for which Mustafa founded a daily Arabic newspaper, *al-Liwa* (The Banner) and a boys' school that bore his own name. Once France and Britain became reconciled in 1904, Mustafa broke with the khedive but continued to court the Ottoman Empire and to promote pan-Islam. He backed Ottoman claims to part of the Sinai Peninsula during the Taba Affair and condemned Britain's harsh treatment of the Dinshaway villagers, accused of assaulting uniformed British troops in 1906. Later in that year he became reconciled with the khedive, who offered support for the creation of Nationalist daily newspapers in English and French. In December 1907 he formally set up the National Party, which elected him as its first president. Stricken with tuberculosis, he took to his bed and died at age 33. His funeral occasioned a mass demonstration of popular grief. He is respected by all Egyptians as a passionate spokesman for independence.

to demonstrate Egyptian loyalty to the Ottoman Empire by hosting a banquet to honor the sultan's accession day. Even in those times few students could have hosted a banquet in Paris without financial aid. For Mustafa this aid came from the khedive.

Mustafa Kamil would devote the rest of his life to securing the British evacuation from Egypt. At that time the Egyptian people were unarmed, unorganized, and, owing to Urabi's defeat in 1882, intimidated by Britain's power. Because of this the young lawyer did not view revolution as an effective means to end the British occupation. He hoped to persuade the British to restore Egypt's independence. However, most British officials had by then accepted the idea of an indefinite occupation and saw no need to heed Mustafa Kamil or even Khedive Abbas.

The French, hoping that a British evacuation would advance their own imperial interests in Africa, showed more sympathy. Mustafa found a French patron, Juliette Adam (1836–1936), the editor of an influential monthly, *La nouvelle revue,* whose pages were opened to Mustafa's cause. He hoped that the German and Austrian governments might join France and Russia in calling on Britain to fulfill its promises to leave Egypt. As for the Ottoman Empire, Egypt's legitimate overlord, Sultan Abdulhamid (r. 1876–1909) not only resented the British occupation but also pressed his claim to the Islamic caliphate in an effort to retain Egyptian loyalty. Mustafa courted his support and exploited it whenever he appealed to Muslim Egyptians.

As well as being a movement aimed at creating an Egyptian nation, nationalism in Egypt could be seen as a Muslim resistance movement against the rule of a non-Muslim power. Sultan Abdulhamid's claim to the caliphate was an element in a wider movement called pan-Islam. This doctrine urged Muslims to unite under the leadership of an Islamic ruler. In the 1890s the only Islamic ruler who could have united even Sunni Muslims was the Ottoman sultan-caliph. Egyptians, 90 percent of whom were Muslim, were susceptible to pan-Islamic appeals, as were India's Muslims. The British worried that any such movement could weaken their empire. The French, with Muslim subjects in Algeria, Tunisia, and Senegal, also feared pan-Islam. So, too, did the Russians, who had conquered vast areas of the Caucasus Mountains and Central Asia. But Ottoman weakness, evident from the 1877 Russo-Turkish War, limited the movement's freedom of action. The sultan welcomed expressions of loyalty from the young Egyptian nationalists. Because he could not confront the Europeans militarily, his policy was to subsidize pan-Islamic and nationalist movements in lands ruled by Russia, France, and Britain.

If the Egyptians had won their freedom from British rule through the actions of the continental European powers (or the intervention of the Ottoman sultan), they would in all likelihood have become dependent on their "liberators." For a true nationalist movement to develop, the Egyptians themselves needed to take action. Khedive Abbas looked to Sheikh Ali Yusuf to arouse Egyptian opinion. Sheikh Ali was the editor of an influential daily newspaper, *al-Muayyad,* which was named for a Cairo mosque built in the early 15th century. A poet and an Azharite with high ambitions but little money, he began publishing *al-Muayyad* in 1889, subsidized by a group of Egyptian Muslims headed by Riyad. When Abbas became khedive, *al-Muayyad* emerged as his palace organ and the mouthpiece for Muslim Egyptian opinion. Mustafa Kamil was one of its writers.

By 1900, though, the Egyptian army, commanded mainly by British officers, had reconquered the Sudan; the French had given up hope of ever ruling in the Nile Valley; and Khedive Abbas, realizing that British occupation of Egypt was likely to endure, began to cultivate ties with the occupiers. As the khedive drew closer to the British, Mustafa Kamil and his followers started to pursue an independent policy. They could no longer count on getting published in *al-Muayyad,* so they founded an explicitly nationalist daily, *al-Liwa.* Now Mustafa wrote on the people's political rights, constitutional rule, and the expansion of public education, even as he continued to attack the occupation.

Khedive Abbas did not want to oust the British if he would then have to share his hard-won powers with a parliament. Thus he no longer wanted to spend his money on the nationalists, who often backed Ottoman or pan-Islamic causes. In 1904, soon after France, in its Entente Cordiale with Britain, agreed not to demand a terminal date for its occupation of Egypt, the khedive and the nationalists broke with each other.

Nationalist Grievances

Perhaps the nationalists could, like the khedive and the French government, have gone along with British rule. The occupation had brought many improvements to Egypt. British engineers had revamped and expanded Nile irrigation, thereby giving the Delta and parts of the Nile Valley enough water to grow three crops a year instead of one. Agricultural output grew steadily as a result. Nuisance taxes had been abolished and other taxes had been lowered, increasing the discretionary income of the Egyptian people. Peasants were no longer flogged or taken away from their families and fields to perform forced labor in other parts of Egypt. Slavery, outlawed (on paper) since 1841, died out. Government corruption almost vanished. Once the financial crisis was over, Europeans resumed investing in Egypt. European entrepreneurship furnished Cairo and Alexandria with most of the amenities of Western cities: gas, electricity, streetlights, piped drinking water, tram lines, and telephones. Many Westerners came to Egypt as tourists and some as permanent residents, protected under the Capitulations from local laws and taxes, but their expenditures enriched the country. Egypt in the first decade of the 20th century was more prosperous than it had been since early Mamluk times.

The nationalist objection was that the Egyptian people were not advancing toward self-rule but, rather, were being treated as tools

Cairo café. The coffeehouse has long been a gathering place for male Egyptians. By the 20th century, cafés provided water pipes and newspapers for their patrons. A child bootblack could help to support his family by shining patrons' shoes. (Library of Congress)

serving British imperial interests. They could grow cotton to sell to the textile mills of Lancashire, they could buy their clothing from the same British firms, but they could not set up their own factories to spin thread, weave cloth, and fashion garments. An Egyptian attempt to set up a textile spinning and weaving factory was quickly squelched by an excise tax on its manufactures. The British scrimped on education long after the financial crisis had passed, never spending more than 3 percent of the Egyptian government budget on schools. Tuition fees at public elementary and secondary schools were higher than those charged by many private schools. Moreover, English was taking the place of French as the main instructional language, and for a long time the British opposed the use of Arabic, even in elementary schools, claiming that it was unsuited to teaching the natural sciences and other modern subjects.

Egyptian ministers were rubber stamps for their British advisers. The longer the troops remained, the greater the number of British advisers appointed to the Egyptian government and army. Cromer repeatedly stated his intention to turn power over gradually to Egyptians, but instead the higher posts went increasingly to his own men. The British advisers, officials, and officers tended to become more insular as their numbers grew and especially once their wives and children came to live with them in Egypt. The British had their own social clubs, from which Egyptians were excluded even as guests, and mingling became the exception, not the rule. The widening social gulf between British and Egyptians led to feelings of mutual incomprehension and hostility.

The Taba Affair and the Dinshaway Incident

Once he broke with the khedive, Mustafa Kamil became even more involved in Ottoman causes. He strengthened his ties with Ottoman Sultan Abdulhamid and used pan-Islam to gain support from the Egyptian people. A key incident was the 1906 Taba Affair. The British had long treated the Sinai Peninsula as part of Egypt, a buffer zone between the Ottoman Empire and the Suez Canal. As the Ottoman government tightened its hold over its remaining provinces, including southern Syria and the Hejaz, the British and the Turks eyed each other's moves warily. When Abbas became khedive in 1892, Egypt turned over the garrisons that Mehmet Ali had established on the eastern shores of the Gulf of Aqaba; at the same time Abbas resisted (with British backing) the Ottoman demand for the Egyptian forts on the western side of the Gulf. In 1906 Ottoman troops built a new fort at Taba, west of the line that the Egyptian government viewed as its border with their empire. The British sent warships into the eastern Mediterranean and threatened a show of force against the Ottoman Empire, which then agreed to demarcate a formal border. That frontier has since come to be known as the "international line," giving most of the Sinai Peninsula to Egypt.

In what may seem an unpatriotic position, the nationalists—indeed, most Egyptians—backed the Ottoman claim against that of their own government. Although a few Egyptians did attack the nationalists for preferring pan-Islam to an Egyptian interest, most opposed the British claim of Sinai for Egypt as serving primarily Britain's own interests. The Taba Affair was an instance of the recurrent struggle in modern Egypt between territorial nationalism and Islamism among politically savvy Egyptians. Muslims everywhere feared the growing encroachment of European imperialism on the lands of Islam and viewed the Ottoman Empire as their sole defender.

The Taba Affair sparked an incident that strengthened the nationalist movement even more. In June 1906 a group of British officers in uniform entered the Delta village of Dinshaway to shoot pigeons. This sport angered the peasants, who kept pigeons as barnyard animals, mainly for their manure. During the hunt a threshing floor caught on fire. The villagers, thinking that the shooting was the cause, rushed at the officers with wooden staves and tried to disarm them. An officer's gun went off, a woman fell wounded (some thought she had been killed), and four other villagers were peppered with shot. The officers panicked and two of them fled. One died of sunstroke as he was running back to his camp. His comrade, finding him in the arms of a peasant who was trying in vain to revive him, assumed that the peasant had killed him and proceeded to beat the peasant to death.

Already alarmed by Egyptian nationalist support for the Ottomans in the recent Taba Affair, the British authorities in Cairo feared an outbreak of what they saw as Muslim fanaticism. They took the Dinshaway Incident to be a premeditated attack on British officers and decided to teach the villagers a lesson. They set up a special court—not part of Egypt's penal system—and tried 52 of the villagers before a panel of five judges, only two of whom were Egyptian. Four of the defendants were sentenced to hanging. Several others were to be flogged or imprisoned. The Dinshaway villagers had to watch as the hanging and flogging sentences were carried out.

The National Party

This atrocity stirred up widespread anger against the British occupation of Egypt. Although British and European liberals were the first to protest, anger spread among all classes of Egyptian society. Many Egyptians, Christians as well as Muslims, flocked to Mustafa Kamil's standard. The widespread revulsion against the Dinshaway sentences led to demands for reform in the British administration and may have hastened Cromer's retirement in 1907. For the first time since the Urabi revolution, many Egyptians became politically active. The khedive made peace with Mustafa. They agreed to set up English and French editions of *al-Liwa* and to turn what had been a secret society into the National Party, open to all Egyptians who wanted the British troops to

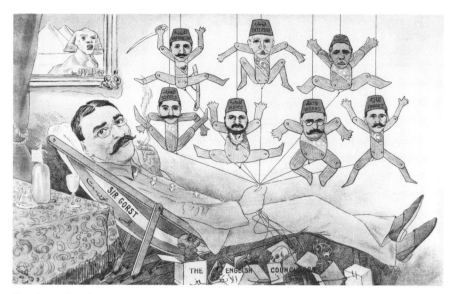

The Cairo Punch *cartoon. Sir Eldon Gorst, Cromer's successor as Britain's consul-general in Cairo, was accused by a humor magazine of manipulating the Egyptian ministers as if they were puppets. Although Gorst really allowed cabinet ministers more freedom than Cromer had, the basic nationalist grievance was that the British were ruling Egypt with no accountability to the Egyptian people.* (Library of Congress)

leave their country. Other Egyptians, mainly landowners and intellectuals opposed to Mustafa's pro-Ottoman and pan-Islamic stance during the Taba Affair, founded the daily *al-Jarida* (The Newspaper) and a rival party, *Hizb al-Umma* (Party of the Nation). Many future political and literary leaders, among them the future "father of Egyptian independence," Saad Zaghlul, and the professor of the generation, Ahmad Lutfi al-Sayyid, joined the latter party. Lutfi al-Sayyid became the editor of *al-Jarida,* which articulated Egypt's interests from a liberal and constitutional viewpoint. Because the National Party claimed to speak for the people, Khedive Abbas and Sheikh Ali Yusuf proceeded to form their own party, *Hizb al-Islah ala al-Mabadi al-Dusturiya* (Constitutional Reform Party), connected to *al-Muayyad* and under palace control.

Britain viewed this proliferation of Egyptian political parties with more amusement than alarm. A later British agent wrote in his annual report home that "party spirit is to them (Muslim peoples) like strong drink to uncivilized African natives." (Lloyd 1933, I, 130) The Liberals had swept into power in Britain in January 1906, but even their left wing was not so opposed to British rule in Egypt as to call for total withdrawal. They did, however, propose to do more to prepare Egyptians for eventual independence. Cromer's replacement, Sir Eldon Gorst (1861–1911), was a subtler man with extensive experience in Egypt as well as in the Foreign Office. He was quite willing to put more Egyptians into responsible posts and to increase slightly the powers of the Legislative Council and the General Assembly. He did not want to meet either National Party leaders or those of the Umma Party, but he promptly began to win Khedive Abbas to his side. The loss of palace support hurt the Nationalists, but they set up their formal party organization and elected Mustafa Kamil president for life. Two months later he died, probably of tuberculosis. He was only 33 years old.

The death of Mustafa Kamil occasioned modern Egypt's first mass funeral demonstration, as civil servants walked off their jobs and students cut their classes to march behind his bier. The demonstration showed the British clearly how popular the National Party had become. But the death of its leader crippled the party. A dispute arose over the succession between Mustafa's brother and his best friend. The Nationalists chose the friend, Muhammad Farid (1868–1919), who was a decent and dignified man but neither a spellbinding orator nor a shrewd manipulator. He had been one of Mustafa's earliest backers. A wealthy lawyer, he could not so easily be controlled by the offer (or denial) of cash subsidies from the khedive or the sultan. But the Nationalists split along several lines: Some wanted to work with the khedive, while others denounced his entente with the British; some favored pan-Islam and firm Ottoman ties, while others wanted to attract or retain the support of Egypt's non-Muslims; and some wanted to win Egypt's independence by fomenting an armed insurrection, while others believed in lawful, nonviolent persuasion.

The party continued to grow for two years, setting up branches in the provincial towns and a clubhouse in Cairo. Mustafa Kamil had founded a private school for boys; now the Nationalists established night schools for workers and consumer cooperatives. Farid supported labor unions and even the first strike organized by Egyptian workers. But the most celebrated Nationalist was Abd al-Aziz Jawish, an Azharite sheikh. Farid appointed him to edit *al-Liwa*. In this role he wrote fiery editorials condemning the Dinshaway executions (articles that united the Egyptian people) and attacking the Copts (articles that divided Muslims and Christians). As Copts and moderate Muslims quit the National Party and its direction became ever more radical and pan-Islamic, some of Egypt's emerging intellectual leaders shifted their loyalty to the Umma Party, Ahmad Lutfi al-Sayyid, and his relatively moderate editorials in *al-Jarida*.

Suppressing the Nationalists

The Egyptian government and its British advisers did fear the National Party's influence on young people. In 1909 the cabinet revived a law requiring all newspapers to be licensed and subjecting those printing inflammatory articles to suspension or suppression. But anti-British papers found that they could evade control by appointing as editors or owners people claiming foreign nationality (hence protection under the Capitulations), thereby weakening the law temporarily.

To raise money for irrigation works, the government in 1909 offered the Suez Canal Company a 40-year extension of its concession (from 1968 to 2008) for 4 million Egyptian pounds (then worth more than U.S. $20 million). The Nationalists opposed this deal because they did not want the canal to remain under indefinite foreign control. Gorst advised the cabinet to submit the issue to the General Assembly, which voted it down almost unanimously. But before the vote was taken, Egypt's prime minister was murdered by a young Nationalist. Subsequent investigation showed that the assassin belonged to a secret society that was forming revolutionary cells throughout Egypt to kill or intimidate Egyptians collaborating with the British. This discovery led to a spate of new laws regulating the press, student political activities, and public meetings. Gorst stopped trying to give power to more Egyptians. Stricken with cancer, he resigned in 1911.

His successor was Lord Kitchener, the man who had quarreled with Khedive Abbas in 1894 and had led the reconquest of the Sudan in 1898. Kitchener took a tough stand against dissidents. The Nationalist leaders now faced severe limitations, prison terms,

Lord Kitchener was Britain's consul-general in Cairo from 1911 to 1914. He is shown here (standing, right) in Port Said, greeting King George V (standing, center), who was transiting the Suez Canal. With them are Khedive Abbas (standing, left) and the Ottoman High Commissioner (seated) in Cairo. (Popperfoto/ Classicstock)

or exile. The faint-hearted quit the party. Muhammad Farid and Sheikh Jawish both sought refuge in Istanbul to continue their struggle. Kitchener was a strong leader, popular in Britain and sincerely eager to improve conditions, especially for Egyptian peasants. Under Kitchener Egypt acquired its first agricultural cooperative banks and its Ministry of Agriculture. Kitchener propounded a new Organic Law in 1913. This let the Egyptians elect delegates to a new, more powerful representative body, the Legislative Assembly, in 1914. Saad Zaghlul was elected vice president of the assembly and emerged as a major opposition leader. Umma Party supporters played a large part in the assembly, while the khedive found himself in relative isolation. Kitchener, who was thinking of removing Abbas from office, was delighted at this result of his policies.

World War I

In 1914 World War I broke out in Europe. Once the Ottoman Empire entered the war on the German side, the British severed Egypt's vestigial Turkish ties and declared a protectorate over the country. Khedive

---

BRITAIN'S DIPLOMATIC REPRESENTATIVES IN EGYPT

H.M. Agent and Consul-General

1879–1883	Sir Edward Malet (1837–1908)
1883–1907	Sir Evelyn Baring, Earl of Cromer (1841–1917)
1907–1911	Sir Eldon Gorst (1861–1911)
1911–1914	Sir Herbert Kitchener, First Earl (1850–1916)
1914–1916	Sir Henry McMahon (1862–1949)
1917–1919	Sir Reginald Wingate, First Baron (1861–1953)
1919–1925	Sir Edmund Allenby, Viscount (1861–1936)
1925–1929	Sir George Ambrose Lloyd, Baron (1879–1941)
1929–1933	Sir Percy Loraine (1880–1961)
1933–1946	Sir Miles Wedderburn Lampson, First Baron Killearn (1880–1964)

Abbas was deposed. One of his uncles, Hussein Kamil (1853–1917), took his place with the title of sultan. On Hussein's death his brother, Fuad (1868–1936), succeeded him. Nationalists still in Egypt were put under house arrest. The Legislative Assembly was adjourned indefinitely and political life in Egypt went into suspension.

The prime minister, Hussein Rushdi (1863–1928), stayed in office on the understanding that the British protectorate would last only until the end of the war. Increasingly, however, the British ran Egypt like a crown colony. Hundreds of Britons, less well trained than their prewar predecessors, were brought in to staff the Egyptian civil service. Thousands of British troops—notably Australians and New Zealanders famed for their assaults on Egyptians and their property when on leave—occupied Cairo, Alexandria, and the Suez Canal zone. Prices skyrocketed. More than 100,000 Egyptians were conscripted to serve as auxiliaries in the Allied armies that used the country as their base of operations against the Ottomans; others had to contribute money, animals, or farm equipment to the war effort. Because of the rising demand for wheat and other grains, restrictions were placed on the amount of land that could be used to grow cotton. Landowners and peasants chafed under these restrictions, and the British lost much goodwill.

Overt opposition to British rule was banned within Egypt. Nationalists in exile kept up their campaign, exploiting wartime opportunities to get financial and moral support from the deposed khedive, the Ottoman government, and its German allies. In Istanbul, Sheikh Jawish helped write the Ottoman sultan's proclamation of jihad, or holy war, against the Allies. Later, in Berlin, Germany, he edited a pan-Islamic monthly magazine, *Die Islamische Welt* and *al-Alam al-Islami* (The Islamic World). Muhammad Farid, who traveled between the Ottoman Empire, Switzerland, and Germany, organized student groups and attended pacifist and socialist congresses. He worked to remind the Germans and Ottomans of the Egyptian nationalist demands for British evacuation and constitutional government.

Immediately following the armistice, conditions changed. The pent-up wartime grievances of the Egyptian people exploded in a nationwide revolution. Demanding the complete independence of Egypt, the revolutionary movement disrupted its government and finally caused the British to give up their protectorate.

7

AMBIGUOUS INDEPENDENCE
(1918–1936)

Wororld War I was, in Woodrow Wilson's words, the "war to end all wars," but its end did not bring peace to the world. Conflicts continued in some countries, and people rebelled in others, but Egypt's revolution took both the British and the Egyptians themselves by surprise. It had been commonly assumed that the Egyptian people accepted British protection, but the revolutionaries demanded complete independence in 1919. The British would eventually make a unilateral declaration of Egyptian "independence," but reserved some points for further negotiation, as Egyptian leaders drew up a liberal constitution. The government of Egypt soon became a three-legged stool: King Fuad, the British, and the Wafd. Everyone became frustrated, as Britain and Egypt struggled to agree on a new status for the latter. Finally, in 1936 the rise of Italian Fascism drove them to accept a 20-year treaty of alliance. Seemingly, independence was at hand.

The 1919 Revolution

The expanded presence of British Empire troops, the increased demand and prices paid for Egypt's agricultural products during World War I, and the high caliber of Egypt's prewar administration had led many foreigners to suppose that the Egyptians welcomed British protection. Indeed, the Egyptian people, except for the exiled Nationalists, had shown few signs of restiveness during the war despite the rising number and falling quality of the British administrators in their country. Preoccupied with making a peace treaty with Germany and its allies after the November 11, 1918, Armistice, the British never thought of ending their protectorate over Egypt.

But the Egyptians thought of nothing else. Their leaders tolerated the British protectorate only as a wartime measure. Prime Minister

Hussein Rushdi and Sultan Fuad (who had succeeded his brother, Hussein Kamil, in 1917) both hoped for greater autonomy from the British. As a peace conference became imminent, Egyptians began to discuss sending a *wafd,* or delegation, that would express their demands to the world. The plan to organize a formal delegation was probably put forth in September 1918 by some Umma Party members who had served in the prewar Legislative Assembly, notably the man whose name is now forever tied to the Egyptian Wafd and the 1919 revolution, Saad Zaghlul.

King Fuad. A great grandson of Mehmet Ali, Fuad had not expected to rule Egypt, but he became sultan in 1917 and king in 1923. He competed for influence with the Wafd and the British. (Harris, *Egypt under the Egyptians*)

Saad had an interesting and varied past. The son of a fairly well-off village headman, he received his early education in mosque schools and at al-Azhar, where he had come under the influence of two of the 19th century's great Muslim reformers, Jamal al-Din al-Afghani and Muhammad Abduh. In the turbulent months leading up to the Urabi revolution, Saad had helped Abduh edit the government newspaper and thus became deeply involved in the revolutionary events of 1882. Just after the British took over, he was arrested and tried for belonging to a terrorist society. After his life was spared, he adopted a safer course of action, going to France to study law.

Upon completing his degree and returning to Egypt, he became a lawyer and then a judge in the national court system. His upward mobility was aided by the patronage of an influential member of the khedivial family, Princess Nazli, and by his marriage to the daughter of Prime Minister Mustafa Fahmi. Both of these prominent figures worked with the British, and Saad became a favorite of Lord Cromer, who advised Khedive Abbas to name him education minister in 1906. In his farewell address in 1907, Cromer singled out Saad: "He possesses all the qualities necessary to serve his country. He is honest, he is capable, he has the courage of his convictions, he has been abused by many of the

Saad Zaghlul (at right). After World War I this respected Egyptian lawyer emerged as the standard-bearer for Egypt's independence struggle. He headed the Egyptian Wafd ("delegation") to the Paris Peace Conference in 1919 and later converted the Wafd into a popular political party. The man beside him is not identified. (Murray Harris, Egypt under the Egyptians)

less worthy of his own countrymen. These are high qualifications. He should go far" (Storrs 1937, 54).

Saad Zaghlul did go far, but not in the direction that Cromer had in mind. Under Gorst, Saad, like many Umma Party members and sympathizers, became disillusioned with British rule. Although he became justice minister in 1910, he left the cabinet two years later because of differences with the other ministers, for he was so outspoken that he often antagonized others. When Kitchener issued the 1913 Organic Law that allowed Egyptians to set up the Legislative Assembly and hold elections, Saad ran and was elected by two separate constituencies. His legislative colleagues elected him vice president of the assembly in January 1914, and he became its leading critic of the government during its few months in session.

When the war started the assembly was suspended and never reconvened, but it had made Saad known to the other members who would found the Egyptian delegation to the postwar conference, the Wafd. During the fall of 1918 Wafd members met frequently to discuss their plans. As soon as the armistice was signed, they requested an appointment with the British high commissioner, Sir Reginald Wingate. Two days later Saad and two of his friends called on Wingate and asked for permission to talk with officials in the British Foreign Office about Egypt's demand for independence. Wingate gave no answer, but he did cable the foreign secretary, Lord Balfour, who replied that his officials were too busy with preparations for the forthcoming Paris Peace Conference to talk with Saad Zaghlul or even with Prime Minister Rushdi. Hussein Rushdi proceeded to resign, and no Egyptian wanted to take his place.

The rebuff angered the Egyptians, who noted that Arabs, Jews, and Armenians were asked to address the conference but that they were not. To refute allegations that Saad's delegation did not truly represent the people, supporters circulated petitions throughout Egypt, and about 100,000 signers authorized the Wafd to speak for them. This act of circulating petitions made the Wafd assume a more formal organization, just as signing them made Egyptians feel more involved in the independence struggle.

As no Egyptian was willing to take charge of Egypt's government, unrest spread throughout the country. The British tried to nip it in the bud by exiling Saad Zaghlul and three of his colleagues to Malta. This infuriated the Egyptian people. Law school students went on strike, followed by government employees, judges, and lawyers. Within a week some Egyptians were looting shops, blowing up railroad tracks, cutting telegraph wires, and burning down buildings. Six British officers were murdered in a railroad car. Street demonstrations, some violent, became a daily occurrence. Dozens of rioters were killed, injured, or arrested. For the first time in history, Egyptian women took part in these demonstrations. Coptic priests mounted the *minbars* of mosques, and Muslim *khatib*s, or preachers, stood in the pulpits of churches to teach the nearly forgotten lessons of national solidarity. The British managed to quell the violence by sending in their troops to reinforce the police, calling on the notables to pacify the rioters, and by sending to Egypt a new high commissioner, General Edmund Allenby (1861–1936).

Allenby promptly called on the Egyptians to submit their proposals for steps to restore tranquility. He also ordered the release of Saad Zaghlul and the other detainees in Malta, freeing them to go to the Paris Peace Conference. It is one of the tragic ironies of Egyptian history that, on the very day when Saad's Wafd reached Paris, the U.S. delegation to the conference issued a statement recognizing Britain's protectorate over Egypt. The Egyptians had hoped that President Woodrow Wilson would champion their claim to self-determination. Instead, they found that no one in Paris cared about them. Demonstrations resumed in Egypt. Allenby struggled to find any Egyptian willing to head the government, as the very real threat of assassination acted as a deterrent.

Meanwhile, the British government announced that it would send a mission to Egypt to examine the causes of the disorders and to report "on the form of Constitution, which, *under the Protectorate,* will be best calculated to promote its peace and prosperity, the progressive development of self-governing institutions, and the protection of foreign interests." The mission was headed by a former official of the Egyptian

SAAD ZAGHLUL MEETS THE
BRITISH HIGH COMMISSIONER

Until 1952 the Wafd celebrated November 13 as the start of the 1919 Revolution, the nationalist uprising that involved more Egyptians than any other. Saad Zaghlul, elected vice president of the Legislative Assembly in 1914, had become the leading opponent of British rule. The demands he made to Sir Reginald Wingate were surprisingly moderate. Note his Suez Canal offer and omission of Egypt's claim to the Sudan. He hoped to be invited to London to negotiate with the Foreign Office, which refused to receive him and criticized Wingate for having done so.

> Sir Reginald Wingate received Saad and two of his friends [at the British Residency on November 13, 1918]. After exchanging greetings and congratulations on the Armistice [ending World War I], Wingate said: "Peace has come and the world is rejoicing after the hardships of war that have burdened it for so long. Egypt will benefit greatly, for God rewards those who are patient. . . ."
>
> Saad replied: "The war was like a fire that has been put out and now only its traces must be cleaned up. I believe that [Egypt] no longer needs emergency laws and censorship of the press and other publications. The people are waiting impatiently for freedom and for an end to the cares that burdened their minds for more than four years."
>
> Sir Reginald promised to write his government about this issue once he reached an understanding with the commander [of the British forces in Egypt]. "The Egyptians must remain calm, be patient, and know that Britain, once it has finished the peace conference, will turn to Egypt and its needs, and the end result will be good."

government, Lord Milner. Most politically aware Egyptians had never wanted the protectorate, did not want to continue it, and now considered their spokesmen to be the Wafd in Paris. The Milner Mission was boycotted by every Egyptian not in the palace or the cabinet.

Milner then negotiated informally with Saad Zaghlul in London in 1920. They drew up a memorandum that would have recognized Egypt's formal independence with an Anglo-Egyptian treaty, a contin-

Saad said: "The Armistice is signed. The Egyptians have a right to worry about their future. There is no reason why they should not know what good Britain wants for them."

Sir Reginald replied: "Don't be in such a hurry and look carefully where you are going. The Egyptians really don't see the long-term consequences." Saad asked him to clarify his words: "Your expression is obscure and I don't understand what you mean by it."

Sir Reginald realized that Saad was offended because he thought that his words were directed at him and started to say that he did not mean Egyptians like him, but rather public opinion in general. He corrected himself: "I meant to say that Egyptian public opinion is not far-sighted." Saad retorted: "I can't accept that, for if I did agree I would undercut my own role. I was elected to the Legislative Assembly by two different Cairo districts, as a genuine expression of public opinion against the opposition of the [Egyptian] government and Lord Kitchener to my candidacy. The same applies to my two colleagues here, Ali Shaarawi and Abd al-Aziz Fahmi."

Following a long argument, Shaarawi said: "We want to be Britain's friend as one free man to another, not as a servant to his master." Sir Reginald shouted in astonishment: "Then you're demanding independence?"

Saad answered: "Yes, we deserve it. Why should we be denied the independence enjoyed by other nations?" A long discussion ensued on Egypt's readiness for independence. Then Saad said: "When Britain helps us gain our complete independence, we'll promise not to aid any other country against her. We'll guarantee her route to India, the Suez Canal, grant Britain the right to occupy it if necessary, and make an alliance with her to furnish troops whenever they are needed against her enemies...."

Source: Abbas Mahmud al-Aqqad, *Saad Zaghlul* (Cairo: Matbaat Hijazi, 1936), 197–198.

ued British military presence, and British financial and judicial advisers. But Saad did not endorse this memorandum; rather, he insisted on referring it to the Egyptian people. Inasmuch as Milner's proposals fell far short of the complete independence demanded by the demonstrators, Egypt's cabinet (anticipating the popular reaction) rejected them. The British cabinet, arguing that Milner had given up too much, also turned down the memorandum.

General Sir Edmund Allenby was one of Britain's few successful generals in World War I.
When in 1919 revolution broke out in Egypt, London sent him to restore order. He freed
Zaghlul to go to Paris and later pressed the British government to declare Egypt's
independence. (Harris, *Egypt under the Egyptians*)

Britain's Declaration of Egypt's Independence

By 1921, though, the British government acknowledged that the Egyptian people would no longer accept its protectorate. Representatives of the two sides would have to agree on what Anglo-Egyptian relationship should take its place. Allenby persuaded his government to let him tell Sultan Fuad that it would negotiate the question with an official Egyptian delegation. Fuad appointed a new government, headed by Adli Yakan (1864–1933), a rival of Saad Zaghlul.

Saad himself returned from Paris to a tumultuous welcome in Egypt. Believing that he alone could parley with the British, Saad stirred up demonstrations against Adli. Adli's negotiations collapsed when Britain insisted on keeping a garrison in Egypt. In Cairo Allenby put together a compromise that he hoped both sides would accept. He proposed having Adli replaced as prime minister by another non-Wafdist politician. At the same time, Britain would recognize Egypt's independence and Egypt would draft a constitution. The British exiled Saad again, this time for more than a year. This act precipitated new strikes, riots, and demonstrations, for Saad had become to most Egyptians a symbol of their national dignity. The British cabinet wanted to dig in and keep the protectorate until the popular agitation ceased, but Allenby went to London and made a persuasive case to the cabinet for declaring Egypt's independence.

On February 28, 1922, the day Allenby returned to Cairo, the British government issued a formal statement terminating its protectorate and declaring Egypt to be an independent sovereign state. But four points were reserved for further negotiations between Britain and Egypt:

1. The security of British Empire communications in Egypt
2. Egypt's defense against foreign aggression or interference
3. The protection of foreign interests and minorities in Egypt
4. The status of the Sudan

The British thus narrowed their area of concern from reforming Egypt to guarding their strategic interests. Egypt had not obtained the complete independence demanded by the Wafd but the partial autonomy that Milner had offered to Saad in 1920 and Curzon to Adli in 1921.

Even if Egypt now enjoyed formal political independence, the country remained almost wholly dependent on foreigners. The Egyptian armed forces would have been too small and ill-equipped to defend Egypt and the Sudan without British assistance. Most of the high-ranking officers were British; Muslim officers were still mainly of Turkish and Circassian descent. Most top government officials were British, European, Syrian, or Armenian. Nearly all public utilities, manufacturing firms, transportation companies, hotels, banks, and insurance companies were owned and managed by foreigners. No Egyptian sat on the Suez Canal Company administrative board. Egypt was home to some 200,000 foreigners, whom the Capitulations still exempted from local laws and taxes.

Egypt's Cultural Revival

Although limits on Egypt's independence remained, signs of a new spirit appeared during and after the 1919 revolution. An Egyptian capitalist named Talaat Harb (1867–1941) founded a giant financial institution, Bank Misr, which set up and financed an Egyptian-owned textile factory, a first step toward Egypt's economic independence. Egypt also made progress toward cultural independence. Egypt's first secular university had been established in 1908 but languished for lack of state support. In 1919 the American University in Cairo was founded and bought its buildings. In 1925 the national university was reorganized as Cairo University and was given its own campus in Giza.

Nahdat Misr (The Awakening of Egypt). This statue, carved by sculptor Mahmud Mukhtar, represents Egypt's revival as a nation. This photograph shows the statue in front of the Cairo railroad station. It was later moved to a mall leading to Cairo University. (Library of Congress)

Egypt also became the leader of Arab popular culture. In 1919 the first recording studio opened in Cairo. During the 1920s several film companies began producing silent movies. Talaat Harb set up a studio complex that helped to make Cairo the Hollywood of the Arab world. During the 1920s a young woman known as Umm Kulthum (1904–75) began a remarkable career lasting half a century as a singer, at first on the stage and at people's private parties, later on radio. Egyptian state broadcasting was launched in 1932; renamed Radio Cairo, its broadcasts soon reached all parts of the Arab world.

Arabic newspapers and magazines proliferated. More books were published in Cairo than in all other Arab capitals combined. Historian Jacques Berque writes about "the generation of 1919"—the group of leading thinkers who emerged after World War I to expand the country's intellectual horizons (Berque 1972, 356). It included Taha Hussein (1889–1973), who applied Western techniques of historical analysis to early Arabic poetry; Mahmud Mukhtar (1891–1934), Egypt's first great Muslim sculptor; Muhammad Hussein Haykal (1888–1956), who wrote Egypt's first novel and a modernist interpretation of the life of Muhammad; Salama Musa (1887–1958), who advocated democratic socialism; Huda Shaarawi (1879–1947), who led Egyptian women in renouncing the veil and female seclusion; and Tawfiq al-Hakim (1898–1987), a prolific and satirical playwright and novelist.

Constitution and Elections

Cultural advances were important, but the political struggles mattered most to educated Egyptians. The document that expressed their highest hopes was the 1923 constitution. It was written, following Britain's declaration of Egypt's independence, by a group of Egyptian legal scholars who modeled it heavily on the Belgian constitution. The Wafd, leaderless while Saad Zaghlul was in exile, had nothing to do with it. Fuad—now king, no longer sultan—called it "that Communist constitution," even though it empowered him to appoint prime ministers, veto legislation, and dissolve parliament. But Allenby, still Britain's high commissioner, promoted it. The Egyptian government accepted the new constitution in April 1923. At last the British agreed to end martial law in Egypt.

Saad and his companions, as well as various Nationalists exiled since 1914, were allowed to return in time to enter the first election for Egypt's new parliament. The Wafd reorganized itself as a political party. Its candidates won 179 of the 211 seats in the Chamber of Deputies.

King Fuad called on the Wafd Party to form independent Egypt's first government, appointing Saad as prime minister.

The Egyptians and the British both wanted to resolve their political differences. Only Saad could negotiate a settlement that most Egyptians would accept. Britain, meanwhile, had just elected its first Labour Party government, which British voters and indeed Egyptians assumed would be less committed to the British Empire than the Liberals or the Conservatives. Not even Labour, though, would give up strategic assets like the Suez Canal. For their part the Wafdists could not stay in power on popular enthusiasm alone. From the Egyptian side Saad faced two threats: Fuad, who detested any parliament not firmly under his control; and the terrorist secret societies, holdovers from the 1919 revolution, which believed that only force could drive the British out.

In November 1924 terrorists assassinated Sir Lee Stack, the commander in chief of the Egyptian army and governor of the Sudan. Allenby was outraged and publicly handed an ultimatum to Saad, demanding an indemnity of 500,000 Egyptian pounds (approximately $2.5 million), a public apology, and the withdrawal of all Egyptian troops from the Sudan, as well as the prosecution of the assassins. Egyptians were galled by Allenby's statement that the murder, which Saad could not have countenanced, was an act "which holds up Egypt as at present governed to the contempt of civilized peoples." The ultimatum also deprived Egypt of the Nile waters that the Sudan needed to irrigate its newly developed Gezira region, which was starting to raise long-staple cotton in direct competition with the Egyptian product. This part especially angered Egyptian landowners and others dependent on the cotton market. Although the Foreign Office had not approved the text of this ultimatum, the British government decided to stand behind Allenby. Saad, who might have rallied the Egyptian people by rejecting its most extreme demands, chose instead to resign. His resignation enabled King Fuad to appoint a caretaker cabinet of his own men. On this sour note the first era of Wafdist rule ended.

Barriers to Egypt's Independence

The emerging pattern in Egypt's politics was that of a power triangle made up of the king, the Wafd Party, and the British. King Fuad wanted to rule autocratically. He used his vast landholdings and his ability to make appointments to the army, the civil service, and the ulama to expand his claque of loyal followers. The Wafd Party enjoyed the support of the overwhelming majority of Egyptian voters. But even nominally democratic elections were marred by large landowners who forced their peasants to vote en masse for themselves or their favorite parties or candidates. The British used the absence of a treaty with Egypt to preserve their influence. They often invoked the 1922 declaration's Four Reserved Points (security of British communications, defense against foreign interference, protection of foreign interests and minorities, and the Sudan) to block any policy or appointment that seemed likely to harm their interests.

There were also lesser Egyptian parties that could not compete with the Wafd for popularity but were able to affect the balance of power within Egypt. The most extreme of these was the National Party, which remained determined to oppose negotiations with the British until all troops were withdrawn from Egypt. The largest minority party, the Liberal Constitutionalists, was made up of supporters of Adli Yakan. They had all belonged to or backed the Wafd in 1919 but had left it because they opposed Saad's overbearing personality or feared his popularity among Egyptians. The Liberal Constitutionalist leaders were mainly landowners and intellectuals who favored the 1923 constitution for the powers it gave them. At times they might work with the Wafd to oppose King Fuad's usurpation of parliament's powers, but from 1926 on they were cooperating with palace politicians to form governments that excluded the Wafdists whom the people had elected. Fuad set up his own group, the Union Party, in 1925. One of Egypt's ablest politicians, Ismail Sidqi (1875–1950), who headed a dictatorial and anti-Wafdist government in the early 1930s, formed one incongruously named the People's Party.

All these parties entered into the triangular power struggle, often to the benefit of the British. Although representatives of several parties negotiated with the British Foreign Office, none reached a treaty that could have won popular acceptance. No cabinet tried to formulate policies to solve any of Egypt's mounting economic and social problems.

Egypt in the 1920s and 1930s was still an agricultural country heavily dependent on the export of long-staple cotton. Improvements in Nile River irrigation were still increasing the amount of land under cultivation, but the population was growing at a faster rate. The distribution of landholdings was becoming increasingly lopsided, and the disparity was widening between a few hundred rich landlords and a mounting number of poor, landless peasants. Crop diversification and industrialization could alleviate these problems only if Egypt managed to find customers

KING FUAD PROMULGATES
THE 1930 CONSTITUTION

Although King Fuad had formally decreed the promulgation of the democratic 1923 constitution, he resented its limitations on his royal powers. He took advantage of the Wafd's failure to reach an agreement with the British government regarding the Sudan to replace that constitution with a new one in 1930. This constitution made the council of ministers (cabinet) responsible to the king, restricted the legislative powers of the elected Parliament, and limited the franchise to male, educated, property-owning Egyptians to weaken the popular Wafd Party. It was to remain in effect until 1936. What follows is his announcement of the change.

We Fuad the First, King of Egypt, having considered our Order, no. 42, of 1923,

And since our most cherished desire and the greatest aim of our determination is to ensure the welfare of our people, in an orderly and peaceable manner,

And taking due note of the experiences of the past seven years and acting in accordance with the necessity of reconciling the basic theories and the conditions and needs of the country,

And having considered the letter and statement submitted to us by the Cabinet on October 21, 1930,

for products other than its long-staple cotton. This overdependence on cotton posed other problems as well: competition from rayon and other artificial fibers, infestation by the boll weevil, and declining output per acre as a result of overwatering and salinization of the fields caused by the ongoing transition from basin to perennial irrigation.

The Egyptian government was spending more money on public education than it did under the British protectorate, but even this had negative side effects. The school system was turning out more graduates than the government and private enterprise could absorb. The result was the unemployment or underemployment of many of Egypt's brightest young people. This in turn created a disaffected intelligentsia and the potential for revolution. Egypt might have tried industrialization to generate more jobs for managers and workers. The first protective tariffs were imposed under Ismail Sidqi in 1930, but the Great Depression reduced the supply of both foreign and domestic investment capital.

Order as follows:

Article 1. The present Constitution will cease to be operative, and shall be replaced by the Constitution annexed to this Order:

The two Houses [of the Egyptian Parliament] existing at present will be dissolved.

Article 2. Subject to the application of Laws 48 and 60, as provided for in the next Article, the new Constitution shall become effective as from the day [the new] Parliament assembles.

Article 3. From the date of the publication of the [new] Constitution and until Parliament assembles, legislative power, together with the other powers assigned to Parliament by virtue of the Constitution shall be vested in us [King Fuad] and exercised by us, in accordance with Articles 48 and 60 of the Constitution, by means of degrees [issued] by us, provided, however, that the provisions embodied in these [decrees] shall not contravene the basic principles established by the Constitution.

Article 4. During the period referred to in the preceding Article, it shall be permissible, for the sake of maintaining public order, religion, or morals, to suppress or abolish any newspaper or periodical, by a decision of the Minister of Interior, following two warnings, or by a decision of the Council of Ministers without a warning.

Both profits and wages fell during the 1930s, and there was little industrialization in Egypt. Overpopulation was becoming a problem, but few Egyptians then saw its threat to their economy and society.

Egyptian politicians put off addressing such issues as these, but everyone wanted to reach a settlement with Great Britain. Allenby's successor as high commissioner, Lord Lloyd, was an imperialist of the old school willing to bring in gunboats to intimidate men like Saad Zaghlul. Lloyd tried to maneuver Egyptian politicians to weaken the Wafd. As long as the Conservatives, who had appointed Lloyd, remained in power in London, Egyptians would not negotiate with Britain. After Saad's death in 1927, Mustafa al-Nahhas (1879–1965) took over leadership of the Wafd Party. When a British Labour government took power in 1929 and the Wafd won a free election in Egypt, Anglo-Egyptian negotiations briefly resumed, but the Wafd's rivalry with the palace led to Nahhas's downfall.

King Fuad appointed as his new prime minister Ismail Sidqi, who dismissed the Wafd-dominated parliament and replaced the 1923 constitution with a new one that concentrated power in his own hands. For five years Egypt was under a virtual dictatorship in which both the Wafdists and the Liberal Constitutionalists boycotted elections. High Commissioner Lloyd's replacement, Sir Percy Loraine, kept a low profile, and there were no Anglo-Egyptian talks. But in 1934 a new high commissioner, Sir Miles Lampson, urged the palace to restore the 1923 constitution and to hold free elections, to form an Egyptian government with enough popular support to negotiate a treaty with the British. After a year of rising discontent King Fuad accepted Lampson's advice and reinstated the old constitution. A caretaker cabinet was formed containing ministers from most of Egypt's parties, and Anglo-Egyptian negotiations resumed.

The Anglo-Egyptian Treaty

By 1936 both the British and the Egyptians were eager to strengthen their ties. A primary cause was the rise in Europe of authoritarian governments. Italy, now governed by the Fascist Party under Benito Mussolini, wanted to join Europe's great powers by gaining colonies. Already ruling Libya (west of Egypt), Italy occupied Ethiopia (east of the Anglo-Egyptian Sudan). King Fuad supported Italy. But most Egyptians, including the Wafd, viewed the Fascists as a threat to their independence and democratic government. In addition, they feared that any war among the European powers might become a replay of World War I, during which Egypt had been used as an Allied military base. If war came an Anglo-Egyptian treaty might enable Egypt to limit British interference. The British, concerned about their deteriorating position in Europe and the Middle East, needed to strengthen their military presence in Egypt. They wanted to deal with Nahhas, the Wafdist leader, because they knew that the Wafd alone could influence Egyptian popular opinion.

In the 1936 parliamentary elections, the Wafd won control of both houses by large majorities. Soon afterward Fuad died and was succeeded by his 16-year-old son, Farouk (1920–65). The two sides started negotiating in earnest and soon reached an agreement on the terms for a 20-year treaty of alliance. The British recognized Egypt's independence, agreed to reduce their troops to 10,000 during peacetime and to limit their bases to the Suez Canal zone, and promised to sponsor Egypt for membership in the League of Nations and to call for the abolition of the Capitulations. The Egyptians accepted a 20-year British occupation of the Canal Zone and allowed British troops to stay in Cairo and Alexandria until adequate barracks, roads, and bridges could be built at Egyptian government expense. Both sides put off any decision about the Sudan's future.

Most observers considered the signing of the Anglo-Egyptian Treaty in August 1936 as the final step toward Egypt's political independence. Representatives of all Egyptian parties except the Nationalists signed the document. Although few Egyptians today recall the treaty favorably, the pact was popular at the time. More popular still was the 1937 Montreux Convention abolishing the Capitulations and phasing out the Mixed Courts over a 13-year period. After 1949, foreigners living in Egypt would no longer enjoy privileges before the law greater than those of the country's own citizens. Britain sponsored Egypt's application for membership in the League of Nations. The Egyptian government was now free to open embassies and consulates in other countries and to make its own domestic and foreign policies.

Need for Reform

For decades most politically active Egyptians had focused on ending the British military occupation of their country. As a result, they had neglected many other problems. In a country where possession of land was the primary source of power, most people owned either no land at all or too little to support themselves and their families. The construction of the Nile irrigation works and improved rail and maritime transport had led to cash crops, especially long-staple cotton, largely replacing subsistence agriculture. If world cotton prices dropped, as they did during the 1930s Great Depression, Egypt's economy suffered. In 1931 the price of cotton fell to one-third of its 1926 level. Small landowners were especially hard hit; between 1927 and 1937 more than 40,000 peasants, unable to pay their taxes, lost their lands. Land rents were so high that, even under optimum conditions, it was hard for tenant farmers to raise enough to pay the landlord and still make an adequate living. The average daily wage for a cotton farmer fell from 8 piasters (40 cents) in 1920 to 2.5 piasters (less than 13 cents) in 1933. Peasants who flocked to the cities to seek work found more jobs in transport and services than in manufacturing, where wages would have been higher.

Egyptians were starting to invest in such industries as textiles, building materials, and food processing, but industrialization remained

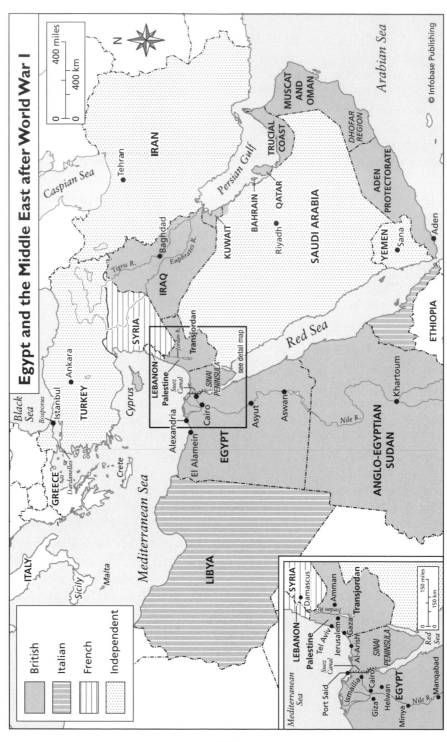

Egypt and the Middle East after World War I

embryonic up to World War II, and most manufacturing firms were still owned by foreigners. Egypt's membership in the sterling bloc tied its economy to that of Britain. Parliament, dominated by landlords and urban lawyers, did limit some land rents during the depression, but it never tried to redistribute landholdings. Land and buildings remained the most popular outlets for investors.

Meanwhile, the income gap between rich and poor Egyptians grew wider. Along with poverty went ignorance and disease. The 1923 constitution had made primary education compulsory, but poor peasants could not pay tuition to send their children to school, because they could not do without the meager income they gained from their children's work in the fields. Mortality rates, especially for rural infants, were among the world's highest. Because of constant irrigation, bilharzia (a parasitic disease) and trachoma (an eye infection) were endemic. Few doctors or nurses lived in rural villages. There were still other causes of bad health conditions. Peasants could not afford piped water, let alone garbage and sewage disposal facilities that might have improved their hygienic conditions. Village ditches and ponds provided most of the water for drinking, cooking, washing clothes and cooking utensils, bathing, washing animals, removing garbage and sewage, and other purposes. Chickens and water buffaloes shared the mud brick huts of the poor. The poorest lacked even houses; some slept in doorways, under bridges, and on railroad rights-of-way. These conditions could not be borne forever. Eventually some were bound to question the system by which the benefits and burdens of citizenship were parceled out. By 1936 Egyptian democracy was on trial.

In retrospect, the signing of the Anglo-Egyptian Treaty was the high-water mark of liberal democracy in Egypt. The 1923 constitution had been restored after five years of government under Fuad. He had died just before free elections swept Egypt's most popular party, the Wafd, into power. His son and successor, Farouk, was adored by the Egyptian press and people. Some even wanted him appointed to the Islamic caliphate, an office that had been abolished in 1924 by Kemal Atatürk, the president of Turkey. Britain's high commissioner (from 1936 its ambassador), Sir Miles Lampson, noted that Farouk was immature and not well educated enough to rule Egypt, but most Egyptian leaders wanted him only as a figurehead. The real power, they felt, should belong to a cabinet responsible to the people's representatives. In 1936 Egyptians looked forward to democracy under a popular king, independence, and social reform. In the years that followed, none of these high hopes would be realized.

8

THE PALESTINE QUESTION AND WORLD WAR II (1936–1952)

By the late 1930s Egypt had to address foreign issues as well as domestic ones. The rise of Nazi Germany and Fascist Italy was undermining the postwar peace settlement in Europe. No country could ignore how the changing European power balance was affecting Britain and France, even in their foreign colonies. Iraq, placed under a British mandate after World War I, had become independent in 1932. The countries mandated to France—Syria and Lebanon—seemed likely in 1936 to follow suit. The two Arab countries most apt to influence these new Arabic-speaking states were Egypt and Saudi Arabia, but the latter was still extremely poor until it began to export oil shortly before World War II. That war and its aftermath would drastically affect Europe's relations with the Middle East and Britain's control over Egypt. One mandated country would become a major focus of world attention, but back in 1936 it was not, so far as most of its inhabitants were concerned, advancing toward independence. This was Palestine.

The Palestine Question

The Palestine question was not a major issue for Egypt until 1936. Palestine had been a part of the Ottoman Empire until it was taken by the British in 1917–18. Shortly before this conquest the British cabinet had issued a statement called the Balfour Declaration. In this document the government pledged to back the creation in Palestine of a national home for the Jewish people. Because the Jews were scattered among many nations of the world, whereas about 93 percent of Palestine's inhabitants were Muslims or Christians who spoke Arabic, the creation of a national home for the Jews would take some time and could require

126

the large-scale transfer of populations. Jews would have to move there from the countries where they were living. Palestine's Arab inhabitants would face an uncertain political status, although the Balfour Declaration did specify that nothing should be done to prejudice their civil and religious rights. Britain's motives for issuing this policy statement remain debatable. Probably it hoped to strengthen Jewish support for the Allied cause in Russia and the United States, to secure British control over the land east of the Suez Canal, and to restrict France's wartime gains to what are now Lebanon and Syria. In later years some Arabs ascribed Britain's support for Zionism to a desire to divide them, or to the Jews' power in British society.

Understandably, Arab Palestinians resisted both the Balfour Declaration and British efforts to carry it out. They looked to neighboring Muslims and Arabs, including Egyptians, for support. As long as the number of Jews entering Palestine was small, the movement to create a Jewish state, called "political Zionism," did not threaten local Arabs. And while most Arabic-speaking countries were being ruled by Britain or France, their leaders could do little to help the Palestinian Arabs to combat Zionism. By 1936, though, conditions were changing. With the rise of Nazi Germany and its fiercely anti-Jewish laws, mounting numbers of Central and Eastern European Jews were trying to flee. In 1917 some 7 percent of the population of Palestine was Jewish. By the late 1930s this figure had risen to about 30 percent. Palestinian Arabs feared they would soon turn into a minority in their own country. In 1936 they set aside the family and religious loyalties that had previously divided them and launched a nationwide revolution against the British and the Zionists. Newly independent Iraq and Egypt tried to help them, politically and economically more than militarily. Often individuals gave more help than their governments.

As Egypt became involved in the Palestine question, Egyptians began to consider Arab nationalism. Until then the Egyptian people had not generally viewed themselves as Arabs. The Arab nationalist idea was associated with the British-backed Arabians and Syrians who had rebelled against the Ottoman Empire during World War I. Egyptian nationalists had viewed this Arab Revolt as an act of treason, for they had wanted the Turks to liberate them from the British. They also regarded themselves as having progressed further toward civilization than any other Arabic-speaking country. Their strongest loyalty was to Egypt. Both Muslims and Copts took pride in their descent from the ancient Egyptians and stressed the pharaonic character of their common culture. But political independence, together with the growing Palestine crisis, gradually reoriented the majority's loyalties from

Pharaonism, as Egyptian nationalism is sometimes called, toward Arab nationalism and Islam.

Egyptian nationalism lost credibility as parliamentary democracy faltered in Egypt after the 1936 election. The Wafdist cabinet, led by Mustafa al-Nahhas, lasted only 18 months before Farouk's advisers engineered its replacement by a coalition ministry made up of party leaders opposed to the Wafd. Ironically, the leaders of the Liberal Constitutionalist Party, which had taken charge of writing the 1923 Constitution, defied that document by joining the anti-Wafd coalition. Farouk turned out to be as dictatorial as his father had been. Owing to his youth he reigned under the influence of his mother and his chief tutor, Ahmad Hasanayn (1889–1946). They were aided by the Wafd's waning popularity. Two of its most capable politicians, Ahmad Mahir (1888–1945) and Mahmud Fahmi al-Nuqrashi (1888–1948), were expelled from the Wafd for criticizing Nahhas. They proceeded to form the Saadist Party, which joined the coalition cabinet. This proliferation of parties, which mainly interested wealthy and educated men (women did not yet have the vote), alienated most of the Egyptian people.

As Egyptians lost faith in European institutions, including parliamentary democracy, many felt drawn to Islamic beliefs and values. Arab nationalist parties and ideologies won only a few followers in Egypt before World War II, but Egyptians of all classes and educational levels joined a revolutionary movement called the Society of the Muslim Brothers. The Brothers rejected parties, parliaments, and constitutions. They wanted to restore the authentic institutions of Islam: the umma (community of Muslim believers), sharia, and the authority of the ulama. Egyptian politicians could not solve the country's pressing domestic problems until they had grappled with foreign policy and ideological issues: Egypt's stance between the democracies and the rising totalitarian states, the Palestine question, and the choice among Pharaonism, Arabism, and Islam.

World War II

Events in Europe almost forced the Egyptian government to adopt a policy on the issue of confronting totalitarian states. As Italy tightened its hold on Libya and Ethiopia, it cast covetous eyes on the Nile Valley. Italian radio transmitters beamed Fascist propaganda into Egypt, where some 60,000 Italian residents helped spread Mussolini's influence. Nazi Germany, meanwhile, was remilitarizing the Rhineland, annexing Austria, persuading Britain and France to concede the Czech-ruled

Sudetenland, and threatening to invade Poland. Although Britain and France did their utmost to appease Hitler, a new European war seemed inevitable. The British wanted to be certain of military bases and support in the now-independent Arab countries.

To lessen the risk of popular opposition in those countries, Britain took a pro-Arab stand on the Palestine question. In May 1939 the government issued a new White Paper that put severe limits on Jewish immigration and land purchases and promised independence in 10 years to a predominantly Arab Palestine. Although Egyptians noticed less the British government's actions in Palestine than London's policy of severing the Sudan from Egypt, the White Paper probably drew them nearer to Britain when World War II started in September 1939.

The major combatants at the beginning of this war were the Allies, mainly Britain and France, against Germany. Most Egyptians did not want to fight on either side, but realism made complete neutrality impossible. If nationalism still alienated them from the British, they knew that kicking their old masters out could clear the stage for new ones. These new masters were most likely to be the Italians, who already held territory on three sides of Egypt. In 1940, once the Germans overran Western Europe and Italy joined the German side, the focus of the war shifted to Eastern Europe and North Africa, regions closer to Egypt. During 1939 and 1940 Egypt was turning into a major base for troops from all parts of the British Empire. Although the Anglo-Egyptian Treaty had limited the number of British troops and bases in Egypt during peacetime, it placed no restrictions in case of a general war. It also did not require Egypt's government to declare war on Britain's enemies. But in Italian and German eyes, the presence of British troops rendered Egypt fair game for attack, invasion, or subversion. Egypt might resist pressure to enter World War II, but, unlike Sweden or Switzerland, it could not avoid involvement completely.

The attitudes of Egyptian politicians and the people shifted as the war progressed. During the first year they expected the British to defeat Germany and cooperated with them, even though their prime minister, Ali Mahir (1882–1960), was a strong nationalist. The fall of France in 1940, the country most admired by Egyptians, came as a shock. Under British pressure King Farouk dismissed Mahir. For the next two years the king and successive ministries tried to minimize Egypt's wartime role. As German troops under General Erwin Rommel took control in Libya and swept across the border into Egypt, many Egyptians called on him to liberate them. Because of the demands of the foreign troops quartered in Egypt, wheat flour and other necessities became scarce.

POLITICAL PARTIES IN EGYPT, 1919–1952

Before and during the period of constitutional government, parties were the most popular form of political organization for the Egyptian upper and middle classes. After the 1952 Revolution the new government banned all political parties.

Communist Party (al-Hizb al-Shuyui)
Egypt actually had several communist groups, of which the largest was al-Haraka al-Dimuqratiya li al-Taharrur al-Watani (HADETO), which appealed to some skilled workers and many middle-class intellectuals, especially minorities.

Liberal Constitutionalist Party (Hizb al-Ahrar al-Dusturiyyin)
Main rival to the Wafd between its founding in 1922 and the 1952 revolution. Strongly committed to secularism and liberalism, the party's main supporters were large landowners and intellectuals.

Muslim Brothers (Jamiyat al-Ikhwan al-Muslimin)
Political movement, technically not a party, formed in 1928 to educate Muslims and promote an Islamic government and society based on the sharia. It had a larger popular following at its height in 1948 than any political party. Banned in 1954, it has been informally allowed to revive since 1970.

National Party (al-Hizb al-Watani)
Party founded by Mustafa Kamil in 1907 to demand the evacuation of British troops from Egypt and a constitution from Khedive Abbas. It was overshadowed by the Wafd after 1919, but it retained some student and professional supporters.

Some Egyptian politicians entered into secret talks with the Nazis. Some officers plotted unsuccessfully to cross the battle lines and link up with Rommel's forces. In Cairo the British burned embassy documents and planned to retreat to Palestine if the Germans took Egypt.

On February 4, 1942, one of Britain's darkest moments, its ambassador took a drastic step to ensure Egyptian cooperation. Countering the king's attempt to replace his pro-British prime minister with Ali Mahir, Sir Miles Lampson ordered British armored cars to surround Abdin Palace and handed Farouk an ultimatum, demanding that he appoint a

People's Party (Hizb al-Shaab)
Small clique organized by Ismail Sidqi in 1930 as a counterweight to the Union Party so that he would not depend totally on palace support. It dominated the government during the first Sidqi era but later merged with the Union Party.

Saadist Party (Hizb al-Saadiyin)
Breakaway faction from the Wafd formed in 1937–38 by Ahmad Mahir and Mahmud Fahmi al-Nuqrashi, claiming to uphold the democratic principles of Saad Zaghlul. It formed several minority cabinets during the era of King Farouk.

Union Party (Hizb al-Ittihad)
Small organization formed in 1925 by King Fuad's supporters to counter the Wafd Party and Saad Zaghlul, it formed a coalition cabinet with the Liberal Constitutionalists and competed with them unsuccessfully for support from the landowning class. It merged in 1938 with the People's Party.

Wafd Party (Hizb al-Wafd)
Originally the delegation that Egyptian nationalists hoped would represent them at the Paris Peace Conference in 1919, led by Saad Zaghlul until his death in 1927 and then by Mustafa al-Nahhas, it was Egypt's most popular party and gained the most votes in any election not rigged by the government. Banned after the 1952 Revolution, it was revived in 1978.

Young Egypt (Misr al-Fatat)
Egyptian nationalist youth movement, especially popular in the 1930s and often thought to be pro-Fascist. It renamed itself the Islamic Nationalist Party in 1940 and the Egyptian Socialist Party in 1946. It was dissolved in 1952.

cabinet that would uphold the 1936 Anglo-Egyptian Treaty. In reality, this meant an all-Wafdist ministry under Mustafa al-Nahhas. The king tried to avoid accepting Lampson's demand, but his alternative was to sign a letter of abdication. He finally gave in.

This action, understandable when German forces were 100 kilometers (fewer than 70 miles) west of Alexandria, traumatized the main actors on Egypt's political stage. King Farouk, shorn of his power, went into moral decline. In the eyes of the Egyptian people the Wafd Party ceased to be the vanguard of nationalist resistance and came to stand for

King Farouk. When he ascended the throne in 1936, he was young, handsome, and immensely popular. After the British forced him to appoint a cabinet he did not want in 1942, he became obese, dissolute, and unpopular. He was ousted by a military coup in July 1952. (Library of Congress)

collaboration with the British. In his memoirs General Muhammad Naguib (1901–84), who later led the 1952 revolution against the monarchy, recalled asking Farouk for permission to resign from the army out of shame for Egypt. Other Egyptian officers, including future leaders Gamal Abdel Nasser (1918–70) and Anwar Sadat (1918–81), grieved over their nation's latest humiliation at Britain's hands. But during the war most Egyptians acquiesced in their situation. They did not like being a base for British, Canadian, Australian, New Zealand, South African, Indian, and even U.S. troops. They resented the rising prices of food, clothing, and housing, but martial law and press censorship muffled their protests. Some wanted a German triumph to free them from British imperialism and the possible threat of Zionism, but most expected little benefit from German or Italian rule. Once the Allies had stemmed the German tide in November 1942 at El Alamein (on Egyptian soil), there was little to gain from supporting Britain's enemies.

Many Egyptians benefited from wartime prosperity. The British government borrowed heavily from Egypt, running up a 400 million sterling pound ($2 billion) debt by 1945. The presence of Allied troops and support personnel created additional demand for Egyptian-made goods and services. More than 200,000 Egyptians were employed by the Allied forces. The entertainment industry throve; especially memorable was the nightclub of celebrated belly-dancer Badia al-Masabni (1892–1974), enjoyed by foreign soldiers and Egyptian men alike. Badia, considered pivotal in changing the Egyptian dance scene, had opened the Casino Opera in 1926, which included comedians, singers, and dancers in its program. Although cotton acreage was again cut back, food prices skyrocketed, enriching landlords whose peasants grew wheat, corn, and rice. The war ended imports of Western manufactures, sparking the growth of local industries. By 1944 Egypt was self-sufficient in sugar, alcohol, and cigarettes, and nearly so in cotton thread, soap, shoes, glass, cement, and furniture. It had also become the hub of a British-formed organization called the Middle East Supply Centre, which tied Egypt's economy to those of other Arab states and opened new markets for its nascent industries.

During the war some British officials urged the Arabs to build political unity on this economic integration. A union of the Fertile Crescent states—Iraq, Transjordan, Palestine, Syria, and Lebanon—was proposed by Nuri al-Said, Iraq's prime minister, in 1943. Fearing that such a union would diminish Egypt's own influence over the Arab world, Premier Nahhas successfully put forth a different scheme, a league of independent Arab states. This looser association, the Arab League, was organized at a conference in Alexandria in 1944. Its formal existence began in March 1945, directed by an Egyptian secretary-general, Abd al-Rahman Azzam (1893–1976). Saudi Arabia and Yemen joined Egypt, Transjordan, Iraq, Syria, and Lebanon in the organization, which vowed to oppose efforts to set up a Jewish state in predominantly Arab Palestine. Most observers saw British encouragement behind the formation of the Arab League, although the initiative came from the Wafd Party. Britain's policy was to focus Egypt's concern on regional economic affairs and blunt its drive to regain control of the Sudan.

Challenges to Democracy after World War II

Although Egypt prospered because of wartime conditions, it should not be assumed that Egyptians were happy. King Farouk remained the symbol of the nation, but his ever more blatant carousing and sexual exploits alienated the people. If Mustafa al-Nahhas and the Wafd still claimed to bear the standard of resistance to British imperialism, they could never evade accusations of having taken power behind British tanks. They were embarrassed when their secretary-general, Makram Ubayd (1889–1961), quit the party and published a searing exposé of Wafd corruption. Egypt may have had the trappings of independence, but in reality it remained a British dependency.

Embittered young Egyptians were losing faith in parliamentary democracy and the prewar political parties and were turning to militant, antidemocratic movements. Even before World War II, many had flocked to the ultranationalist group Young Egypt, whose members took paramilitary training and adopted a Fascist salute. Its leader, Ahmad Hussein (1911–82), professed a strong admiration for Hitler and Mussolini. During and after the war Young Egypt recast itself as the Islamic Socialist Party and continued to stir up demonstrations. Egypt's hitherto obscure Communist Party scored propaganda gains while the USSR was a British ally between 1941 and 1945 and could spread propaganda in Egypt. It won support among the growing number of unionized industrial workers.

The most popular movement was the Society of the Muslim Brothers, whose members became notorious for their well-organized demonstrations, terrorist actions, and political assassinations. They set up schools and welfare institutions in villages and urban slums, winning the support of Egypt's poor. They organized massive rallies protesting British rule in Egypt and the Sudan. When the United Nations voted to partition Palestine (against the wishes of its Arab majority) into Jewish and Arab states in 1947, the Muslim Brothers would be the first Egyptians to volunteer to fight on the Arab side.

The Egyptian government, during the early postwar years, tried to persuade the British to revise the 1936 Treaty, which governed relations between the two countries. The peoples of Asia and Africa were demanding the same freedoms, democracy, and national independence for which the Allies had fought in World War II. In 1945–46 Egypt did not experience a popular revolution like that of 1919, but unrest was rife. Ahmad Mahir was assassinated in February 1945, only four months after he became prime minister. An attempt was made on the life of Mustafa al-Nahhas in November of that year, and Amin Uthman (b. 1900), an advocate for cooperation with the British, was murdered in January 1946. On February 9 of that year, a student demonstration got out of hand when Egyptian police opened a drawbridge on which students were marching. Many demonstrators fell into the Nile and as many as 20 lost their lives. Riots and protest marches became a daily occurrence as students for the first time made common cause with labor unions. On February 21 students and workers together stormed the British army barracks in Ismailia (now Liberation) Square and the soldiers opened fire, killing 23 and injuring about 120.

The people of Egypt chafed at being treated like an independent country in name but like a British colony in practice. Britain's new Labour government understood Egypt's concerns and withdrew its troops from Cairo and Alexandria, concentrating them in the Suez Canal zone. After India and Pakistan became independent in 1947, however, the British viewed Suez as their imperial lifeline. The canal remained important, they argued, for Gulf oil shipments and for their defense, and so it became the largest military base outside the Communist bloc.

Successive Egyptian governments tried to minimize Britain's presence in Suez and to gain control over the Anglo-Egyptian Sudan. Since the British had expelled all Egyptian troops from the Sudan after the 1924 assassination of Sir Lee Stack, joint rule there had been a fiction, although the 1936 Treaty did allow Egyptian troops to return. Britain was in fact governing the Sudan as a private colony. If the Egyptians wanted to be independent of Britain, the British asked, why should the Sudan be an Egyptian colony? Egypt argued that it had been paying for the conquest and administration of the Sudan and that the two countries had to unite because of their common dependence on the Nile. Late in 1946 British foreign minister Ernest Bevin and Egyptian prime minister Ismail Sidqi, who had formed his second government in early 1946, drafted a treaty that would have provided for the complete withdrawal of British forces from their Suez Canal base by 1949 and acknowledged "the framework of unity between the Sudan and Egypt under the common crown of Egypt." But it also called for preparing the Sudanese for self-government. This compromise was vehemently opposed by the Wafd; by the Sudanese Umma Party, which wanted independence from Egypt; and by British Conservatives appalled at Bevin's concessions to Egyptian nationalism. After Bevin denied, in the House of Commons, that he had handed the Sudan to Egypt, Sidqi resigned and the treaty was never ratified. Sidqi's successor, Saadist Party leader Mahmud Fahmi al-Nuqrashi, carried the Sudan issue to the UN Security Council in summer 1947. Unable to justify freeing the Sudanese from Britain only to subject them to Egyptian rule, the member states urged the two countries to resume negotiations. The UN decision was a defeat for Nile Valley unity and for Egypt.

It was also in 1947 that Egypt took a step that would eventually destroy both the monarchy and the 1923 constitution. King Farouk met with representatives of Syria, Lebanon, Iraq, Transjordan, Saudi Arabia, and Yemen and agreed to commit Egypt's forces to war against any plan to partition Palestine and to create a Jewish state there. The Arab leaders expected to win easily any such conflict. Later events would prove them wrong, however, and many of their regimes did not survive their shameful defeat. Egypt's regime would ultimately share their fate.

Some argue that the old regime might have implemented a program of economic and social reforms that would have addressed Egypt's real ills: poverty, illiteracy, and disease. An American adviser, Kermit

Roosevelt, urged Farouk to launch an Egyptian New Deal from Abdin Palace (Copeland 1969, 63). One reason this policy was never adopted is that the royal family owned one-tenth of Egypt's arable land, the major source of wealth and power in an agrarian society. Even if Farouk had given up his land and real estate holdings, he could hardly have persuaded the other heirs of Mehmet Ali and Ismail to follow his example. Egypt had growing numbers of doctors, lawyers, economists, teachers, and other educated people. Nearly all agreed that the gap between the richest and the poorest Egyptians would have to be narrowed. Still, the landowning politicians in government posts, in the judiciary, among the ulama, and in the clergy—and of course those in parliament—would all suffer if Egypt's lands were reallocated.

Defeat in Palestine

If the state could not meet people's material needs, the palace hoped to distract them with foreign adventures. The decision to commit the Egyptian army to fight in the 1948 Palestine War was made not by the Saadist cabinet but by King Farouk himself, under the influence of a Lebanese journalist, Karim Thabit. Farouk's main motive for going to war was to prevent Amir Abdallah of Transjordan from seizing Palestine if the Arabs won. Prime Minister al-Nuqrashi, his cabinet, and the Egyptian general staff argued that the army was not ready to fight. But many other Egyptians favored intervention. The UN decision to partition Palestine and hence to create the Jewish State of Israel affronted Muslim and Arab opinion everywhere. The Muslim Brothers started recruiting volunteers even before Britain's withdrawal from Palestine and Israel's declaration of independence precipitated the war in May 1948. The Arab League had resolved to go to war against Israel.

The Egyptian army's performance in the Palestine War was humiliating. So ill-prepared was Egypt's general staff that it needed to borrow road maps of Palestine from an American car dealer in Cairo. General Muhammad Naguib later recalled hiring 21 trucks from Palestinians to move his troops from the Sinai to Gaza. Farouk insisted on making strategic decisions, ignoring repeated warnings from his ministers that his mistress was passing his orders along to Israeli spies.

The first force sent into Palestine consisted of two brigades of Egyptians and Sudanese infantry, fewer than 3,000 men. Although they penetrated well into the Negev Desert in the early days of the war, they did not score the victories that Farouk's adviser Karim Thabit vaunted in his press releases and that were broadcast over Egyptian state radio.

In his war memoirs Gamal Abdel Nasser (Egypt's future leader) alleged that the Egyptian general staff had made no plans for feeding the troops, caring for the wounded, reconnoitering enemy positions before battle, drawing up a strategy for the Egyptian soldiers' advance, or preparing fallback positions in case of a retreat. For the general staff, it was a political war, not one of military strategy.

During the first cease-fire, ordered by the United Nations, both sides combed Europe's used-weapons markets, but Israel replenished its arms more effectively with the timely aid of Czechoslovakia. Once the fighting resumed, the Israelis pushed back their enemies on all fronts. The various Arab forces, far from coordinating their plans, often fired on one another. The largest and best equipped were the armies of Transjordan and Iraq; both countries were ruled by Hashimite kings, whom Farouk viewed as his hereditary enemies (Hashimites are members of the family of the Prophet Muhammad). Transjordan's Arab Legion was especially well trained. Its commander, an Englishman named Sir John Bagot Glubb, wrote in his memoirs that Egypt often undercut the Arab Legion. Iraq's army performed poorly. The Israelis did surprisingly well, capturing and holding lands in Palestine not allotted to them by the UN partition plan.

One serious consequence of the Arab armies' failure was the exodus of most Palestinian Arabs from their homes. Most Zionists believe that they fled voluntarily, or on orders from the Arab leaders (Schechtman 1952, passim), but recent scholarship has shown that Israel devised a strategy to expel them (Morris 1987, passim). Some fled to lands within Palestine that remained in Arab hands, the areas now known as the West Bank and the Gaza Strip. Others went to neighboring Arab countries other than Egypt, for the Nile Valley was already too crowded to admit more than a few thousand refugees.

There was little for the Egyptian people to cheer about. Their great army, as touted by Farouk, Azzam (the secretary-general of the Arab League), and Karim Thabit, had proved to be a hollow shell. The Israelis would have invaded the Sinai Peninsula but for Britain's threat to invoke the 1936 Anglo-Egyptian Treaty (the very pact the Egyptians hated) to defend the canal. An Egyptian delegation negotiated an armistice agreement with Israel. The other Arab states gradually followed suit but attacked Egypt's leaders for letting them down. Egypt administered but did not annex the lands around Gaza, which was crowded with angry Palestinian refugees. Two thousand Egyptian soldiers had been killed, more were wounded, and many were missing. Their officers, especially those who had spent time in the field, were embittered against the king, his court, parliament, and the old regime in general. They sought someone to blame for Egypt's unexpected defeat. Many leading politicians, some of them close to the king, were accused of selling defective weapons to the army. The arms scandal was one more nail in the coffin of Egypt's parliamentary democracy.

The Last Days of Democracy

Because Egypt had a bewildering array of parliamentary parties, most cabinets were coalitions of politicians from several parties and factions. The only popular party was the Wafd. Indeed, its members viewed the Wafd not as a party but as the embodiment of the Egyptian nation. It had become notorious, however, for corruption and administrative incompetence. The Liberal Constitutionalists, Ismail Sidqi, the Saadists, and the Wafdist Bloc had all left the Wafd. A few politicians, such as Ali Mahir, managed to remain independent, but most were caught in the maelstrom of partisan rivalries, which left them little time or energy to devote to their country's real needs. Young Egypt still espoused extreme nationalism; it was effective mainly in league with other groups, such as the National Committee of Workers and Students formed during the 1946 student demonstrations. The Communists were divided into at least four factions that appealed mostly to the educated members of ethnic and religious minorities: Jews, Greeks, Armenians, and Copts. Because the USSR and its satellites supported Israel against the Arabs in 1948, communism no longer appealed to rank-and-file Egyptians. Farouk, his entourage, and some Westerners still feared the spread of communism, but the Muslim majority despised its atheistic doctrines and did not care to make common cause with minority groups.

The Society of Muslim Brothers

In contrast, about half a million Muslims had joined the Society of the Muslim Brothers by 1948. The society stayed aloof from parties, but it was politically active in its call for a return to Quranic values and traditional Muslim institutions. The organization reached its apogee during the Palestine War, in which the Brothers distinguished themselves as volunteer soldiers and auxiliaries. By 1948 it had 2,000 branches in Egypt, most of which ran schools, clinics, and various welfare institutions. It had a women's auxiliary section, appropriately named the Muslim Sisters, and a youth movement, 40,000 strong, called the Rovers. It had also spawned a dreaded Secret Apparatus, a militant wing that bombed movie theaters and assassinated politicians, judges, and police officers. The leader, or supreme guide, Sheikh Hasan al-Banna (1906–49), was respected for his religious principles even as he was feared for his violent Secret Apparatus. Some Egyptians hoped for a coalition between the Muslim Brothers and other power centers, such as the Wafd or the palace; many foreigners believed the society to be in the pay of Germany (during World War II) or Britain (after the war).

The group was starting to falter, however. During the Palestine War, while Egypt was under martial law, Prime Minister Nuqrashi outlawed it for its revolutionary activities. Hasan al-Banna countered by having Nuqrashi assassinated in December 1948. In this stressful time Farouk appointed a tough cabinet that began arresting the Brothers and seizing the society's assets. Hasan al-Banna was not imprisoned, but in February 1949 he was murdered, probably by government agents. By July 4,000 Brothers were in prison. A series of trials ensued. The most notorious was the "Jeep Case," named for a government-captured vehicle filled with documents that incriminated the Brothers for attacking Jewish property in Cairo, allegedly to foment an Islamic revolution in Egypt. In spite of heavy state pressure to execute the defendants, the judges acquitted some and gave others light jail sentences, due to insufficient evidence. The society appealed its dissolution in 1951 and the government had to restore its funds and property. But the repressive measures of 1949 had weakened the society. Even the election of a new supreme guide with strong palace connections did not reinvigorate the Muslim Brothers at that time.

The 1950 Elections

During the dark days following the Palestine defeat, one ray of hope for Egypt was the government's decision to hold parliamentary elections in January 1950. The Wafd took part in the elections and again won most of the seats, but with only 40 percent of the vote. For the next two years, Egypt was again governed by Mustafa al-Nahhas at the head of the Wafd Party. This government put through a number of major reforms intended to better the welfare of Egypt's workers and peasants. The education minister, well-known writer Taha Hussein, abolished fees for the state secondary and technical schools. Dr. Ahmad Hussein (1902–84) (no relation to Taha Hussein or to the Ahmad Hussein who led Young Egypt) extended social service centers to many of the villages. For the first time the government set up a social insurance program for widows, orphans, and disabled and aged persons. The Wafd even offered to distribute a million *feddans* (1.038 million acres) of state land to poor peasants, but it did not follow through. At last the government seemed to address Egypt's real problems.

Meanwhile, the Wafd resumed its campaign to oust the British from Egypt and the Sudan. Negotiations were difficult. The civil war in Greece (1946–50), the loss of Palestine, and the outbreak of the Korean War (June 1950) all strengthened Britain's determination to keep its Suez Canal base, manned by 80,000 troops and holding equipment and supplies worth more than a billion dollars, lest war break out between the Soviets and the West. But the Egyptians felt that their main enemy was not the USSR but Israel. If they must fight an anticommunist war, they wanted better terms than they were apt to get from an unpopular alliance treaty that let British troops remain on their soil and might enable London to interfere in their politics.

Britain also seemed to respond more to the demands of the Sudan's Umma Party for self-rule than to Egypt's desire for Nile Valley unity, driven by its dependence on that river's waters. In 1947 British administrators in Khartoum had prepared a draft constitution for the Anglo-Egyptian Sudan, creating a popularly elected legislature. The Egyptian government, fearing that the British presence would bias the elections toward the Umma and against the pro-Egyptian Ashiqqa Party, opposed this constitution and ignored subsequent Sudanese elections. The Sudan's separation from Egypt now seemed inevitable. Direct negotiations and UN debates had not helped Egypt's cause.

In October 1951 Nahhas unilaterally renounced the 1936 Anglo-Egyptian Treaty and declared Farouk king of Egypt and Sudan. The radical nationalists could now claim that the presence of British troops in the Suez Canal region was illegal and could be opposed by force. Egyptian workers at the British camps went on strike, customs officials held up the clearance of goods destined for the base, longshoremen balked at unloading British supplies, and tradesmen refused to sell their merchandise or their services. British troops retaliated by occupying the roads and bridges near the canal area, as well as the Suez customs house. The Egyptian government summarily dismissed its British employees and openly encouraged students, workers, and auxiliary police to become fedayeen (Muslims who sacrifice themselves for a cause) and to attack the British troops on the Canal.

On January 25, 1952, the British besieged and sacked the police headquarters in Ismailia, one of the main trouble spots. More than 50 Egyptians were killed. The next morning hundreds of auxiliary policemen, who were gathered at Cairo University, met students affiliated

Shepheard's Hotel. Long the most fashionable hotel in Cairo, it was destroyed by fire during Black Saturday, January 26, 1952. (Library of Congress)

with the Muslim Brothers, the Wafd, and Young Egypt, and marched into downtown Cairo. An argument started in Badia's Casino Opera between some of the demonstrators and an off-duty policeman, who was sitting with a woman and drinking whiskey. Enraged, the demonstrators set the casino on fire. Soon mobs spread out through the Westernized downtown, carrying cans of kerosene and igniting such landmarks as Shepheard's Hotel, Groppi's restaurant, and many other buildings that symbolized foreign economic and cultural influence. If any wind had been blowing that day, most of Cairo would have burned to the ground. More than 30 people perished, hundreds were injured, and 400 buildings were destroyed. Property damage ran to $500 million. After several hours' delay, during which mobs looted the burnt-out shops, the army restored order, martial law was declared, and the fires were put out. Then King Farouk, who had done nothing to stop the rioters, dismissed the Wafdist cabinet.

No one has ever proved who started "Black Saturday." It was probably not the Society of the Muslim Brothers, which was still recovering from its earlier repression and its reputation for fanaticism. Some suspected that Young Egypt had started the burning of Cairo, but that other groups, street gangs, and individuals had quickly joined in. Farouk may have sent in some of his agents to prove the Wafd's incapacity to govern. Some Egyptians accused the British of using the fire to discredit all of Egypt's nationalist movements and to oblige the Egyptian government to invite Britain's troops back in to restore order. The consensus is that no one group was solely responsible. Black Saturday was the collective expression of many Egyptians' hostility to Western wealth, power, and cultural influence. It also exposed the bankruptcy of the old regime. Farouk's reign lasted just six more months. During this time he appointed four different cabinets, some of which were headed by honest and energetic men. Cairo was under a dusk-to-dawn curfew for several months. Some of the looters were arrested and tried. The public prosecutor's office tried to find out who had started the fire. In a final attempt to win popular support, Karim Thabit had one of the ulama proclaim Farouk a descendant of the prophet Muhammad. Farouk also tried to strengthen his hold over the officers of the armed forces by concentrating his loyalists against the dissidents. But he had few options left; his regime was doomed, and popular discussion centered on when it would be overthrown, and by whom.

9

MILITARY RULE AND ARAB NATIONALISM (1952–1961)

The Egyptian people are proverbially easy to govern. Because 99 percent of Egypt's people live in the Nile Valley or Delta, they are within easy reach of their rulers. Their culture values obedience to persons in authority. But sometimes an incompetent ruling elite exhausts the patience even of the Egyptians and once conditions permit, as previous chapters have shown, revolution erupts. As King Farouk grew more inept, the Wafd and its rival parties more corrupt, and parliamentary democracy more irrelevant, a rebellion became inevitable. But who would lead the Egyptians? Many looked to the Muslim Brothers, some to Young Egypt, and a few to the Communists. Few expected the army to act. Its 1948 defeat in Palestine by a smaller, seemingly ill-equipped Israeli force shamed all Egyptians. Yet as revolutions broke out in Yemen in 1948 and in Syria in 1949, and after King Abdallah of Jordan (as Transjordan had been renamed in 1949) was assassinated in 1951, a forceful change of Egypt's government seemed imminent. Many secret societies within Egypt were plotting to overthrow Farouk. The one that succeeded was the Free Officers, a cabal of some 300 commissioned Egyptian officers.

The Egyptian Officers' Cabal

One of the unexpected results of the 1936 Anglo-Egyptian Treaty was the opening of the Egyptian Military Academy, hitherto a school for pashas' sons, to secondary-school graduates who passed a competitive examination. This change led to a rise in the quantity and quality of the entering cadets. These young men, ambitious for themselves and their nation, often came from modest backgrounds. In the late 1930s many of them supported Hasan al-Banna of the Muslim Brothers, arch-nationalist General Aziz Ali al-Misri (1879–1965), or Prime Minister Ali Mahir's nationalist war minister, Salih Harb. Then, according to Anwar Sadat, some of them secretly pledged to drive the British from Egypt. The decisive event was Lampson's ultimatum to Farouk on February 4, 1942, which Sadat described in his memoirs as "a date our generation cannot forget," when Mustafa al-Nahhas lost the respect of the Egyptian people for agreeing to become prime minister "literally at gunpoint" (Sadat 1977, 32). After that the young officers felt that Egypt's welfare depended on destroying all points of the power triangle: the Wafd, the king, and the British.

Several inside accounts purport to tell the true story of when the Free Officers' society was formed; Sadat's version stresses his early involvement, but Gamal Abdel Nasser and his friends claim that they were the founders. The personal association of Nasser, Sadat, and such other young officers as Zakariya Muhyi al-Din (1918–   ) and Abd al-Hakim Amir (1919–67) began before World War II, but they probably organized their group just after the Palestine War. Sadat wrote that it was organized into cells of five officer or civilian members, each of whom was expected to form another cell. A minimum of 20 cells made up one section. According to Sadat each section had a defined task: fund-raising, recruitment, security, terrorism, and propaganda. Overall direction was supplied by a 12-man revolutionary committee headed by Nasser, whose appointment as an instructor at the Military Academy enabled him to spot likely recruits. As individuals the Free Officers had contacts with various parties or revolutionary societies, including the Muslim Brothers, Young Egypt, and the Communists. As a group, though, they chose to work without ties to other organizations.

The Free Officers had no ideology. The following six points, put forth by the secret society in 1951, would remain their guiding principles long after they had taken power: (1) destroying the British occupation and its Egyptian supporters, (2) eliminating feudalism, (3) ending capitalism's domination of political power, (4) establishing social equality, (5) forming a strong popular army, and (6) establishing a "healthy democratic life." These points were open to various interpretations: liberal, nationalist, and Marxist. They were not a detailed blueprint for governing the country.

At first the Free Officers planned to take over the government in 1954. They advanced their timetable after Black Saturday revealed the incompetence of the old order. Realizing that their relative youth might weaken their authority in the eyes of the Egyptian people, they sought a senior officer to serve as their figurehead, finally choosing General Muhammad Naguib.

The 1952 Revolution

More influenced by what was happening in the army than by events in the rest of Egypt, the Free Officers decided to move their revolution up to early August 1952. They then advanced their plans to the night of July 22–23, when they learned that the king was convening his generals to move against them. The actual power seizure, carefully planned by Nasser, proved easy. But there were a few hitches: Sadat had taken his family to a movie (he knew that a coup was imminent, but not the exact date and time), and a policeman stopped Nasser's car because of a burnt-out taillight. By 3 A.M., though, the revolutionaries had taken all the key military posts in Cairo, with only two casualties. Most Palace and high government officials had gone to Alexandria for the summer, but that city, too, soon fell. In fact, there was almost no resistance at all. King Farouk asked the U.S. and British embassies to help stop the coup. Both refused. After debating whether to kill Farouk, try him, exile him, or keep him as a constitutional ruler, the Free Officers agreed to let him abdicate in favor of his infant son and to leave Egypt. A three-man regency council was set up, but all power was held by the Free Officers.

Several writers, notably Miles Copeland, Gail Meyer, and William Stadiem, assert that Nasser and the Free Officers were put in power by the U.S. Central Intelligence Agency (CIA). They argue that the Americans, fearing a Communist takeover, wanted to turn power over to army officers who, having been British trained and traditionally apolitical, were apt to be pro-Western (Copeland 1970, 52–74; Meyer 1980, 40–44; Stadiem 1992, 12–16). More likely, though, the coup's timing surprised the CIA, like nearly everyone else. However, the agency quickly made contact with the new regime and later helped it to fend off power bids by the Muslim Brothers, the Communists, and the old political parties.

The young officers soon realized that ruling Egypt after the revolution would not be so easy. Divided, Egyptians were egotistical and vengeful, with no vision of national reconstruction. As Nasser wrote in *The Philosophy of the Revolution*: "Every man we met sought nothing else but the destruction of another man. And every idea we heard aimed at nothing else but the demolition of another idea" (Nasser 1955, 22). Once Farouk had sailed into exile, the Free Officers handed the premiership over to an old-regime politician, Ali Mahir, whom they admired for his patriotism, planning to return to their barracks. Nahhas returned from a European vacation to say that the Wafd wanted new elections under the 1923 constitution to confirm its hold over parliament and public opinion. The Free Officers responded by ordering all political parties to purge themselves of corrupt politicians, including Nahhas. The Muslim Brothers insisted that the Quran was Egypt's constitution and demanded veto power over any laws passed by the new regime.

In early August the textile workers at Kafr al-Dawar (near Alexandria) rioted in the name of "the peoples' revolution," seized the factory buildings, set fire to several, and damaged the machinery. The new regime clamped down on them, killing eight, trying the ring-leaders, and putting two of them to death. This glaring contrast with the bloodless coup against the king shocked the Egyptian Left. So did the new regime's creation of a state security department to combat communism and Zionism. The Free Officers dismissed Ali Mahir and named a watchdog body, the Revolutionary Command Council (RCC), to oversee the government. A few competent old-regime politicians, such as Sayyid Marei (1913–93), a Saadist member of the old Chamber of Deputies, found their way into the new order; most waited until they saw how the wind was blowing. The Free Officers named a capable finance minister who adopted stringent measures to balance the government budget.

Among the accomplishments of the Free Officers, the first and most revolutionary was their September 1952 land-reform decree. It limited to 200 *feddans* (about 208 acres) the amount of agricultural land that any individual was allowed to own. Though not a new idea, this time it was enforced. The lands belonging to ex-King Farouk and his relatives were confiscated and redistributed to landless peasants. Other land-tenure abuses were outlawed. A major change was the abolition of family *waqfs*, Muslim endowments that had been used to keep estates within a family from being broken up under the Quranic inheritance laws. These reforms weakened the large landowners, but the government was committed to reimburse them for their confiscated property. Some of Egypt's destitute peasants became small landowners for the first time, but they would have to pay for the lands they received. These reforms weakened the power base of the Wafd and other old-regime parties. The land reform may have been a revolutionary step, but its ends were conservative, not radical. Sayyid Marei took charge of organizing this agrarian reform program (Springborg 1982, 139–151).

Hoary political issues, especially Egypt's relationship with Britain, had to be addressed. In 1952 British troops still guarded the Suez Canal, a link in the West's chain of defenses against the USSR. Most Egyptians wanted them to leave. Talks with Britain resumed a month after the military coup. The Sudan, nominally an Anglo-Egyptian condominium, remained in fact a British colony. Unlike Egypt's prerevolution politicians, General Naguib, who was born in Khartoum and related well with the Sudanese people, accepted their right to decide whether they wanted complete independence or unification with Egypt. In February 1953 Egypt agreed to a Sudanese plebiscite, thus removing one cause of Anglo-Egyptian antagonism. Egypt hoped that it would eventually persuade the British to give up their Suez Canal base. Naguib even hinted that Egypt might make peace with Israel. The new regime seemed patriotic, but not xenophobic.

The Free Officers' regime hoped to maintain order, promote national unity, and shun radical policies. Addressing Egyptian and foreign journalists, the homely, pipe-smoking Naguib stressed his commitment to civil liberties and to free elections under the 1923 constitution. He and his young officers were technically educated and middle class. Only after they had consolidated their power and realized the extent of Egypt's problems would the Free Officers truly turn into revolutionaries, as their own propaganda would later depict them.

Naguib vs. Nasser

The Free Officers took pride in their solidarity, but there was an inherent tension between the society and the general whom they had designated as their titular leader, Muhammad Naguib. Their real leader was Gamal Abdel Nasser, the son of a postman in Alexandria, the grandson of peasants in Beni Murr, a village near Asyut, and one of the first cadets admitted to the Military Academy on the basis of a competitive examination. His eventual successor, Anwar Sadat, wrote in his memoirs that on July 27 the Revolutionary Command Council debated whether the new Egypt would become a military dictatorship or remain a democracy. By a seven to one vote, the RCC leaders chose dictatorship. Incensed by their choice, Nasser stormed out of the room and went home. Afraid of ruling without him, one of the officers ran after him and persuaded him to return, promising democratic rule for Egypt.

It is a strange story, for Nasser, once he took over full executive power two years later, would rule for the next 16 with no regard for parliamentary democracy. But it does show the dilemma facing the Free Officers.

GAMAL ABDEL NASSER
(1918–1970)

Unlike Naguib, who had been born in Khartoum to a Sudanese mother, Nasser was a pure Egyptian. Although he was actually born in Alexandria, because his father came from Beni Murr, a village near Asyut, young Gamal spent his summer vacations there and later liked to identify himself as coming from Beni Murr. He identified closely with Upper Egypt, resenting the stereotype of Upper Egyptians as strong but stupid hicks. Living with an uncle in Cairo, Nasser received most of his schooling there. A fervent nationalist, he marched in many schoolboy demonstrations. Upon graduating in 1936 from one of Cairo's leading secondary schools, he tried to enter the Military Academy but was rejected. Entering law school instead, he reapplied for officer training in 1937 and completed the program in 18 months. After he was commissioned, he served in Upper Egypt, the Sudan, and El Alamein and taught at the Military Academy. Nasser was a chess player in his spare time, and his methodical organization of the Free Officers movement, the revolution, and Naguib's fall from power demonstrated his talents as a tactician. He served as deputy prime minister in 1953 and as prime minister from 1954 to 1956, when he was elected president in a national plebiscite in which there were no other candidates. He became hugely popular for his commitment to Arab nationalism and his attempts to defy the West. His claims to fame include his purchase of Czech (actually Soviet) arms in 1955, his nationalization of the Suez Canal Company in 1956, the unification of Syria with Egypt as the United Arab Republic in 1958, and his attempt to create Arab socialism between 1961 and 1967. His defeat by Israel in the June 1967 War discredited his policies, but he continued to lead the other Arabs in confronting Israel in the War of Attrition (1969–70). He died in September 1970. Many other Arab leaders, especially Muammar Gadhafi and Saddam Hussein, tried unsuccessfully to imitate his Arab policies and leadership style.

The Egyptian people wanted to have a democratic government. The 1923 constitution, whatever its faults, guaranteed civil liberties and the people's right to self-rule. It conferred sovereignty on the regency council, but free elections, with universal male suffrage, should be held for a new parliament. The winner of such a vote would probably be the Wafd Party, because of its appeal to rural landlords who could make their tenant farmers and hired laborers vote for Wafdist candidates. Such a regime would not end corruption or restore order. Egypt needed strong, decisive leadership to solve its problems. But repudiating democracy would anger its educated elite, the press, students, labor unions, and the foreigners whose support the revolutionaries still needed.

The Free Officers' solution to this dilemma was to pay lip service to democracy but to rule by decree. Egypt would have cabinets made up of civilian politicians. Behind them, though, sat "secretaries-general" from the Revolutionary Command Council who observed the ministers as the advisers had done during the early days of the British occupation. Naguib ordered the parties to get rid of their corrupt elements. Only the Wafd resisted purging itself, but it was the sole party with a real constituency. The others vanished once Parliament was dissolved in December 1952. Most of the members of Young Egypt embraced the new regime, whose pronouncements reflected their views. The Muslim Brothers assumed that their officer contacts, one of whom was Sadat, would guarantee their influence over the new regime. The society did indeed win privileges denied to the parliamentary parties. When the officers shelved the constitution and put off elections, they banned all parties and confiscated their assets. The Muslim Brothers, however, remained free to agitate for their program. Old-regime politicians were barred from public office, tried by a revolutionary court using exceptional judicial procedures, and sentenced to prison terms. No one was executed. Military censorship curtailed but did not deny people's rights to free speech.

During the first year of the new regime, Egyptian and foreign observers admired the Free Officers' energy and efficiency. All agreed that reforms were vital, corruption must be rooted out, and Egypt should negotiate with the British for a peaceful evacuation of their Suez Canal base. But people began asking whether the Revolutionary Command Council would give up its power to a civilian government. In June 1953 the RCC ended the monarchy. Naguib became Egypt's first president, as well as its prime minister and RCC chairman. He had become popular in his own right. Most of the younger Free Officers stayed out of the limelight and made the critical decisions. As the date for a new constitution kept receding, Naguib seemed to be Egypt's political reformer in a military uniform.

The 1952 revolution had been a classic army coup, not a popular uprising. If the Free Officers wanted to gain and hold the people's support, they had to appeal to groups and individuals whose interests and attitudes often clashed with their own. Some officers had family or personal ties with the royal family, big landowners, old-regime politicians, Young Egypt, the Muslim Brothers, Communists, the trade unions, or various foreign embassies. As long as these ties strengthened the RCC's power over the government and the people, Nasser tolerated and even exploited them. But once the RCC was clearly in control, it could no longer share power with its rivals. Naguib stood for a pluralistic polity, in which the RCC would compete for the minds and hearts of the people with the Wafd, the Muslim Brothers, and the Communists. Nasser disagreed. If the Egyptians wanted their country to be strong and respected, all power would have to be concentrated in the RCC. Even if some of its members had loose ties with competing power centers, the RCC was independent of them all. Now that the monarchy and the old parties had been abolished and the landowning class weakened by land reform, the RCC no longer needed the rival movements. Instead Nasser resolved to build a new popular consensus behind the officers.

Although the Egyptian army enjoyed little prestige, especially since its loss in Palestine, the RCC set up a mass movement called the Liberation Rally. Its organizers tried zealously to enlist workers and students, but its strongest backers were the very Muslim Brothers whose organization were competing with Nasser for popular support. Within the government RCC members took over the major ministries from civilians. Nasser became deputy premier and interior minister. He soon gave up the latter post, but he made sure that his allies dominated the cabinet and that his closest friend, Abd al-Hakim Amir, took command of the armed forces. Amir's chief aide, Shams Badran, purged the officer corps of Nasser's opponents.

The Muslim Brothers, fearing that they too would be deprived of their power and influence, got up mass demonstrations in January 1954 to commemorate the Egyptian guerrillas killed by the British in the Suez Canal zone two years earlier. They were challenged by the Liberation Rally at Cairo University, leading to a brawl and many injuries and arrests. The RCC promptly banned the society, but the Muslim Brothers had been outlawed before and might well revive, as they still enjoyed strong support. Naguib became the standard-bearer for their hopes. Naguib opposed Badran's purge of the officer corps and Nasser's measures against the former party leaders. He thought that the other RCC members were flouting his leadership and that Nasser was turning the press against him. On February 23, 1954, he resigned as RCC chairman and president. Several of his supporters followed suit.

At first, Nasser hit back, putting Naguib under house arrest, but mass demonstrations obliged him to rescind this act. Realizing that

Cairo Tower. Built between 1957 and 1961 on land taken from the Gezira Sporting Club, it has become a symbol for modern Cairo. It is 187 meters (608 feet) high and affords an excellent view of the city, especially at night. (Shutterstock)

Naguib commanded widespread support and that many Egyptians were clamoring for a return to constitutional government, Nasser made a tactical retreat. After three days he asked Naguib to resume his posts. He promised to dissolve the RCC by July and to hold free elections for an assembly that would write a new constitution. Naguib's restoration was celebrated by a mass victory rally during which he invited a leading Muslim Brother to join him at the podium, a possible sign of Naguib's true loyalties.

It looked as if Naguib had won, but he underestimated Nasser's ability to mobilize the support of the Free Officers, the state security forces, and his trade union allies. Nasser was a master tactician, willing to withdraw at first in order to advance later. While Naguib went to Sudan for the ceremonial opening of its new parliament, Nasser spoke to union leaders and convinced them that Naguib's opposition to the RCC threatened the revolution. By late March he had lined up his Liberation Rally members to demonstrate against Naguib. Nasser then became premier and purged the pro-Naguib ministers. He reneged on promises to abolish the RCC and to hold elections for a constituent assembly by July. Naguib's leading supporters were jailed or exiled and Nasser emerged as Egypt's dictator. Naguib remained as a figurehead president.

Journalists and scholars have written (Copeland 1969, 171–178; Eveland, 91–97) that the CIA, notably Kermit Roosevelt, facilitated Nasser's takeover. One concrete form of U.S. aid was a suitcase containing $3 million that Roosevelt dispatched to one of Nasser's aides. Although fiercely against taking bribes, Nasser kept the money to embarrass the donors. He used it to build a decorative tower, topped by a revolving restaurant and a blinking antenna, officially named the Cairo Tower but sardonically called *al-waqif Rusfel* (Roosevelt's erection) by Egyptians. In 1954 he worked with the Americans, who preferred the dour colonel to the smiling General Naguib, who they thought enjoyed Communist backing. Washington wanted Egypt to join an anti-USSR pact and to make peace with Israel; Nasser wanted the Americans to pressure the British to give up their Suez Canal base. Their cooperation was temporary and tactical.

Anglo-Egyptian Agreement and the Baghdad Pact

The Egyptian people cared most about getting the British out of Suez. The two sides held lengthy negotiations over the terms of the evacuation. Even after Britain had conceded that the West's defense needs could not be met by occupying lands belonging to a hostile people, it still wanted to retain technicians at the base in case a general war broke out with the Communist countries. Both Britain and the United States urged Egypt to join an anti-Communist military alliance similar to NATO. Nasser rejected these conditions. He argued, with good reason, that his domestic opponents would attack him for agreeing to put Egypt under several occupying powers, including the British. If Egypt needed defense, it was against Israel. Even if communism threatened Egypt as much as Zionism did, which he doubted, the greater menace would be an internal revolution, not an invasion from the USSR, more than a thousand miles from Egypt's shores. Contemporaries observed that, for the British, it was harder to evacuate the Suez Canal than it had been to grant independence to India and Pakistan.

At last British and Egyptian negotiators reached an agreement. Ratified in October 1954, it provided for the evacuation of all British troops from the Suez Canal within a 20-month period. For the next seven years Egypt would let Royal Air Force planes land in Suez Canal zone airbases and British civilian technicians maintain the base facilities. Britain would have the right to reoccupy the canal in case of an armed attack by an outside power against any Arab League member or Turkey. The inclusion of Turkey, which belonged to NATO and was more directly menaced by the USSR than Egypt or any other Arab state, seemed to tie Egypt to the West's defense system. Egypt's Communists and Muslim Brothers both assailed the pact, as did many less ideological nationalists who rallied behind the tattered standard of President Naguib, now powerless against the RCC. Many said the pact pushed the British out the front door but let them in through the rear.

Nasser nearly paid for the 1954 agreement with his life. A week later, while he was speaking in Alexandria, eight shots were fired, but they missed him, and he managed to go on. The police quickly caught the assailant and his accomplices, who turned out to be Muslim Brothers. The revolutionary court was promptly reactivated and the conspirators were tried and executed, as were several of their leaders. Then the Egyptian government began a long campaign to wipe out the Muslim Brothers, including its branches, schools, and welfare institutions. The society had put down deep roots in Egypt and several other Arab countries; Nasser's vendetta against it ranks among his least popular policies. Naguib was put under house arrest, and the presidency of the republic was declared vacant. Old-regime politicians, Communists, Muslim Brothers, and other dissidents filled the prisons. After 1954 there was no legal opposition to Nasser's rule.

The military junta, like any government, needed legitimacy. Legitimacy is the ability of leaders to command their subjects' voluntary obedience. Nasser might have argued that his government should be obeyed because it was building Egypt's economy, but economic development seemed too slow for a revolutionary regime. The country's fiscal policies from 1952 to 1955 were conservative. Technical assistance, from the United States, Britain, and the United Nations, was modest.

People are most apt to obey a military junta if it is able to defend the country. The most obvious menace to Egypt was Israel. Even though Egypt had a larger land area, more soldiers, and a population 10 times greater than that of Israel, it was ill equipped to withstand an Israeli attack. It needed arms, but the United States, France, and Britain had reached an agreement in 1950 not to arm the Arabs or Israel. Several U.S. aid missions had visited Cairo, but up to the 1954 agreement, British opposition deterred the Americans from selling weapons to

Egypt. Even after that treaty Israel's supporters in Congress argued against arms sales to any enemy state. The Egyptian government did explore ways to make peace with the Jewish state. Cairo wanted the repatriation of Palestinian Arab refugees, mainly those in Gaza who were chafing under Egyptian administration, and an Israeli concession to create a land bridge across the Negev Desert to Jordan. Israel wanted to have peace with its strongest Arab neighbor.

The cause of peace was not helped by a covert operation of several Israeli agents to blow up U.S. cultural institutions in Cairo and Alexandria in 1954 in an attempt to damage Egypt's relations with the United States and Great Britain. The agents were arrested by the Egyptian police, put on trial, and executed. The ensuing scandal in Israel led immediately to the return of Israel's first prime minister, David Ben-Gurion, from retirement to the defense ministry. He called for a firm Israeli response to military actions (or threats) by any neighboring Arab state. On February 28, 1955, Israel's army raided Gaza, retaliating against attacks by Egyptian-trained Palestinian fedayeen. This raid exposed the weakness of Egypt's army. Four days earlier Iraq and Turkey had formed an alliance—joined later by Britain, Pakistan, and Iran—that came to be called the Baghdad Pact.

The Gaza raid and the Baghdad Pact presented a double challenge to Nasser. He now intensified his quest for arms, looking first to Britain and the United States, but neither government was willing, without conditions, to sell him the arms he wanted. His reprisals against Israel, therefore, took the form of intensified Palestinian fedayeen raids. As the tension grew, he also stepped up economic measures against Israel, seizing Israel-bound cargoes on ships transiting the Suez Canal. As for the Baghdad Pact, Nasser argued that it served the interest, not of the Arab countries, but of Western imperialism in the Arab world. The inclusion of Iraq, the most powerful and influential Arab state next to Egypt, meant that the Hashimites in Baghdad and Amman challenged Cairo's preeminence and undermined Arab solidarity.

Nasser's prestige soared when he attended the first nonaligned Afro-Asian summit, held in Bandung, Indonesia, in April 1955. He was welcomed as a hero (for persuading the British to quit Suez) by such leaders as Indonesian president Sukarno, Indian prime minister Jawaharlal Nehru, and Chinese prime minister Chou En-lai, whom he was meeting for the first time. They also encouraged him to buy arms from Communist countries if Britain and the United States refused to sell enough to meet Egypt's needs. Nasser came to view himself and Egypt as actors on the international stage. Voice of the Arabs, a program of Radio Cairo, broadcast propaganda into other Arab countries discrediting their leaders, if they were already independent, or inciting them to overthrow their colonial masters.

Communist Arms and the Aswan High Dam

Even though Egypt had spearheaded forming the Arab League in 1945, Egyptians rarely thought of themselves as Arabs. Nasser had never seen another Arab country, except the Sudan, and knew few Syrians, Iraqis, or other Arabs personally. However, this heady combination of Arab nationalism and anti-imperialism raised Egypt's dignity and self-esteem. Nasser became a hero, especially in the eyes of frustrated youths in other Arab countries. As his troops trained fedayeen to raid Israel, and as Voice of the Arabs' transmitters broadcast anti-Zionist propaganda, Nasser became a hero to the Palestinians. Therefore it was easier for Nasser to make large arms deals with Communist countries than to buy smaller quantities from Britain or the United States. In September 1955 Egypt announced an agreement to buy up to $200 million worth of weapons from Czechoslovakia, to be paid for by exporting Egyptian cotton. Only later did it become known that the real seller was the USSR. The arms sales, larger than any ever made in the Middle East, nullified the 1950 agreement among the United States, France, and Britain to limit such sales. Now an Arab-Israeli arms race began in earnest. France speeded up weapons sales to Israel and assailed Nasser for stirring up anti-French feeling in Tunisia, Morocco, and especially Algeria, where 1 million European colonists faced a bloody rebellion by 10 million Algerian Muslims. The deal also signaled a more visible Soviet role in Middle Eastern politics. Nasser ignored American pleas to cancel the arms deal. He was determined, after the Gaza raid, not to be humiliated by Israel again.

Although Western countries were estranged from Egypt by their support for Israel, they could provide more economic aid than the Communist states. Aside from strengthening his armed forces, Nasser's surest path to legitimacy was to implement projects that showed his determination to develop national pride. One such showcase project was the Nile Corniche, or shore drive. Cairenes had long been cut off from portions of the river by princely palaces, Britain's embassy in Garden City, and the British army barracks, whose lands extended to the water's edge. The completion of the Corniche and the replacement of the barracks by the Arab League Headquarters and the Nile Hilton Hotel inspired civic pride and gave ordinary Egyptians a river

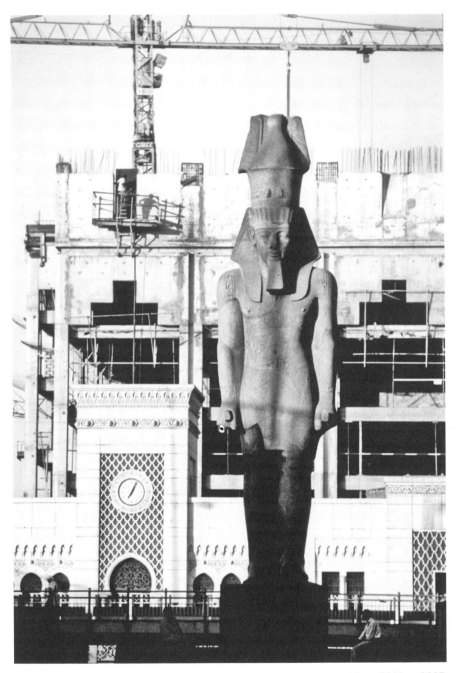

Ramesses II statue. Originally erected in Memphis, this 83-ton statue stood from 1955 to 2007 in the main square before the Cairo Railway Station. Due to traffic congestion and air pollution, it has now been moved to a site near the Giza pyramids. It will eventually be incorporated into a new museum of Egyptian antiquities. (Dick Doughty/Saudi Aramco World/PADIA)

promenade and a big public square in which to mingle on hot summer nights. In addition, a huge statue of Ramesses II was moved from its ancient site and erected in front of Cairo's main railroad station, with a big fountain cooling the public square. It replaced another statue, *Egypt's Awakening,* the best-known work of sculptor Mahmud Mukhtar, which was moved from the station to grace the head of an avenue of trees leading to Cairo University.

But the project that came to symbolize Egypt's reawakening was the High Dam at Aswan. One of Britain's greatest achievements in Egypt had been to extend large-scale, year-round irrigation throughout the Nile Valley. Since the reign of Mehmet Ali, dams, canals, and water-raising devices had increased the area of Egyptian lands that could grow two or three crops in one year. The British had built a dam at Aswan, completed in 1902 and later raised twice, that had made perennial irrigation possible in much of Upper Egypt. The country had also benefited from various river projects in the Sudan. By the 1950s, though, if the region's agricultural output was to keep up with its rapid population growth, most engineers recommended building still more dams to store and regulate the Nile water.

The plan most experts preferred before the 1952 revolution was the Century Storage Scheme. It proposed the creation of additional reservoirs, mostly on the White Nile and its sources, to hold enough water to ensure year-round supplies to Egyptian and Sudanese farmers, regardless of the height of the flood, which depended on how much water flowed down the Blue Nile. The plan would have made Egypt dependent on public works projects located in Sudan. Once it became clear that the two countries would probably not unite, the Century Storage Scheme would have subjected Egypt to the goodwill of an independent Sudan.

The alternative plan was to build a much larger Aswan dam wholly within Egypt, creating a reservoir large enough to hold a year's flood waters. No longer would Egypt's farmers fear that the Nile flood was too high or too low to sow and harvest their crops. Such a dam would also enable the Nile to irrigate at least a million more *feddans* (1.038 million acres) of farmland and to generate sufficient hydroelectric power to meet all of Egypt's electricity needs. The High Dam project had been advocated by some engineers before the 1952 Revolution, but the Free Officers soon seized on the idea and made it the centerpiece of their plans. It would be large and could be built in a decade. Though engineers foresaw technical problems in the High Dam project, the main obstacle was financial. Egypt was too poor to pay the billion dollars that

Aswan Dam. Completed in 1902, this dam was enlarged between 1907 and 1912 and then again between 1929 and 1934 to provide water for the perennial irrigation of Upper and Middle Egypt. Its reservoir was never adequate for a high Nile. In 1955 Nasser's government proposed to build the High Dam. (Torben Larsen/Saudi Aramco World/PADIA)

most experts expected the dam to cost. Large foreign loans would be needed to build the dam. The risks were far too great for private investors or even for a single government to undertake.

Therefore, Egypt turned to the International Bank for Reconstruction and Development (World Bank) for financial assistance. Its director cautiously favored the project and sent World Bank engineers and economists to make a feasibility study. In December 1955 it offered a package deal: a $200 million loan for the first phase of construction, combined with $56 million in grants from the United States and $14 million from Britain. The two countries would also lend more money to help finance the project's later phases. The offer depended on Egypt's agreeing to the conditions placed on the U.S. and British grants. These terms included close Western scrutiny and control of Egypt's economy, no new arms purchases, open bidding for contracts (excluding any Communist countries), and prior agreement with Sudan over allocation of the Nile waters. Nasser's government did not want to accept a package deal reminiscent of the Dual Financial Control; he hinted that Egypt would seek offers elsewhere, hoping that the Soviets might rise to the bait. Egypt was trying to get the superpowers to outbid each other for its support.

Egypt knew that the West was making a political offer to counter the rising Communist influence on Egypt and other Arab states after the Czech arms deal. Both Syria and Yemen had followed Egypt's example by buying Communist arms, ending the West's monopoly. Rioting mobs (inspired by Radio Cairo) greeted Britain's representative when he visited Amman late in 1955 to sign up Jordan for membership in the Baghdad Pact. Nationalist opposition in that country dissuaded King Hussein's (1935–99) government from joining Iraq in the anticommunist treaty. A few months later, while Britain's foreign secretary was visiting Nasser, Hussein publicly dismissed Sir John Bagot Glubb, the British commander of Jordan's Arab Legion. Amman was under a pro-Nasser if constitutionally chosen government. The French were fighting a bitter war in Algeria against Muslim rebels who were being backed by Cairo. With Tunisia, Morocco, and Sudan all gaining independence in early 1956, the tide of Western imperialism was receding in the Arab world. Nasser and the Communists seemed to be filling the void it had left behind.

U.S. secretary of state John Foster Dulles regarded the world as divided between the democratic nations and the Communists, with no true neutrals. He viewed with alarm Egypt's leftward drift, especially when Nasser recognized the Communist regime in China. Meanwhile, Congress, whose approval would have been needed for the U.S. government's part in financing the High Dam, raised objections about the danger to the cotton-growing southern states (here Congress erred, for the High Dam was supposed to help Egypt diversify export crops), the project's long-term costs, and Egypt's hostility to Israel. When Egypt's ambassador in Washington, Dr. Ahmad Hussein, finally secured Nasser's consent to the U.S. offer despite its objectionable conditions, on July 18, 1956, Dulles replied the next day that the deal was off.

The Suez Crisis

Withdrawing the High Dam offer was a huge diplomatic blunder. Nasser was furious over what he regarded as a calculated insult. His response came a week later. In a speech on the fourth anniversary of Farouk's abdication, as Nasser repeated the code name "Lesseps," Egyptian military and naval units occupied the offices, wharves, and other facilities of the Suez Canal Company. Nasser then announced the nationalization of the Suez Canal Company, saying that the canal tolls would pay for building the High Dam. No previous Nasser speech had ever received

Suez Canal Company. The Egyptian headquarters of the company was in Ismailia (the company's main headquarters was and is in Paris). Its board of directors was mainly French, with British government representatives and, as of 1951, four Egyptians. On July 26, 1956, Gamal Abdel Nasser announced the nationalization of the Egyptian assets of the Suez Canal Company, a move hugely popular in Egypt. (Library of Congress)

such an enthusiastic response, for the Suez Canal symbolized the West's exploitation of Egypt. Its governing board, still mainly French, had virtually excluded Egyptians from its management. To France, the canal was the last vestige of its role in Egypt's economy. To the British, it had been their imperial lifeline during two world wars, and they had defended it as tenaciously as if it were their home territory. To the Arabs, Nasser became an instant hero for defying the imperialist West. The United States cared mainly about navigation rights and the possible influence of Nasser's action on Panama, with its canal.

Few Westerners recalled that the Suez Canal was legally Egyptian, a fact recognized since it was built and confirmed most recently in the 1954 Anglo-Egyptian Agreement. The company had been chartered in Egypt, though its head office was in Paris. The right of governments to nationalize companies within their borders, if they compensate shareholders, is recognized under international law. Nasser's act was, nevertheless, loudly praised or stridently condemned for its symbolic significance.

Reactions elsewhere were varied. The French and British press and the public urged invading Egypt and to stop Nasser before he took control of the whole Arab world. Zionists stressed Egypt's arms buildup, the crescendo of fedayeen raids and of Radio Cairo propaganda against Israel, and the likely use of the canal to blackmail the West. Westerners doubted that the Egyptians had the technical expertise or discipline to manage the Suez Canal. Neither Britain nor France could invade Egypt immediately to seize the canal. U.S. president Dwight Eisenhower, campaigning for reelection, insisted that Washington would not support military action without congressional approval. He and Dulles called for a diplomatic response. Western Europeans, who imported most of their oil on ships transiting the Suez Canal, wanted it placed under international administration. A conference was held in London, but Egypt refused to send representatives, and India and the USSR blocked unanimity on a resolution calling for international control of the canal. The 18 nations that did support that plan sent a delegation to Cairo, headed by Australia's prime minister, hoping to persuade Nasser, but he firmly rejected internationalization. Dulles proposed to set up a Suez Canal Users Association (SCUA) to collect the tolls. Nasser rejected that idea, too. Egypt offered to negotiate. French, British, U.S., and Egyptian diplomats agreed to meet in Geneva in late October to reach a compromise, but the first two governments still threatened to regain the canal by force.

The Egyptians did not flinch. They set up the Suez Canal Authority, headed by Colonel Mahmud Yunis, to replace the old Canal Company administration. When most of the European pilots, who had guided convoys of ships through the canal, walked off their jobs, hoping to shut it down, Yunis managed to bring in replacements from Communist and neutral countries and to train enough Egyptian pilots to keep it running. Tolls did not become extortionate. Egypt offered to pay stockholders for the value of their shares, as determined by their selling price on the Paris stock exchange just before nationalization was announced. In short, the country proved that it could manage the canal as well as the company had done. There was no need to put the Suez Canal under international control.

Britain and France reacted by preparing for war. Fearing Nasser's influence over his people, Iraq's pro-Western leader, Prime Minister Nuri al-Said, would have supported the European powers but for their collaboration with Israel. France, angry at Nasser for aiding the Algerian revolution, was arming Israel heavily. Israel's Ben-Gurion wanted to attack Egypt to stop the fedayeen raids and to wipe out its military potential before it learned how to use the new Communist

NASSER'S SPEECH NATIONALIZING THE SUEZ CANAL COMPANY (JULY 26, 1956)

... The Suez Canal is an Egyptian canal built as a result of great sacrifices. The Suez Canal Company is an Egyptian company that was expropriated from Egypt by the British who, since the canal was dug, have been obtaining the profits of the company.... The annual canal revenue is 35 million Egyptian pounds. From this sum Egypt—which lost 120,000 workers in digging the canal—gets one million pounds from the company.

It is a shame when the blood of peoples is sucked, and it is no shame that we should borrow for construction. We will not allow the past to be repeated again, but we will cancel the past by restoring our rights to the Suez Canal.... We will build the High Dam, and we will obtain our rights. We will build it as we wish, and we are determined to do so. The 35 million pounds which the company collects each year will be collected by us.... When we build the High Dam, we will be building the dam of prestige, freedom, and dignity, and we will be putting an end to the dams of humiliation. We announce that the whole of Egypt is one united national bloc. We will fight to the last drop of our blood ... for the sake of our motherland.

... Today we restore these rights, and I declare in the name of the Egyptian people that we will protect these rights with our blood and soul. The Suez Canal was one of the edifices of oppression. Now our funds are coming back to us.... With our sweat and our tears and with the lives of our martyrs and their skulls in our memory, we can protect this country.

The people will stand united as one man to resist imperialist acts of treachery. We shall do whatever we like. When we restore all our rights, we shall become stronger and our production will increase. At this moment, some of your brethren, the sons of Egypt, are now taking over the Egyptian Suez Canal Company and directing it. We have taken this decision to restore part of the glories of the past and to safeguard our national dignity and pride. May God bless you and guide you in the path of righteousness.

weapons. His protégé, General Moshe Dayan, met with British and French leaders to coordinate an attack on Egypt.

On the very day when British, French, U.S., and Egyptian diplomats were to have met in Geneva to strike a compromise deal over Suez, Israeli paratroopers landed at the strategic Mitla Pass, deep in Sinai, and

Israeli ground forces spilled across the border into the Gaza Strip and the Sinai Peninsula. Although the Egyptians had known that Israel was mobilizing its reserve troops, they had expected it to attack Jordan, and so they fell back in shock. On the following day an ultimatum came from London calling on Egypt to withdraw its forces to 10 miles (16 kilometers) west of the canal so that the British could secure the Suez Canal Zone, as provided for in the 1954 Anglo-Egyptian Agreement. Egypt refused. British planes started bombing targets in Cairo, Alexandria, the Canal Zone, and the coastal region, while an immense Anglo-French armada steamed slowly into the eastern Mediterranean. Nasser vowed that Egypt would never surrender, but he pulled the army out of Sinai to prepare for a European invasion.

Britain and France had misjudged their ability to rally support against Nasser. Even though U.S. politicians were nearing the end of an election campaign, Eisenhower decided to risk losing the votes of Israel's supporters by demanding its withdrawal and condemning the European attacks. Even while the USSR was crushing a revolt in Hungary, its leaders threatened to bomb London, Paris, and Tel Aviv if the "Tripartite Aggression" against Egypt did not stop. Many members of the British Commonwealth opposed the attack; India and Pakistan assailed it in the strongest possible terms, as did London's Arab allies, Iraq and Jordan. British Prime Minister Sir Anthony Eden decided to abort the attack just as British and French troops were going ashore at Port Said to capture the canal. Nasser would later exalt the heroic resistance of Port Said's citizens to the invaders, but their heroism was due partly to his army's hasty withdrawal from the city, partly to Eden's failure of nerve, and mostly to the superpowers' joint condemnation of the invasion. British and French troops lingered in Port Said for seven weeks. The Israelis occupied Sinai a little longer. Canada's foreign minister proposed stationing a UN Emergency Force in Gaza and in strategic Sinai points, such as Sharm al-Sheikh, letting Israeli ships use the Gulf of Aqaba. The UNEF was duly authorized, and the United States pressured Israel to withdraw its troops.

For Nasser the Suez War was a military defeat but a political triumph. He lost most of his new jet fighters, Egypt's post revolutionary army lost some credibility, and Israel's military reputation was enhanced. But it also showed the Egyptians that Nasser could stand up to British pressure. Even if no diplomat said so publicly, Britain had clearly hoped to overthrow Nasser's regime, but without knowing who would replace him. Other Arabs now viewed Nasser as the foremost foe of both imperialism and Zionism. The Suez War weakened British and French influence throughout the Middle East, raised U.S. prestige slightly, and improved the USSR's reputation greatly. Many British and French subjects who had spent their entire lives in Egypt were expelled without their property, as were most Jews, even if they were anti-Zionist Egyptian citizens. The nationalization of British and French companies in Egypt after the Suez War set a precedent for many later seizures or sequestrations of private property. Egypt boycotted British and French goods. It broke diplomatic relations with the two countries and persuaded other Arab states to do so. It renounced the 1954 Anglo-Egyptian Agreement. As for the canal itself, Egypt had sunk enough ships to make it impassable; it then would not let the United Nations clear it until all British, French, and Israeli invaders had withdrawn.

Despite the clamor and strife over Aswan and Suez, in June 1956 the people got to vote on the new constitution that had been promised for years. The document set up a government with a strong presidency and a new consultative assembly in the place of the abolished parliament. Egyptian women were finally allowed to vote and hold public office. Political parties were banned. Having served to legitimize Nasser against his foes in March 1954, the Liberation Rally had later faded away. Nasser called for a new popular organization, the National Union, which was to serve Egypt by mobilizing support, gathering ideas, discovering political talent, and sending government directives down to villages and neighborhoods. The 1956 constitution was also the first to proclaim that Egypt belonged to the Arab nation, an idealized community of all Arabic-speaking countries.

Egypt and Arab Nationalism

This proclamation helped the government to spread its influence from the Atlantic Ocean to the Persian Gulf, but it was also the cause of new troubles for Egypt. Nasser's commitment to Arab nationalism, denounced in the West as a ploy to grab Arabia's oil fields, was sincere. His pursuit of Arab unity, however, was in response to the expectations that Arabs everywhere now placed on him. If Nasser could confront Israel and two major imperialist powers to defend Egypt's dignity and the Suez Canal, then Palestinians expected him to dictate policy to Jordan's King Hussein; Syrians belonging to Arab nationalist parties wanted him to rescue them from both CIA and Communist plots; and Lebanese Muslims hoped he would free their country from Maronite Christian control. Nasser often told reporters that he did not act—he only reacted to the moves of others. The leader of an independent country needs to formulate policies, as Nasser would later learn. The United States, too, learned by trial and error how to formulate its Middle East policy. The Eisenhower Doctrine, passed by Congress in January 1957, offered economic and military aid to any Middle Eastern country facing aggression from a state controlled by "international Communism." Some governments accepted the U.S. offer, hoping to fight Nasser's influence, not communism. In April Jordan's King Hussein confronted a group of rebellious army officers, ousted his Arab nationalist cabinet, and established a royal dictatorship that defied the will of his mainly pro-Nasser Palestinian subjects. Later that year Syria asked for Soviet help against threats made by Turkey. Then the Syrian government, led by the Arab socialist Baath Party, asked to unite with Egypt before its few but highly disciplined Communists could take control. Nasser insisted on an organic unification of Egypt and Syria. In February 1958 they formed the United Arab Republic (UAR).

The new UAR raised Arab hopes in neighboring countries, notably among Palestinians and young people, embarrassing their governments. Civil war broke out in Lebanon. The pro-Western side accused Nasser of aiding the rebels with propaganda, agents, and arms. Then a revolution toppled the monarchy in Iraq and set up a military regime that professed socialism and Arab unity, patterned on Nasser's UAR. The Iraqi Revolution led to the landing of U.S. Marines in Lebanon (under the Eisenhower Doctrine) and to the airlift of British paratroopers to Jordan. The Western powers pursued their strategic interests while claiming to fight communism, but they wanted to weaken Nasser. They failed. By late 1958 Nasser seemed to tower over the Arab world. After King Saud of Saudi Arabia reportedly bribed a Syrian Nasserite to assassinate Nasser, Saudi Arabia turned Saud's powers over to his brother Faisal, who was presumed to be an Arab nationalist. The U.S. occupation enabled Lebanon to end its civil war by electing a new president acceptable to the UAR. Sudan, too, had a military coup, but its new regime proved not to be Nasserite. Iraq's new rulers decided that Arab nationalism did not require them to join the UAR and hence to turn over their oil revenues to Cairo.

In the course of seeking Arab hegemony, Egypt ignored its real problems of overpopulation, undercapitalized agriculture and industry, and inadequate technicians. Arguments arose among Egyptians on whether they were really Arabs; the UAR had initially stirred up more fervor in Damascus than in Cairo. Syrians viewed themselves as cleverer than Egyptians. Their leaders, especially the Baath Party, assumed they would manipulate the less ideologically sophisticated Egyptian colonels.

Nasser for his part was amazed at the power of Syria's capitalists and the simplicity of their government, whose accounting system he termed no better than that of an Egyptian grocery store. Before long Egyptian officers, administrators, accountants, and technocrats poured into Syria to reform what was now the UAR's northern province, as though it were their latest colony. This was not what the Syrians had wanted.

Liberal democracy had vanished throughout the Arab world. Parliamentary government had been discredited as a game for palace hangers-on, rich landowners, capitalist merchants, and shrewd lawyers. Nasser's propaganda treated Egyptian nationalism as outmoded. The competing ideologies, Arab nationalism and communism, were both supranational. The idea of uniting all Arab countries appealed to many citizens, partly as a modern version of the old idea of pan-Islam. Pan-Arabism seemed even better. It did not exclude Arabic-speaking Christians. It would combine oil-rich countries having few people, such as Saudi Arabia, with populous ones poor in petroleum, such as Egypt. For the past millennium Arabs had served as a doormat for foreign invaders: Turks, Crusaders, Mongols, French, and British. Now independent, except for Algeria, Palestine, and a few fringes of Arabia, Arab peoples wanted to join together to become rich, strong, and respected. This was the gist of Nasser's speeches and press interviews at the time.

The Communists accused Arab nationalists of romanticizing their past and not planning for their future. The class struggle alone enabled societies to progress from slavery to feudalism to capitalism to socialism. Arabism might oust Western imperialism and destroy its lackeys in some countries, they said, but it could not develop free peoples. Because Nasser had banned all parties except the National Union and had jailed Egypt's Communists, Arab nationalism ruled in Cairo. But Iraq's revolutionary regime, having denounced the Baghdad Pact, steered between Arabism and communism, turning Nasser against Iraq and (briefly) the USSR.

In October 1958 the USSR had promised the aid needed to start building the Aswan High Dam. The Communist states had strengthened their ties with the UAR. Yet a few months later Nasser was exchanging brickbats with Soviet leaders, ostensibly over ideology but really over who could influence Iraq. The UAR resumed diplomatic relations with Britain, and U.S. ties warmed up slightly. As long as the UAR depended on the Communists for its weapons and replacement parts, though, the West had little influence in Cairo. The UAR still refused to let ships carrying Israel-bound goods transit the Suez Canal. When New York longshoremen refused in 1960 to unload an Egyptian freighter, Arab-American ties grew colder.

Influenced by the Syrian Baathists, the UAR began in 1960 to strengthen its commitment to socialism, nationalizing more foreign-held property and placing public utilities, banks, and newspapers under state control. Another harbinger of change was the Egyptian government's first published five-year economic plan. Egypt had become independent, and the processes of nation building were now controlled by a native Egyptian acting for the Egyptian people. For the people of Egypt, Nasser's policies brought a mix of good and bad. On the one hand, free press and assembly were squelched, students' excess energies were diverted from politics to soccer and ballet, and censors scrutinized incoming books, magazines, and letters. On the other hand, most workers were making more money, people were better housed, and more children were going to school and receiving medical care. More than half a million *feddans* (519,000 acres) of farmland had been redistributed to needy peasants. The Aswan High Dam, started by Soviet and Egyptian engineers in 1959, promised even higher living standards in the future. Egypt was respected now by other countries.

Nasser's incorruptibility impressed Egyptians and foreigners alike. His devotion to Arab unity won him support from Arabs everywhere, especially from Palestinians. Most Arabic-speaking peoples believed that the union of Egypt and Syria would be the first step toward a wider federation of all Arab states; Yemen (then still a monarchy) chose to federate with the UAR. Nasser's ability to play the superpowers against each other, which he called "Positive Neutrality," won aid for Egypt from both the United States and the USSR—and respect from the other new nations of Asia and Africa. Students from many of these countries flocked to its universities, gaining lasting impressions of Egypt as a country worthy of emulation. It seemed that Nasser's quest for national dignity and strength had succeeded.

10

ARAB SOCIALISM
(1961–1971)

The regime of the Egyptian officers began as a nationalist revolution with no general ideology. Nasser was essentially pragmatic; he deliberately shaped his program around the needs of the moment. The officers gradually realized, though, that they needed guiding principles to solve Egypt's social problems. Nationalism alone was not a sufficient social philosophy.

Perhaps the missing element was the political theory of the Islamic *umma,* buttressed by the sharia (the rules and laws of Islam) and the once-powerful Sufi brotherhoods that had been weakened during 150 years of state-imposed Westernization. Modern Egyptians had earlier expressed their desire for these traditional institutions by joining and supporting the Society of the Muslim Brothers, but this group had been ruthlessly extirpated by Nasser's government—ostensibly for having tried to assassinate him, but actually for challenging the primacy of the state. Nasser looked elsewhere and came up with what soon would be called "Arab socialism." It would be the defining characteristic of Egypt's political life from 1961 to 1971, even as the country tried to strengthen its ties with other Arab states and suffered a stunning defeat at the hands of Israel in June 1967. During this time its outside guidance came mainly from the USSR and other Communist countries, not from the West.

Socialism in Egypt

The ideological development not only of Egypt but of most Asian and African countries has been shaped by the power, wealth, social institutions, and ideas of Western Europe and North America. If the peoples of Asia and Africa have at various times viewed Britain and France, or Germany and Italy, or the United States and the Soviet Union, as militarily strong, economically prosperous, and socially cohesive, they have also chosen to adopt the organizing ideas, as well as the material goods and other attributes, that have made them so. The presence of European merchants in Egypt helped to promote a capitalist form of economic organization, together with the ideas of individual freedom and parliamentary democracy associated with liberal capitalism. The power of the British occupation to manipulate the Egyptian government stirred up nationalism. The challenge of the USSR and other Communist states to the West's pre-1956 hegemony in the Middle East lent an attractive luster to the ideas of socialism.

"Socialism" has many meanings. It can mean state ownership of factories and other means of production, workers' participation in the management of industries, national policies aimed at equalizing personal incomes, state economic planning, or charitable actions by individuals to share their material goods. In predominantly Muslim states, such as Egypt, it is rarely used in the purely Marxian sense, for Muslims can never deny the primacy of the one God above mundane material interests, nor can they accept a historical dynamic based on a struggle between classes. In Egypt the term *socialism* has commonly been applied to state ownership and management of the means of production. In that sense it is hardly novel, for the factories of Mehmet Ali and Ismail (not to mention their irrigation works, which were later extended by the British) were state enterprises. Even such nascent capitalist enterprises as Bank Misr had sought and received government subsidies and tariff protection before the 1952 Revolution.

Most of the Free Officers were not socialists. The 1955 Bandung Conference first brought Nasser into contact with Asian socialist leaders. The 1956 constitution pledged the government to strive for social justice by raising living standards and providing old age benefits, public health, and social insurance, but free enterprise and private property were also respected. In 1957 several state planning agencies were established, notably the Economic Development Organization, with authorization to set up new companies and to dispense state funds to existing firms. Land reform continued, as more *waqfs* were turned over to needy peasants, followed by reductions of peasant payments and landlord compensation for the lands that had been redistributed earlier.

The formation of the United Arab Republic in 1958 brought Nasser and his fellow officers into contact with a more developed socialist ideology than any they had known before. Syria's Baath Party was the first Arab movement to attempt a synthesis of nationalism and socialism. Its leaders were at first among the staunchest advocates of union with Egypt, although they became disenchanted when Nasser abolished their party along with all the others. However, it left major traces, including the slogan "Freedom, Socialism, Unity," which the United Arab Republic adopted for itself. During its three years of existence, the UAR tried to develop a distinctively Arab interpretation of socialism. Traditional Arabism had stressed the pre-Islamic virtues of generosity to the poor, hospitality to visitors, and subordination of each person's interests to those of his or her tribe. Islam itself could be seen as socialist, or at any rate egalitarian, in its injunctions to be charitable toward the orphaned and the needy and in its institution of *zakat*, a tithe on each Muslim's income or property. Egypt's early nationalists had assailed foreign ownership of their utilities and factories, a grievance corrected by Nasser's nationalization decrees after the Suez War. Now the people saw and resented the widening economic gap between such oil-rich countries as Saudi Arabia and those poor in petroleum and natural gas like the UAR. If the Arabs combined their military and political power, they would share their economic resources to create a strong state that could guarantee a decent living standard to everyone.

As a first step, the UAR in 1958–59 required new industrial firms to be licensed, barred any person from being a director of more than one corporation, placed 13 public utility companies under the state audit department, nationalized the large banks, subjected most newspapers and publishing houses to the National Union, and drew up its first five-year plan, which expressly aimed at doubling the national income in 10 years. These small steps toward socialism led to the great leap known as the July Laws of 1961. Featured among those laws were (1) the regulation of most industries; (2) the nationalization of such businesses as textiles, tobacco, pharmaceuticals, shipping, and all banks and insurance firms not already under state ownership; (3) income redistribution, whereby no Egyptian could receive an annual salary above £E 5000 (then worth $11,500) and incomes above £E 10,000 were to be taxed at 90 percent; and (4) land reform, under which the maximum individual landholding was reduced from 200 to 100 *feddans*, with the excess to be distributed among landless peasants, and all future peasant loans would be free of interest. The real July Revolution took place in 1961—not in 1952.

The effect of these laws, and of those that Nasser would enact during the rest of his presidency, was the weakening of the Egyptian bourgeoisie and the destruction of what had been the domination of the large landowners. Unable to oppose Nasser and his policies, many sent their money—or their children—out of Egypt. The industrial workers were now somewhat better off than ever before. They were guaranteed a minimum wage (although it remained abysmally low) and various fringe benefits, such as health care and disability payments. A few became leaders in the state-controlled labor unions or members of the boards of directors in the companies for which they worked. Some peasants benefited from the land reforms, although they could barely come up with minimal payments for the lands they had acquired. Rural cooperatives that shared supplies and equipment helped, though their efficiency suffered as a result of their ties to the government bureaucracy. There were still many landless peasants, however, working for daily wages on lands owned by others.

Public education at all levels expanded rapidly, but school buildings and teaching staffs could not keep up with the burgeoning numbers of pupils, and so educational standards fell below their prerevolutionary levels. But improved school discipline reduced the number of days lost to political demonstrations. Egypt's private schools, long the training ground for the elite, were reduced in number and increasingly subjected to state regulation. Government employees rose drastically in number, especially after so many manufacturing, financial, and commercial firms were nationalized. Nasser's 1962 guarantee of a government job for every university graduate also swelled the bureaucratic ranks. Salaries for civil servants were low, as was productivity. Subsidized housing, health care, and old-age and disability pensions were offered as fringe benefits.

One unforeseen result of the new Arab socialist laws was Syria's secession from the UAR in September 1961. Many explanations have been given for this breakaway: intrigues by other Arab regimes or foreign powers, low salaries paid to UAR government officials and military officers relative to what Syrians had been accustomed to earning, Syrian resentment over the imperial attitudes of many Egyptians working in Syria, years of poor harvests and higher food prices, and disillusionment with Arab nationalism once it became clear that Iraq and other oil-rich states would not join the UAR. Syria had not only more doctrinaire socialists than Egypt but also more recalcitrant capitalists who hated the July Laws. Although chagrined by Syria's defection, Nasser did not try to retake the country by force, nor did he block its readmission to the Arab League. Egypt still called itself the United Arab Republic, but it severed its federation with Yemen.

Nasser did conclude, though, that the National Union had failed to mobilize UAR citizens behind him. He claimed that it had been infiltrated and corrupted by reactionaries. In October 1961 he proposed a

National Congress of Popular Forces to form a revolutionary organization that would be the "highest political authority" in the country: the Arab Socialist Union (ASU). The Congress would be open to workers, peasants, intellectuals, professionals, military men, and owners whose property was not based on exploitation. Students and women were also to be represented. To the Congress, which met in May 1962, Nasser presented a new National Charter. It summarized Egypt's modern history, explained why Arab socialism had become the country's guiding ideology, stated the ASU's aims and organizational framework, and reiterated the UAR's basic domestic and foreign policies. It advocated equal rights for men and women. For the first time Nasser accepted family planning as necessary to combat Egypt's overpopulation. For six weeks the Congress debated the charter and even criticized some of Nasser's policies. The National Charter was passed unanimously.

On all domestic fronts—political, economic, intellectual, and social—Egypt now committed itself to an ambitious modernization program that could be achieved only if it remained at peace with its neighbors and attracted aid from abroad. Fortunately, with the USSR building the High Dam, the United States selling wheat for Egyptian pounds, and other countries giving aid independently, modernization just might succeed.

The Arab Cold War

Egypt's relations with other Arab countries, not to mention Israel, were more problematic. In the wake of Syria's secession from the UAR, Nasser felt isolated within the Arab world. Iraq under its revolutionary leader, Abd al-Karim Qasim (1914–63), was as fierce a rival as it had been under its Hashimite kings. Jordan and Saudi Arabia, as monarchies, opposed republican socialism. Lebanon had recovered from its 1958 civil war and its leaders practiced untrammeled Arab capitalism. Syria was assailing Egypt in the Arab League. Tunisia and Libya had long opposed Nasser, and Morocco under King Hasan II was aligning itself with them. Algeria's independence in June 1962, after a bitter eight-year war against French rule, was the sole bright star in the Arab firmament, for President Ahmad Ben Bella (1918–   ) was firmly allied with Nasser.

In September of that year Yemen's aged imam died. A week later an army mutiny in Yemen's capital overthrew his son. Egypt promptly recognized its new junta, headed by General Abdallah al-Sallal (1917–94). When the deposed imam took to Yemen's mountains to stir his tribal loyalists into fighting back, Egypt sent advisers, arms, and troops to help Sallal's republicans. Saudi Arabia's regent, Faisal (1904–75), viewed Nasser's aid as an attempt to gain influence in the Arabian Peninsula. So, too, did the British, still ruling southern Arabia. Before long Saudi Arabia and Britain were aiding the Yemeni royalists, and Egypt was ensnared in a five-year civil war.

Nasser gained new allies early in 1963 when successive military coups brought Baathists to power in Iraq and Syria. The new regimes petitioned Nasser to start talks to revive the United Arab Republic. The three countries, despite their leaders' shared commitment to Arab unity and socialism, differed on the terms of their union. Nasser argued that Egypt, with its larger population and longer adherence to Arab social-ism, deserved more power. He distrusted the Syrian Baathists, accusing them of having sabotaged the earlier UAR. He liked Iraq's new leader, Abd al-Salam Arif (1921–66), who had broken with Qasim in 1958 to promote Arab unity, suffered exile and imprisonment, and now emerged as a Nasserite. But even Iraq's Baathists rejected Nasser's no-party dic-tatorship, so Egypt put off this new federation. By year's end the three countries were estranged. To quote an Arab proverb: "I can protect myself from my enemy, but God defend me against my friends."

The cause of Arab unity was better served by its enemy's actions than by those of its friends. Israel had begun its National Water Carrier Project, tapping Lake Tiberias to irrigate farms and bring water to its cities, towns, and new settlements. In 1954 President Eisenhower had sent a special envoy to the Middle East to promote a plan for developing the Jordan River valley and sharing its waters among Israel, Jordan, and Syria. The Arab states, while approving its technical aspects, rejected the plan politically because it would mean recognizing Israel. In 1963 Israel began diverting what would have been its share of Jordan River waters under the plan, much to the alarm of its Arab neighbors. In January 1964 Nasser called a summit meeting of all Arab kings and other heads of state. He managed to convince the other leaders that they were not ready to fight Israel. They agreed to study ways to divert the Jordan River's sources in Syria and Lebanon so that Israel could not take the Arabs' water, but the summit achieved nothing concrete. The leaders also agreed to set up a group to be known as the Palestine Liberation Organization (PLO). This would concentrate the political clout of the Palestinian Arabs, deflecting their pressure from themselves. In May 1964 Palestinian delegates met in Jordan-ruled Jerusalem and founded the PLO under the presidency of a Nasserite Arab nationalist. These actions enhanced Nasser's stature as an Arab leader but did little to unify the Arabs or liberate Palestine.

EXCERPTS FROM THE NATIONAL CHARTER OF THE ARAB SOCIALIST UNION, 1962

The National Charter was drafted by Nasser's staff and submitted to the National Congress of Popular Forces on May 21, 1962. It combined ideas of European socialism with Arab nationalism, which Nasser claimed to lead. Widely disseminated in Egypt and other Arab countries once it was formally adopted on June 30, 1962, it is now largely forgotten. This excerpt forms a part of the preamble.

The Arab revolution that is currently both the implement and a reflection of the Arab struggle must arm itself with three forces that will enable it to win its battle of destiny:

First, consciousness based on scientific conviction derived from enlightened thought and free discussion, untainted by the forces of fanaticism and terrorism.

Second, free movement adapted to the changing circumstances of the Arab struggle, provided that this movement observes its objectives and moral ideals.

Third, clear perception of the objectives, never losing sight of them, never being carried away by emotion or diverted from the high road of the national struggle.

Early in 1964 the UAR adopted a new constitution and held elections for the local, provincial, and national councils of the Arab Socialist Union, as well as for the reorganized National Assembly. All Assembly delegates had to be over 30 years old and able to read and write. At least half had to be workers or peasants, a lofty goal for a country most of whose adult population was illiterate. The ASU mainly mobilized the people and recruited local leaders; its National Assembly's powers were purely consultative. The country's new laws still took the form of "republican decrees." By now many of the Free Officers were leaving the UAR cabinet, because they opposed Nasser's Arab socialism, wanted more freedom, or saw greater opportunities for advancement outside the government. The new ministers were mostly civilian technocrats who lacked an independent power base. The executive branch, too,

> The great need for these three forces arises from the particular circumstances of the Arab revolutionary experiment, under whose influence it takes control of the course of Arab history.
>
> Today the Arab revolution is called upon to strike a new path before the objectives of the Arab struggle. Ages of suffering and hope have shaped the objectives of the Arab struggle. These objectives, which truly express the Arab national conscience, are:
>
> Freedom
> Socialism
> Unity
>
> ... Today, freedom has come to mean freedom of the nation and freedom of the citizen.
>
> Socialism has become both a means and an end, namely sufficiency and justice.
>
> The road to unity has become the popular call for the restoration of the natural order of a nation that was torn apart by its enemies against its will and its interests, and the peaceful endeavor to promote this unity 'and its unanimous acceptance as a crowning achievement.
>
> Source: Adapted from Sami A. Hanna and George H. Gardner, *Arab Socialism: A Documentary Study* (Leiden, Netherlands: E. J. Brill, 1969), 344–345.

had become a rubber stamp for Nasser. Several distinct secret services protected the UAR against spies—or dissidents.

Egypt's Estrangement from the West

Soviet leader Nikita Khrushchev finally visited Egypt in May 1964 to celebrate the completion of the first stage of the High Dam. During his visit he argued with Nasser and his colleagues over their belief in Muslim values and Arab nationalism as opposed to Marxian scientific socialism. But Soviet aid, whether economic or military, kept coming, whereas U.S. wheat sales got bogged down in politics, especially once Lyndon Johnson succeeded John F. Kennedy as president. Disputes with Washington over an internal power struggle in the Congo led to a protest by African students in Cairo that destroyed the American library there. Just days later Egyptian jets shot down a U.S. civilian plane that had strayed into the country's airspace without authorization. Then Nasser, misconstruing a talk between U.S. Ambassador Lucius Battle and Egypt's minister of supply over the terms for renewing the wheat sales agreement, said in a public speech that if the Americans resented his policies, they could "drink from the sea," the Egyptian equivalent of "Go jump in a lake." Such incidents delighted Egypt's Communists, American Zionists, and anyone else opposed to friendly U.S.-Egyptian relations. U.S. grain sales sputtered; as the USSR tried to take up the slack, Egypt edged toward the Communist camp. West German arms sales to Israel, followed by diplomatic recognition, drove radical Arabs to recognize East Germany. The Middle East became more polarized than it had ever been before.

Foreign observers believed that Nasser's government was split between a doctrinaire, pro-Communist wing led by Ali Sabri (1920–91) and a pragmatic, pro-Western one personified by Zakariyya Muhyi al-Din (1918–   ). In reality both men espoused various cold war positions during their political careers. Nasser conflated loyalty to Pan-Arabism and the Egyptian state with himself. By 1964 even Nasser's fellow Free Officers, while in his presence, cautiously said what they thought he wanted to hear.

Ali Sabri, as prime minister from 1962 to 1965, administered Nasser's program of modernization via Arab socialism. When Zakariyya replaced him, Ali became a senior vice president and the ASU leader. Prime Minister Zakariyya was less interested in Egypt's cold war stance than in its budget and balance of payments, both of which had run deficits for years. Zakariyya took a fateful step when he let Egyptians emigrate freely abroad. Each year since 1965 up to half a million Egyptians have gone to other Arab countries or to the rest of the world, sometimes to seek greater freedom but usually to make more money. In 2000 their remittances would provide $3.74 billion in foreign exchange, a boon to Egypt's balance of payments, but its loss of entrepreneurial and technical skills has been incalculable.

Zakariyya's government did not relax the police-state atmosphere. The Muslim Brothers, after a decade of severe repression, had been released from prison in 1964 and allowed to resume their propaganda. Their undiminished ability to win support in Egypt and other Arab countries alarmed Nasser, who would brook no dissent from his Arab socialist program. By the end of 1965 their leaders, notably their most respected writer, Sayyid Qutb (1906–66), were back in jail. In a show trial he and several other Brothers were convicted of plotting against

Nasser, condemned to death, and hanged in August 1966, horrifying Muslims everywhere. As for the Communists, both the pro-Soviet and Maoist parties dissolved themselves in 1965 and joined the ASU, where they tried to shape public opinion. Setting up the Vanguard Organization, Youth Organization, and Higher Institute for Socialist Studies pushed the ASU to the left. Pro-Western Egyptians, if they had not left the country, kept quiet; many had already lost their property or their positions.

Nasser's relations with the Saudis, even after Faisal officially succeeded King Saud in 1964, remained tense, mainly because of the Yemen civil war, which was still tying up 70,000 Egyptian troops. Faisal and Nasser reached an agreement to end their involvement and settle the war, only to have it dissolve amid mutual recriminations. Late in 1965 King Faisal visited the shah of Iran, and the two rulers issued a joint statement calling for an Islamic pact to combat elements and ideas alien to Islam, by which they meant socialism, thereby alienating Nasser further.

Drift toward the June War

Of all the troubled countries in the Middle East, the least stable was Syria. The Syrians who had taken power in March 1963 were a coalition of Nasserite and Baath Party pan-Arabists. By year's end the Baath alone held power and vowed never to sacrifice its existence or its principles to join a Nasser-led union. In February 1966 a cabal of officers belonging to a radical Baathist faction seized power in Damascus. Most of these men belonged to the religious minority called the Alawites and tried to prove that they were as patriotic as the Sunni Muslim majority by fiercely opposing Israel. The number of border incidents rose, for Syria was arming, training, and organizing a new Palestinian guerrilla group called Fatah to attack Israel from Jordan. Israel retaliated with a massive raid on the Jordanian village al-Samu in November 1966, but many Israelis felt they should have punished Syria as the instigator of the attacks.

Days earlier, hoping to control the new Baathists, Nasser had made a defense pact with Syria. The new alliance did not calm the Syrians; in April 1967 tensions with Israel mounted. An aerial dogfight between Israeli warplanes and Syrian MiGs, fought within view of Damascus, brought down six Syrian planes while all Israeli fighters returned to their bases. Relying on its Egyptian pact, Syria called for war against Israel. Neither Egypt nor Israel could afford a war. Egypt had exhausted its hard-currency reserves and could no longer buy spare parts to operate its factories or to fly its United Arab Airlines passenger jets. Israel was in a recession, and more Jews were leaving than entering the state. But at a time when Jordan and Saudi Arabia were taunting Nasser for hiding behind the skirts of the United Nations Emergency Force (UNEF) in Sinai, Israel's army was raiding al-Samu, and its fighters were downing Syrian MiGs, he could not keep quiet. Accepting Soviet reports about an Israeli buildup at the Syrian border, Nasser decided to send troops to Sinai. As Egypt's radio stations began competing with those of the other Arab countries to threaten the Jewish state, Israel started calling up its reserves and preparing for what it believed would be a war for its survival.

Nasser and his Soviet advisers should then have spent more time on strategy and less on tactics. With its best soldiers still in Yemen, Egypt needed to make itself look stronger than Israel without ever firing a shot; it could not really destroy the Jewish state. Instead Nasser asked the UNEF to pull back from its strategic posts in Gaza and Sinai. Rather than haggle with Egypt, the UN secretary-general hastily withdrew his entire force. Once Egypt's army faced the Israelis directly, Nasser proclaimed a naval blockade across the Tiran Straits, which passed through Egyptian territorial waters, against Israeli ships and cargoes. Even if few Israeli naval or merchant vessels actually used the Gulf of Aqaba, the blockade threatened Israel's oil imports from Iran. Both Israel and the United States objected. U.S. troops were largely mired in Vietnam. The Americans hoped either to defuse the issue diplomatically or to test the blockade by sending ships to Israel's port of Eilat.

No country wanted a war. Both Egypt and Israel promised not to fire the first shot, the UN Security Council met almost continuously, and various secret efforts were made to avert an armed conflict. The U.S. and Egyptian governments discussed sending their respective vice presidents to each other's capitals to work out a face-saving deal.

The June 1967 War

Diplomacy failed. Nasser's speeches and interviews aroused Israeli Jews' deepest anxiety—that he planned to wipe them out. No one heeded his insistence that Egypt would not start the war. While Egypt's forces remained on a peacetime footing and its planes were lining up on their bases, Israel's general staff drafted a plan to defeat the Arabs. Early on June 5 Israeli fighter planes, flying below Arab radar, swooped down on its enemies' airbases and wiped out four-fifths of the military aircraft of

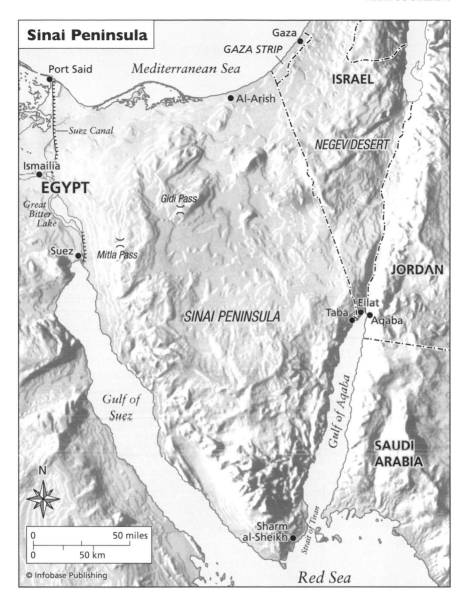

Egypt, Syria, and Iraq. Without air cover Egypt's forces could not stop the Israelis, who in three days took the Gaza Strip, all of Sinai, and at least 5,000 prisoners. Some officers deserted their troops. About 20,000 soldiers died, more often from thirst and exposure than battle wounds. Egyptians believe that the Israelis tortured and shot Egyptian POWs near al-Arish. Israel bombed an American naval ship, the USS *Liberty*,

179

killing 34 and wounding 170 sailors, to prevent it from gathering intelligence in the area.

On June 8 Egypt accepted the Security Council's call for a cease-fire in place, as Israel's troops occupied the east bank of the canal. Alleging that U.S. planes flew air cover for Israel, Nasser broke diplomatic relations with Washington, while the USSR broke with Israel. If Nasser had acute economic problems before the June War, he was now confronted by a worse political crisis. He had misled his people and all the other Arabs to expect that Egypt, despite Israel's preemptive strike, would win the war. His vaunted arsenal of medium and light bombers, MiG-21 fighters, SAM-2 missiles, tanks, artillery, and rifles, for which Egypt had promised to pay billions of dollars in commodities or hard currency, had turned to smoking ruins. With his army clearly defeated, Nasser decided to resign.

In a televised speech he admitted losing the war, assumed total responsibility for defeat, and announced that he would give up all his posts. The new leader would be Zakariyya Muhyi al-Din. The speech sparked mass demonstrations, most of them spontaneous, as men and women filled the streets, singing nationalist songs and begging Nasser not to quit. At first he resisted the people's entreaties but finally withdrew his resignation after the National Assembly unanimously asked him to stay in office. The mandate enabled Nasser to dismiss his best friend from his post as commander of the armed forces and to jail other officers for mismanaging the war.

No War No Peace

Nasser never lived down his defeat. Egypt's armed forces had been destroyed, its enemy had captured Sinai with its oil wells and strategic control of the Suez Canal, and its economy was in shambles. Egyptians forgave Nasser, the symbol of their national dignity. But many grumbled against his regime once they realized how many of their sons had fallen in the war and how some of their officers had fled the battlefield. Egyptians began to criticize the Soviets and urged the Palestinians to retake their own land.

As for Israel, Arab radio threats to destroy the state had been at least put off, and the lands it controlled had tripled in size. Egypt had made those threats not to carry them out but to impress other Arabs. Israel denied that it had waged war to expand its territory; it called for peace negotiations and recognition. Perhaps it also wanted new leaders in Cairo, Amman, and Damascus. Above all, it wanted security. It got none.

As the UN Security Council reached an impasse and the General Assembly held an inconclusive session, Moscow went back to arming the Arab states while calling for a peaceful resolution to the conflict. But Washington was no longer willing to repeat its 1956–57 demand for an unconditional Israeli withdrawal from Sinai. In fact, Nasser's relations with the United States hit an all-time low. Preoccupied with the Vietnam War, Johnson wanted the Arab states to make peace with Israel. Most of the defeated Arabs, however, chose to buy more Soviet arms and to renew the struggle. Meeting at Khartoum in August and early September, the Arab heads of state agreed to aid Egypt financially and adopted a policy of "the Three Noes": no negotiations, no recognition, and no peace with Israel.

Egyptians and Israelis were already firing across the Suez Canal, which had been closed since the war began. Egypt sank the Israeli destroyer *Eilat*. Israel retaliated by blowing up the Suez oil refinery. Egypt had to evacuate 700,000 civilians from Port Said, Ismailia, and Suez. The search for peace was more urgent than ever. In November the UN Security Council adopted Resolution 242, which in essence called on Israel to return captured lands to obtain peace with the Arabs, but its wording was ambiguous. Israel was to withdraw its forces from "territories occupied in the recent conflict," but not (in the English version) *all* territories. The resolution stressed "the inadmissibility of the acquisition of territory by war." It would recognize the right of "every state in the area," implicitly including Israel, to "live in peace within secure and recognized boundaries." It guaranteed freedom of navigation through international waterways, e.g., the Gulf of Aqaba and the Suez Canal. It demanded a "just solution of the refugee problem," thereby fueling Israeli arguments that Jews fleeing from Arab countries were just as entitled to fair treatment as the Palestinian refugees. That clause angered the Palestinians, who no longer cared to be viewed as mere refugees but wanted their own nation-state in Israel's place. Jordan, Egypt, and Israel each accepted Resolution 242 on its own terms. The secretary-general then dispatched Swedish diplomat Gunnar Jarring to talk to them about implementing it.

Jarring's mission failed. Both sides got new arms and resumed sporadic fighting. The most notable development in 1968 was the emergence of the Palestinian fedayeen, mainly Fatah, a guerrilla group led by Yasir Arafat (1929–2004), which joined the Jordanian regulars in repulsing an Israeli raid east of the Jordan at a village called Karameh. The Palestinian guerrillas became heroes in an Arab world disillusioned with its regular armies after the 1967 "setback." Potentially, though, the Palestinians challenged Nasser and other leaders for the support of their citizens.

The survival of Nasser's regime and its resistance to Israel attest to the underlying strength of the Egyptian nation. The people could endure austerity measures, a necessity owing to their tottering economy. Luckily for them, the 1967 cotton and rice harvests were abundant, and more oil was discovered south of Suez. Saudi Arabia and Kuwait would subsidize Egypt so that Nasser would not seek a separate peace with Israel. In return he withdrew his troops from Yemen, which stanched a drain on Egypt's resources.

In 1968, for the first time since 1954, workers and students demonstrated independently of the regime and its mobilizing organization. Nasser's police had curtailed student political activity, outlawing unauthorized demonstrations, petitions, leaflets, and magazines posted on walls. It had tried to co-opt student leaders into its Liberation Rally, National Union, Arab Socialist Union, Youth Organization, and finally its Vanguard Organization. Apart from these groups, all university students belonged to the Student Union, a social and recreational group supervised by teachers holding administrative veto powers that young people naturally resented.

Nasser. A colonel in the Egyptian army, Gamal Abdel Nasser masterminded the coup that ended the monarchy and turned Egypt into a republic. He became the leader of Arab nationalism, especially between 1956 and 1967, and tried to institute socialism in Egypt, especially after 1961, with a corresponding rise in the influence of the USSR and its allies. (Associated Press)

The first call for students to act came from a demonstration by Helwan workers against the lenient sentences passed by the military court on the air force · leaders accused of negligence in the war. Due to an ASU mix-up, the police tried to stop an authorized demonstration by munitions workers on February 21 (Egypt's Students' Day). Scores were wounded in the ensuing melee, in which some students took part. Thousands of Cairo and Alexandria University students demonstrated, the police turned out in force, and there were numerous arrests and injuries. The student leaders went on to present their demands to the National Assembly, occasioning a debate about the lenient sentences of the air force officers, the Helwan workers' demonstration, and the repressive actions of the security police. The youths also wanted to end secret intelligence and teachers' surveillance and other repressive measures against them, and to have laws passed guaranteeing political freedoms. After Nasser met with the student leaders, he accepted some of their demands and announced what became his March 30 Program, promising to liberalize Egypt's government. Most of his promises were never kept.

The War of Attrition

Meanwhile, the Egyptian government wanted the Israelis removed from the Suez Canal's east bank, whether peacefully or by force. Nasser faced a dilemma. If Egypt fought the Israelis while the Soviets replenished the arsenal it had lost in the war, he could not get the offensive weapons needed to drive the Israelis back. Many suspected that the Kremlin was prolonging the state of no-war-no-peace to tighten its control over Egypt. If Egypt wanted the Israelis to hand back Sinai, it would have to enter direct talks, recognize Israel, and forgo its claim to lead the Arab countries. Nasser viewed this option as a capitulation to the Johnson administration, which seemed to have abandoned the Arabs. The UN was snarled by the two sides' conflicting interpretations of Resolution 242 and by the superpower rivalry. Richard Nixon's electoral victory in November 1968 raised Egypt's hopes for a change. Talks among the U.S., Soviet, British, and French foreign ministers hinted at an imposed solution, but no agreement was reached.

Instead, Palestinian raids into Israel from Jordan and Lebanon intensified, as did Israeli reprisals. The shooting across the Suez Canal also intensified. In March 1969 Nasser declared a "War of Attrition" against Israel. His strategy was to make the cost of the occupation to Israel in human lives and manpower losses unbearably high, or perhaps to convince Washington that it must force Israel to withdraw from Sinai. This strategy proved costly for Egypt. Israel launched a "war of nerves" that included demonstrations of its ability to send tanks up and down the Suez Gulf coast, capture a new Soviet radar installation from a Red Sea island, buzz Cairo at dawn with jet planes, and drop bombs on a military factory in Maadi and a school in the Delta. Unable to win the Arab support that he wanted at the Rabat summit meeting of December

1969, Nasser flew to Moscow to seek additional SAM-3 missiles and more military advisers. By April 1970 aerial dogfights were taking place high above the Suez Canal, amid Israeli claims that Soviet pilots were flying the Egyptian MiGs. The War of Attrition was costly for Israel, too, and it ended with a peace initiative by U.S. secretary of state William Rogers.

The Rogers Peace Plan

Rogers' Plan, first proposed in December 1969 and revised in June 1970, called for a cease-fire in the War of Attrition, reactivating the Jarring mission, and carrying out Resolution 242. Jordan, then Egypt, and finally Israel accepted a 90-day cease-fire.

Despite Nasser's ineradicable reputation for hostility to Israel, his acceptance of the Rogers Peace Plan was his final effort to put the Palestine problem into the deep freeze. Egypt's ambitious policies in Yemen and Palestine had drained the nation's economy and left Nasser depending on both the Communist countries and royalist Saudi Arabia, a difficult balancing act. Nasser viewed Israel as the tool used by successive U.S. administrations to force a "Pax Americana" on the Middle East. But indirect negotiations, sponsored by the superpowers, were an acceptable step toward the peace Egypt needed. For months Nasser advised Syria and other frontline Arab states that they could not win a full-scale war with Israel.

Most Palestinians were unconvinced. They feared that Egypt would make peace at their expense. Yasir Arafat, who now headed the Palestine Liberation Organization, was fighting Jordanian King Hussein's government and opposing the Rogers Peace Plan. The fedayeen stepped up their activities. On September 6 a splinter group hijacked four passenger jets and took three of them to an abandoned airstrip near Amman, where they held their passengers hostage and demanded the release of Palestinians jailed in Europe. This action directly challenged King Hussein. His troops replied by bombarding Palestinian refugee camps and Amman neighborhoods. Meanwhile, Israel broke off talks with the Jarring mission because Egypt had moved its newly acquired SAM-3 missiles up to the canal, an act it justified by noting that Israel had entrenched its forces behind the Bar-Lev Line.

Peace talks, however indirect, between the Arabs and Israel had to await a truce between Jordan and the Palestinians. Syria threatened to invade Jordan, an act likely to bring either the United States or Israel to Hussein's aid. Nasser convoked an Arab summit meeting in Cairo and made an exhausting effort to reconcile Hussein with Arafat. After escorting Kuwait's emir to the Cairo Airport, Nasser went home, lay down, and died.

Sadat Succeeds Nasser

Nasser had been diabetic for years and had suffered a heart attack in 1969, but his death came as a shock to the Egyptian people. Millions turned out in the Cairo streets, sobbing, shouting slogans, and following his flag-draped coffin to its final resting place in what was renamed the Gamal Abd al-Nasser Mosque in Heliopolis. His vice president, Anwar Sadat, was his constitutional successor, but no one expected him to remain in power. He was seen as a political lightweight.

Behind Sadat's back, several of Nasser's friends contended to succeed him. During Nasser's last year, when ill health made him take prolonged vacations, several "power centers" had filled the vacuum. Men with direct ties to Nasser seemed to be displacing the remaining Free Officers. The new Nasserites were pro-USSR, authoritarian in their governing style, and hostile to a peace with Israel. They accepted Sadat's nomination by the National Assembly and approval by the ASU and the Egyptian people for the presidency, in accordance with the 1964 Constitution. But by controlling the secret police, the main ministries, and the information network (their centers of power), they would ease Sadat out and carry on Nasser's program.

At first they seemed to have guessed correctly. Sadat was nominated and elected by a majority of Egyptian voters. He pledged to continue Nasser's policies, extended the cease-fire several times, and offered to reopen the Suez Canal if the Israelis would pull their forces back a few miles. When Israel refused, he warned that 1971 would be the "year of decision" and began public war preparations. He let the cease-fire run out, put his troops on full alert, ordered a partial blackout in Cairo, and asked for more Soviet arms to renew the war against Israel. He reached a tentative agreement to form a federation of Libya, Syria, and Egypt. But in early May he suddenly dismissed Ali Sabri as vice president, just before Secretary of State Rogers arrived in Cairo to revive the Jarring mission and the peace plan that bore his own name. A week later, apprised of his foes' plot, Sadat took over the army and dismissed all the Nasserites.

Sadat thus confirmed his hold on the presidency and began dismantling his predecessor's regime. He stopped using wiretaps and tape recorders to spy on government officials and released many dissidents who had been placed under house arrest in Nasser's time. Even though Sadat signed a friendship treaty with the USSR in May 1971, he assumed a more neutral stance between the superpowers. The tide of Arab socialism was ebbing.

Most people think these policy changes began when Nasser died, but the Arab defeat in the June War had set events in motion. After the war Nasser had accepted Saudi and Kuwaiti subsidies at the 1967 Khartoum summit, his government agreed to Resolution 242, and it entered indirect talks with Israel under the Rogers Peace Plan in 1970. The transition would not be complete, though, until Sadat found a decisive moment to redeem Egypt's honor in battle.

11

ANWAR SADAT
(1971-1981)

Sadat ruled, almost unopposed, from May 1971 until October 1981. Although he turned out to be as dictatorial as Nasser, the less obtrusive character of his government made Sadat's regime seem more democratic. Outsiders assumed, therefore, that the Egyptian people's lives became less tense and driven than they had been under his predecessor. Because Sadat dramatically reversed Nasser's policies toward the superpowers, socialism, and the conflict with Israel, he was highly lauded in the West. But his place in the hearts and minds of his own countrymen has not been so secure. Egyptians hailed Sadat's leadership when Egypt's army successfully challenged Israel in the October 1973 War, welcomed his loosening of socialist controls on the economy, and cheered Sadat when he returned from his trip to Jerusalem to talk peace with Israel. However, when he was assassinated during a military parade in October 1981, most Egyptians did not mourn his passing.

Sadat's Early Years

Originally from the Delta village of Mit Abu al-Kum, Sadat spent most of his youth in Cairo in what in traditional Muslim society was the lowly position of second son of his father's second wife. Like Nasser, he climbed the social ladder by becoming an army officer. The two became friends in 1938 when they were both stationed in Manqabad, where Sadat claims in his memoirs to have started the secret society that Nasser later led. One of the most ardent Free Officers, Sadat spent time in jail and was even discharged from the officer corps for his subversive activities. He was implicated in the 1941 attempt to smuggle Egypt's popular nationalist general, Aziz Ali al-Misri, through British lines to the German general Erwin Rommel. In 1942 he helped Nazi agents in Cairo to make contact with Muslim Brothers and extreme national-

Anwar Sadat. Vice president at the time of Nasser's death, Anwar Sadat was initially thought to be a political lightweight, but he struck out against his rivals in June 1971 and soon pared back Arab socialism and demanded the withdrawal of Soviet advisers from Egypt in 1972. (Associated Press)

ists, but got caught and sent to prison. Accused of conspiring to kill Amin Uthman in 1946, he was jailed again but finally acquitted. He wanted to blow up the British embassy in 1948 and to hang King Farouk and his courtiers in front of Abdin Palace in 1952. Nasser restrained him.

During Nasser's presidency Sadat was among his most visible henchmen. His account of the 1952 Revolution, written in French and English as well as Arabic, was among the first to see print. He also wrote a laudatory children's book about Nasser. He broadcast the revolutionary manifesto over Radio Cairo on July 23, 1952, and announced Nasser's death on September 28, 1970. It was Sadat who edited the government daily *al-Gumhuriyya* (The Republic), served as secretary-general for the Islamic Congress, chaired the National Assembly, and performed other jobs for Nasser; rarely did he hold any power. Though other RCC members drifted away from Nasser, Sadat stood by him until the end. He earned from his colleagues the sardonic name *Bikbashi Sah-sah* (Colonel Yes-Yes) for dissimulating his differences with the leader. Nasser rewarded this fidelity by naming him vice president in 1969 but did not want him as his successor.

After eight months of shared leadership, during which most experts predicted that Nasser's closest supporters would ease Sadat out of office, he staged his Corrective Revolution on May 15, 1971, taking uncontested control of Egypt. People were relieved when Sadat purged Nasser's "centers of power." The new president had outgrown his conspiratorial youth and hence—unlike Nasser—no longer cared to spy on opponents or tap their telephones. Huge bonfires of secret police tapes illumined Sadat's pledge to respect civil liberties.

Meanwhile, Sadat praised the USSR for assisting Egypt's development. He invited the Soviet president to attend the inaugural festivities for the Aswan High Dam and signed the Soviet-Egyptian Treaty of Friendship and Cooperation. At the same time he harped constantly on Egypt's need for more arms and extended Nasser's tentative contacts with the

West. This policy shift was partly in response to the U.S. search for a comprehensive Arab-Israeli settlement under the Rogers Peace Plan, but it also reflected the anti-Communist stance of Saudi King Faisal. When the Communists nearly took power in Sudan, Egypt's government was alarmed. Sadat felt almost as vulnerable as his upstream neighbor. Also, by 1971, Egypt's officers were becoming more professional and less eager to serve the Kremlin as the vanguard of socialism.

Sadat and the Soviets

Sadat paid lip service to Nasserism while edging away from Nasser's policies. He went to Moscow in October 1971, seeking more arms to renew the war with Israel. He signaled to Washington that 1971 would be the "year of decision," in which either the Arabs and Israel (under U.S. pressure) would make peace on the terms stated in UN Resolution 242 or the War of Attrition would resume. He was disappointed when Israel and the United States ignored his offer to reopen the Suez Canal in return for a partial Israeli pullback in the Sinai. But 1971 ended with neither progress toward peace nor renewed war with Israel. The Indo-Pakistani War, fought in December 1971 over the secession of East Pakistan, which became Bangladesh, provided an excuse to delay fighting Israel; it also angered Sadat that India received new Soviet weapons that Egypt could not buy. He felt that Moscow was using arms sales to control Egypt, just as Nasser had accused the West of attaching strings to its 1955 aid offers. The chasm between Sadat and the Kremlin widened. The latter wanted to slow down the arms race by reaching a détente with Washington. It saw the fall of Ali Sabri and the "centers of power" as a warning signal that Egypt would desert the kind of Arab socialism that could have turned into communism.

Sadat's proposed "Federation of Arab Republics," comprising Syria, Libya, and Egypt, alarmed the Soviets, especially because Libyan leader Muammar Gadhafi (1942–   ) craved an organic union between Egypt and Libya. So much did the new Libyan leader admire Nasser's role as leader of the Arab revolution that he offered to put his country and its burgeoning oil wealth under the control of Nasser's successor. Cairo gossip predicted that Gadhafi would try to replace Sadat. At the time the Kremlin saw the young Libyan leader as a threat to its influence, although he had already successfully removed British and U.S. bases from Libyan soil. The Soviets had hoped for Sadat's cooperation in the pro-Communist Sudanese coup of July 1971; they got the opposite. Egypt resented Moscow's imperious demands for more bases on

Egyptian soil and the Soviets' refusal to admit high-ranking Egyptian officers into some bases they already had. Soviet-manned equipment in Egypt could be operated only on orders from Moscow. Soviet technicians, lacking any common language with the Egyptians they were training, often treated them with contempt. The Soviets' popularity had been great when Nasser called them in after the 1967 war, but it had vanished five years later. Like the British and the Americans before them, the Soviets failed to heed Egyptian nationalism. Sadat decided, therefore, to expel most Soviet technicians from Egypt, effective July 17, 1972. Those who stayed would work under Egyptian command. Although the Soviets kept their naval bases, the number of Soviet military personnel in Egypt was reduced from 20,000 to fewer than 1,000. Most of the advanced weapons under their control were also withdrawn. Moscow accepted all of these terms but rejected Sadat's request for high-level talks. Both sides recalled their ambassadors, and Sadat asked discreetly about buying arms in Western Europe. When Palestinians killed 11 Israeli athletes at the Munich Olympics in 1972, however, anti-Arab feeling increased in the West, and Egypt put off trying to buy Western arms. Sadat renewed ties with the Soviets, extended their naval facilities, and resumed buying weapons from them. USSR technicians started returning to Egypt; by April 1973 Sadat, in an interview with *Newsweek,* could claim that the Soviets "are providing us now with everything that's possible for them to supply. And I am now quite satisfied." He also stated that Egypt was ready to end the current deadlock by resuming its war with Israel. He hinted to others that Egypt was planning to raid the occupied Sinai Peninsula. Israel called up some reserve troops. No war ensued. Others ignored Sadat.

The October War

The sudden attack launched by Syria and Egypt on the Israel-occupied territories on October 6, 1973, was, as Sadat had planned, a shock to the Americans. Intermittent war scares had broken out ever since the 1970 cease-fire, and Sadat had given ample notice of his intentions, but most outside observers thought the Arabs were unprepared to fight against Israel. If Sadat were to start a war, military experts said that Israel would totally crush the Arab armies.

Sadat took the risks and made his preparations for four reasons. First, Egypt's economy could no longer endure the state of no-war-no-peace. The government had spent $8–9 billion (more than Egypt's annual gross domestic product) since 1967 to rebuild and retrain its armed forces. Unable to buy U.S. grain with Egyptian pounds, it had to spend its scarce hard currency to buy wheat on the world market. There were no tourism dollars or Suez Canal tolls after 1967. By 1973 Egypt's real money supply was nearly exhausted.

Second, the country was demoralized. Faced with years of military service upon graduating, Egyptian students in Cairo and other university towns had demonstrated against Sadat in 1972 and early 1973. A group of mothers held a mass protest in the Ezbekia Gardens. Government corruption was spreading, and some thought it went straight to the top. The officers and soldiers on the front grew tired of being kept on constant alert. New laws tightened censorship on books and periodicals. Many writers were jailed on falsified charges. Harsh sentences were imposed on rumormongers. Sadat even tried to outlaw political jokes.

Another reason for the war was that Sadat feared losing the material and moral support that Egypt had been receiving from other Arabs, especially the oil-exporting states. The Palestinian Arabs were increasingly restive. The fedayeen committed terrorist acts against Israelis at home and abroad; Israel replied with reprisals against Palestinians and their backers. Israel's downing of a Libyan passenger jet over the occupied Sinai, which caused more than 100 deaths, outraged Arabs and increased the pressure on Sadat to take revenge. Unable to commit Sadat to a date for unifying Libya and Egypt, Gadhafi led a well-publicized mass march to Cairo, demanding war against Israel.

The fourth reason for starting the war was that Sadat needed the superpowers' respect and cooperation. Although the USSR had resumed selling arms to Egypt, by 1973 it was seeking other Arabs as allies. The U.S. government, having taken its troops out of Vietnam, was distracted by the Watergate scandal. American attempts to mediate between Israel and the Arabs had stalled. At the same time, U.S. arms sales to Israel were rising, suggesting that Israeli and U.S. policies were converging. During September 1973 a tough election campaign led Israeli politicians to compete for votes by calling for new Jewish settlements in the occupied lands, including Sinai.

Given these conditions, Sadat bought more arms from the USSR and proceeded to strengthen Egypt's ties with the nonaligned countries, the Organization of African Unity, and the leaders of the other Arab states. He paid special attention to Syrian President Hafiz al-Assad (1930–2000), who, though no less militant than his precursors, had opened new links with the West. The two met several times to devise joint strategies for a war on Israel. They agreed to divulge their plans to Jordan's King Hussein, who did not feel ready to fight, and to Saudi

EGYPT AS SEEN BY NAGUIB MAHFOUZ, 1973

The Egyptian novelist Naguib Mahfouz (1911–2006), who won the Nobel Prize in literature in 1988, depicts in this excerpt from his novel *Karnak* (1974, published in English in 2007) a discussion among a group of Egyptian men sitting in a Cairo café shortly before the October War on what they saw as the options facing their country regarding Israel.

—*"A peaceful settlement is also possible."*

—*"The only possible solution is that which is dictated by the great powers."*

—*"Negotiation means surrender."*

—*"Negotiations are a necessity. All the nations negotiate—even America and China and Russia and Pakistan and India."*

—*"Peace means that Israel would dominate the entire area."*

—*"Why should we fear peace? Were we swallowed up by the English and French?"*

—*"If the future proved that Israel is a 'good state' we would coexist with her and if it proved the reverse we would eradicate her as we eradicated the crusaders' state before."*

—*"The future belongs to us. Look at our numbers and our wealth . . ."*

—*"Our real battle is a civilizational battle. Peace is more dangerous to us than war."*

Arabia's King Faisal, whose support they needed. Owing to Gadhafi's erratic behavior, he was not informed, even though he still craved an organic union between Egypt and Libya. To throw off its enemy, Egypt twice held war maneuvers on so large a scale that Israel mobilized its armed forces at great expense. Then Sadat lulled the Israelis by stating that he would attend the UN General Assembly session in October.

Egypt and Syria agreed on a plan for a simultaneous attack on the Sinai and the Golan, to take place on October 6. This date happened to be both the Jewish Day of Atonement (Yom Kippur) and the Muslim anniversary of the Battle of Badr, Muhammad's first victory over the Meccan pagans. The Egyptians wanted to attack at dusk so that the sun would be behind them and a nearly full moon would illumine their canal crossing; the Syrians wanted to invade the Golan Heights early in

—"Let us then demobilize the army and rebuild ourselves."

—"Let us declare our neutrality and ask other states to recognize it."

—"What of the Fedayeen? You ignore the real catalyst in the situation."

—"We have been defeated and we must pay the price and leave the rest to the future."

—"The real enemy of the Arabs are the Arabs themselves."

—"Everything depends on the unity of the Arabs in the effort."

—"Half the Arabs . . . were victorious on the fifth of June [1967]."

—"Let's begin then with the internal situation. There is no escape."

—"Great. Religion, religion is everything."

Naguib Mahfouz. Winner of the Nobel Prize in literature in 1988, Mahfouz wrote many novels, stories, and film scripts depicting life in Egypt. (Portrait by Lauren Uram/Saudi Aramco World/PADIA)

Source: Fouad Ajami, "The Humanist in the Alley, Naguib Mahfouz, 1911–2006," The New Republic, September 25, 2006. Available online. URL: http://www.tnr.com/doc.mhtml?i=20060925&s=ajami092506&c=2. Accessed on September 16, 2006.

the morning, when the sun would be in the Israelis' eyes. They settled on 2:00 P.M. The deception worked. Having grown accustomed to false alarms, Israeli intelligence did not pick up on the Arab threats, maneuvers, or greater frontline troop concentrations until the day before the attack. Most Egyptians and Syrians, too, were taken by surprise.

The coordinated Arab attack was effective. On both fronts the Israelis, outnumbered and outgunned, fell back in confusion. Egyptian soldiers had rehearsed setting up pontoon bridges and moving their equipment until they could cross the Suez Canal blindfolded. Armed with bazookas and fire hoses, backed by Soviet MiG fighters and the latest SAM-6 and SAM-7 missiles, five Egyptian divisions crossed the canal and pierced the Bar-Lev Line, although it had been raised in places to a height of 38 feet (12 meters). Within a day they had penetrated 6 miles (10 km) beyond that line. The troops hoped to capture the strategic Gidi and Mitla passes.

Given Israel's strategy of first repelling Syria, the Egyptians could have easily advanced before Israel could bring its full might to bear against them. According to General Saad El-Shazly, Egypt's five divisions needed time to consolidate their gains. By the time they got orders to advance to the passes, the central division had become vulnerable to an Israeli counterthrust. Mohamed Hassanein Heikal (1923–   ), then Sadat's information minister but later one of his severest critics, writes that Syria had relied on Egypt's ability to reach the passes so that its army could finish taking the Golan Heights. But Sadat was only looking for a foothold in Sinai that would lead to U.S. pressure to bring Israel to the bargaining table. He was thinking of a quick victory to redeem Egypt's dignity, not of a drawn-out war that could tempt the superpowers to intervene.

Once the Israelis had driven the Syrians off the Golan Heights, they could concentrate enough forces in the Sinai to reverse the tide of battle. On the war's 11th day, while Sadat and Israeli prime minister Golda Meir (1898–1978) were giving well-publicized speeches to their respective parliaments, the Israel Defense Forces found a weak spot between Egypt's second and third armies, pierced through it, reached the canal, and crossed it just north of the Great Bitter Lake. While the superpowers hastened to rearm their Middle Eastern client states, the cutting edge of the fighting entered Arab territory, with Cairo and Damascus both only an hour's drive from Israel's frontline troops.

The USSR needed a cease-fire before Egypt and Syria lost the arms it had sent them. U.S. secretary of state Henry Kissinger flew to Moscow, where he and Foreign Minister Andrey Gromyko drafted a cease-fire resolution that provided for negotiations among the belligerents "under appropriate auspices." Passed by the UN Security Council, it was due to take effect on October 22. It did not. Each side accused the other of violating the cease-fire. The Israelis tried to encircle the city of Suez and isolate Egypt's Third Army, while the Egyptian units tried to break out of the circle. It took two days and another Security Council resolution to end the shooting.

Although the Egyptians hailed their crossing the Suez Canal as a great victory and as the work of Sadat's strategic genius, the real Arab victory was the ability of the petroleum-exporting states, led by Saudi Arabia, to quadruple prices and reduce production, thus threatening Western Europe and Japan with severe oil shortages just at the outset of the winter heating season. Output was to be reduced by 5 percent each month until Israel withdrew from all the lands it had occupied in the 1967 and 1973 wars and recognized the Palestinians' right to self-determination. The Arab oil exporters proclaimed a total embargo against the United States for its massive arms airlift to Israel and against the Netherlands for facilitating weapons shipments. The psychological effect of this oil diplomacy was devastating. Common Market members rushed to befriend the Arabs, back their demands for Palestinian state-hood, and distance themselves from Israel. This postwar trend explains why, even though the Israelis had penetrated farther into Arab lands than ever before, they were grieving while the Arabs were rejoicing. Even so, the oil weapon would probably not have worked without the backing of Iran, which raised both its prices and its output to take advantage of the Arab oil embargo. Sadat's victory was real, all the same. Now he had reopened the issue of Sinai and the other territories occupied by Israel. He had confounded his Arab detractors, who had formerly dismissed him as a hapless windbag.

Sadat's triumph was played out concurrently on two planes—one worldwide, the other domestic. On the international level he restored the Arab-Israeli conflict to center stage; every country, large or small, near or far, had a stake in its outcome. Both superpowers showed the depth of their involvement by the value of the arms they furnished to the combatants and by their efforts to manipulate events to advance their own strategic positions. President Nixon put all U.S. forces on red alert just after the cease-fire to intimidate the USSR, which was report-edly shipping nuclear-tipped missiles through the Turkish straits. The more immediate cause was a Soviet proposal to set up a joint patrol with the United States to police the uneasy cease-fire between Egypt and Israel, and it was reported that Soviet troops had already entered Egypt for this purpose.

Kissinger and the Peace Process

With Israeli troops west of the Suez Canal and Egyptians east of it, the fighting could resume at any time. Kissinger went to the Middle East hoping to organize a peace conference. His first meeting with Sadat was cordial, and the prospects for a peace settlement brightened. Sadat had to extricate his Third Army, which was surrounded by Israeli troops. Kissinger agreed to press Golda Meir's government to let Egypt truck in food and other nonmilitary supplies. Israel and Egypt, hoping to avert renewed fighting on the front, agreed to hold direct talks in a tent pitched at Kilometer 101 on the Suez-Cairo road. Both countries accepted the Soviet-American joint invitation to attend a peace conference in Geneva, to be convened in late December. Because the Palestine Liberation Organization had not been invited, Syria refused to attend, but the Geneva Conference met anyway. After one day, the conferees agreed to an indefinite adjournment to negotiate a separation of Egyptian and Israeli forces.

Kissinger mediated the indirect negotiations between Egypt and Israel in January 1974, starting what came to be called shuttle diplomacy between Jerusalem and Cairo, to hammer out a separation-of-forces agreement. By forgoing his demand for an immediate Israeli pullback to the pre-1967 border, Sadat managed to secure Israel's withdrawal to a line 6 miles (10 km) east of the canal, corresponding to Egypt's farthest advance during the war. After Kissinger brokered a comparable agreement between Israel and Syria, Nixon visited Egypt. American-Egyptian ties improved dramatically, starting with the exchange of ambassadors and the resumption of U.S. aid, both of which had been suspended since the June 1967 war.

The Reaction against Arab Socialism

The political honeymoon between Washington and Cairo coincided with Sadat's other major policy change, which he called *al-infitah* (opening). During the heyday of Nasser's Arab socialism, major business firms owned by Egyptian citizens as well as by foreigners came under state ownership or sequestration. These assets were valued at 2 billion Egyptian pounds (about $3 billion at the time). Nasser's Egypt was not a fully Marxist state. Most Muslim and Christian Egyptians rejected communism, and Arab nationalism could not be reconciled with the class struggle. Surviving pockets of private enterprise included farming, retail sales, and construction. Arab socialism no doubt weakened Egypt's capitalists, but many owned enough land and real estate to support themselves. Reducing the maximum individual landholding to 50 *feddans* (52 acres) in 1969 had hurt some people, but an owner could maintain a comfortable living standard from that amount of land, especially if he or she grew specialty crops like fruit and vegetables, kept honeybees, or raised livestock. Arab socialism had also created a new bourgeoisie, a class of managers that had arisen in the state-owned enterprises and had sometimes found ways to milk the treasury for their own benefit. Sadat viewed the rising wealth of the oil-producing Arab states as a rich source of capital. He also hoped to lure back some of the Egyptian capital, if not its owners, that had fled abroad because of Nasser's Arab socialism.

The October War enhanced the value of Arab oil and Egypt's attractiveness as a country in which to invest the proceeds. It also made Sadat popular in Egypt for the first time; Egyptians listened when he announced new initiatives, and civilian morale rose. Egypt could rebuild Port Said, Ismailia, Suez, and the other cities on the western side of the Suez Canal. Reconstruction was a bonanza for Egyptian builders. Egyptians compared Nasser, whose policies had brought not only two defeats in 1956 and 1967 but also a standoff in 1970 that had made Egypt heavily dependent on the USSR, with Sadat, who took credit for the crossing, the oil embargo, and Kissinger's ability to coax the Israelis to pull back. This comparison produced an anti-Nasser reaction that enabled Egypt to renounce war against Israel as an instrument of national policy, to rebuild ties with the United States, and to open the country to free enterprise and foreign investors. The new attitude was expressed in the revelations of veteran writers Tawfiq al-Hakim in *Awdat al-wa'y (The Return of Consciousness)* and Naguib Mahfouz in *Karnak,* depicting Nasserite oppression and torture.

The earliest expression of these changes appeared in the government October Paper. While feigning loyalty to Nasserite principles, including socialism and Arab nationalism, it argued that their application must adapt to changing times. Nasser's achievements would be preserved, but certain "deviations" of the late 1960s would be corrected by an "opening" to the new international economic environment. A few years later Sadat went further and effectively dismantled the Nasserite heritage.

The strongest argument for *infitah* was Egypt's apparent economic revival. Its obvious aspect was an immense construction boom in the canal cities that enabled their residents to return after six years of exile. Cairo and Alexandria, too, were bursting out in new construction. As Egypt's population surpassed 40 million in 1977, plans were resurrected for building satellite towns in desert lands near Cairo or the Delta. Another sign of *infitah* was the return of foreign banks to do business in the new Egypt. Until then the largest loan that Egypt had ever received from the World Bank was for $60 million to widen the Suez Canal; in 1974–75 it would receive $227 million. Private foreign investment came mainly from the Arab states and Iran, which spent more of their new oil wealth on real estate than farms and factories, but Sadat also coaxed money out of the rulers of Saudi Arabia and Kuwait. In 1976, when Egypt fell behind in repaying its short-term debts, the Arab states formed a consortium, the Gulf Organization for the Development of Egypt, which lent $1.475 billion on easier terms than the World Bank. Another project was the construction of an oil conduit running from

Cairo traffic jam. Vehicular traffic has choked the streets of Cairo and other Egyptian cities, especially since Sadat's infitah policy enabled more Egyptians to own cars. (Dick Doughty/Saudi Aramco World/PADIA)

the Gulf of Suez to the Mediterranean, parallel to the canal, called the Sumed Pipeline. Built by Italian contractors and owned jointly by Egypt, Saudi Arabia, Kuwait, the United Arab Emirates, and Qatar, it was completed in 1977. It can carry up to 2.5 million barrels of oil per day.

However, *infitah* failed to attract as many U.S., European, and Japanese investors as Sadat had hoped for. Its main beneficiaries were the Egyptian bourgeoisie, some of whom celebrated their return from the Nasserite wilderness by spending their money on urban land, new villas, apartments, and hotels. Rarely did they invest in such productive enterprises as factories. Many imported expensive cars, which further clogged the already infamous traffic of downtown Cairo and Alexandria. Sadat courted their support: The Cairo Governorate spent much to build new bridges and overpasses that would benefit the minority of its population who could afford to own cars or ride taxis, while neglecting the need of the majority for improved public transport, especially in the poorer quarters.

For the peasants, *infitah* meant an end to land reform, deteriorating service from the rural cooperatives and health centers, and declining terms of payment for the crops they produced. Though Egypt had exported cereal grains for almost its whole history, under Nasser and

Sadat it became a net importer. Indeed, Sadat's new policy made Egypt a net exporter of its own people; peasants as well as engineers, doctors, teachers, plumbers, and electricians left for wealthier Arab lands to earn higher wages. Given Egypt's annual 2.5 percent population growth rate, emigration was a short-term benefit; in the long run it separated families and created new income disparities and shortages of skilled workers and farmers. Workers in private firms gained more from *infitah* than those in public-sector companies, which were losing money. As the government promised to employ every university graduate, price inflation outpaced salary raises for its clerks, teachers in schools and universities, librarians, and doctors and nurses in public clinics and hospitals.

Peace with Israel

If Sadat could settle Egypt's conflict with Israel, his people hoped to be relieved from the heavy cost of the five wars they had fought and the ongoing arms race against Israel. Although Sadat still paid lip service to Arab nationalism, he moved toward an Egypt-first policy more consonant with his country's rapprochement with the West. The watershed came in September 1975, when Kissinger returned to perform his last feat of shuttle diplomacy: the second Sinai accord. In return for Israel's further troop withdrawal to the Gidi and Mitla passes, Egypt renounced war as a means to settle the Arab-Israeli conflict and agreed to limit its troops and tanks on the regained lands east of the canal and Gulf of Suez. Although Kissinger and Sadat argued that step-by-step diplomacy was gradually restoring to Egyptian control lands that it had lost in war, notably the Sinai oil fields, Sadat's critics argued that Israel had driven a hard bargain and that the real price Egypt would have to pay was its loss of leadership over the Arabs.

But that role, too, Sadat's supporters argued, had been devalued by the internal quarrels of Arab rulers and factions. Their decision in 1974 to make Yasir (Yasser) Arafat's PLO the sole power that could negotiate for the Palestinians, just when that group was backing terrorist attacks against civilians in Israel, disrupted the Israeli-Arab peace process. The assassination of Saudi King Faisal and the outbreak of civil war in Lebanon added to the general picture of Arab political instability. Egypt should have learned from its 1962–67 involvement in the Yemen civil war to avoid Arab quarrels, but Sadat committed Egyptian forces to fight in Oman against the leftist Dhofar rebels and to raid Libya to intimidate Gadhafi, after their proposed union had foundered.

The difference was that Nasser had fought in Yemen to help a republican military junta to replace a traditional monarchy, but Sadat used Egypt's armed forces to aid the West and its backers. Naturally, the USSR reduced and then canceled military aid, amid recriminations against Sadat for moving Egypt into the imperialist camp. Sadat blamed the Soviets for withholding weapons and spare parts and refusing to let Egypt put off repaying its debts to them. At the end of 1975, Egypt's inflation rate exceeded 30 percent, foreign investment was lagging, the government was borrowing on the short term at rates up to 17 percent per annum, and the total amount it owed to the USSR exceeded $7 billion. In March 1976 Sadat renounced the 1971 Treaty of Friendship and Cooperation, then closed Soviet naval facilities in Egypt, and finally announced that he would put off paying $1.5 billion owed to the USSR for past arms purchases. These acts were bound to antagonize the Kremlin.

Worsening relations with the USSR did not guarantee better ones with the Americans. Washington's commitment to Israel and its own apparent instability during the Watergate scandal deterred Sadat from seeking closer U.S. ties. Sadat did not welcome Jimmy Carter's election to the presidency in 1976, because the Democratic Party traditionally favored Israel and because he liked Secretary of State Kissinger. Sadat also feared Carter's search for a comprehensive Arab-Israeli settlement that would involve the Palestinians and the USSR.

Early in 1977, though, Sadat had to counter a domestic challenge. Egypt's rising debts led to burdensome repayments, which by this time amounted to more than half the value of Egypt's total annual exports. The International Monetary Fund (IMF), trying to help Egypt strengthen its economy, suggested cutting government subsidies on consumer goods. The policy of subsidizing low prices for bread, rice, sugar, tea, cooking oil, bottled gas, kerosene, and a few other necessities had begun in World War II to ease the lives of the poor. But the policy had taken on a life of its own. By 1976 Egypt was importing more than half the wheat its citizens consumed, and the government had to allot huge sums to pay for these imports while depressing bread and flour prices to artificially low levels. Because of its rising foreign debt Egypt could no longer manage its economy as it might have liked. The government ended subsidies on goods that the poor did not need, such as beer, refined flour, granulated sugar, French bread, and macaroni, and reduced them on bread, cooking oil, broad beans, and lentils. The announcement of these changes sparked Egypt's fiercest rioting since 1952. Mobs rampaged through downtown Alexandria and Cairo, pillaged boutiques of their expensive imported goods, torched the ASU headquarters, and tried to break into Abdin Palace, where Sadat had one of his offices. The army was called in to quell the riots. More than 150 Egyptians were killed in three days of rioting. People protested against *infitah* not because it was liberal, but because it increased inequality.

The government's immediate response was to restore all the food subsidies and to increase them, no matter what the cost to Egypt, to fend off further disturbances. This policy became one of the real reasons behind the huge aid provided by the United States since 1979. Sadat also called for a plebiscite with questions so worded as to give the appearance that he received unanimous support. He also set about planning his most spectacular act on the international stage—a journey to Jerusalem. No Arab leader had ever openly talked to an Israeli counterpart, let alone gone publicly to Israel, since the creation of the Jewish state in 1948. Sadat had told reporters that he was not about to recognize Israel or make peace without the concurrence of the other Arabs. In early 1977 Israel held an election that was won, to the surprise of both Egypt and the West, by Menachem Begin, the ultranationalist leader of the Likud coalition. Even so, Egypt's border war with Libya in July 1977, the rising tide of Muslim extremism that took the life of the *waqfs* minister, and the Carter administration's attempts to bring the USSR and the Palestinians into the peace process led him to this dramatic policy shift.

Speaking before the People's Assembly on November 9, 1977, Sadat announced that, in his search for peace with Israel, he was prepared to go to the ends of the earth, or even to the Knesset in Jerusalem. When asked later by U.S. TV journalist Walter Cronkite and a congressional delegation whether he had meant to be taken seriously, Sadat affirmed his willingness to negotiate directly with Begin's government. When Cronkite asked Begin how he would react to such an initiative, he replied that he would gladly invite Sadat to visit Israel to make peace. Within two weeks, ignoring pleas by many Arab countries and some members of his own cabinet that he not go, Sadat made the one-hour flight from Cairo to the David Ben-Gurion Airport. He was greeted by Israel's president, prime minister, and the whole cabinet. On his one-day visit, Sadat laid a wreath at the tomb of the unknown Israeli soldier, prayed at al-Aqsa Mosque, and made an eloquent speech to the Knesset. Even though his peace terms were the same ones he had been stating all along—Israeli withdrawal from all occupied lands and self-determination for the Palestinians—the fact that Sadat had come to Israel and recognized its existence dramatized his desire for peace and obliged Begin to make comparable concessions. He never did.

EXCERPT FROM SADAT'S SPEECH TO THE ISRAELI KNESSET, 1977

. . . Peace cannot be worth its name unless it is based on justice and not on the occupation of the land of others. It would not be right for you to demand for yourselves what you deny to others. With all frankness and in the spirit that has prompted me to come to you today, I tell you that you have to give up once and for all the dreams of conquest and give up the belief that force is the best method for dealing with the Arabs.

You should clearly understand the lesson of confrontation between you and us. Expansion does not pay. To speak frankly, our land does not yield itself to bargaining; it is not even open to argument. To us the nation's soil is equal to the holy valley where God Almighty spoke to Moses, peace be upon him.

We cannot accept any attempt to take away or to accept to seek one inch of it, nor can we accept the principle of debating or bargaining over it.

I sincerely tell you also that before us today lies the appropriate chance for peace. If we are really serious in our endeavor for peace, it is a chance that may never come again. It is a chance that if lost or wasted, the resulting slaughter would bear the curse of humanity and of history.

What is peace for Israel? It means that Israel lives in the region with her Arab neighbors in security and safety. Is that logical? I say yes. It means that Israel obtains all kinds of guarantees that will ensure these two factors. To this demand, I say yes.

Beyond that we declare that we accept all the international guarantees you envisage and accept. We declare that we accept all the guarantees that you want from the two superpowers or from either of them or from the Big Five or from some of them. Once again, I declare openly and unequivocally that we agree to any guarantees you accept, because in return we shall receive the same guarantees.

In short, then, when we ask what is peace for Israel, the answer would be that Israel lives within her borders, among her Arab neighbors in safety and security, within the framework of all the guarantees she accepts and which are offered to her.

But, how can this be achieved? How can we reach this conclusion that would lead us to permanent peace based on justice? There are facts that should be faced with courage and clarity. There are Arab territories that Israel has occupied and still occupies by force. We insist on complete withdrawal from these territories, including Arab Jerusalem. . . .

Many outside observers feared that Sadat would be assassinated during or right after his trip to Jerusalem, as many Palestinians were furious at him for going there. On his return to Cairo, however, he received a tumultuous welcome. Many Egyptians clearly wanted peace with Israel, especially on the terms Sadat had stated in his speech. The Marxist Left and the Islamist Right dissented. Two foreign ministers resigned in rapid succession. The only Arab governments that openly approved were those of Sudan, Morocco, Oman, and Jordan. Most Western governments and peoples hailed this new peace initiative. The Carter administration, taken by surprise, quickly backed Sadat and scrapped its plans to reconvene the Geneva Conference and to seek a comprehensive settlement including the Palestinians.

Sadat promptly convened an international peace conference at Mena House near the Pyramids. Only Israel and the United States attended. Begin returned Sadat's visit on December 25, but they made no progress toward peace. During January 1978 the two sides set up military and political committees to work on the technicalities of a peace treaty. The sticking point was Sinai. Begin had offered unequivocally to hand back the peninsula but wanted to retain the Jewish settlements there, whereas Sadat wanted them evacuated and returned to Egypt. The Palestinians under Israeli occupation posed issues, but less so for Sadat than for other Arab leaders. Many Egyptians had come to feel that the Palestinians did not appreciate the sacrifices made for them in five wars against Israel. Other Arab states felt that Egypt ignored the financial backing they had given since 1967. Libya hosted a summit meeting, attended by Algeria, Iraq, the PLO, South Yemen, and Syria, to set up a "Steadfastness and Rejection Front," opposing Sadat's initiative.

The Jerusalem initiative led to some domestic changes in Egypt. The government had been toying with a more pluralistic political system, starting in 1976 by creating three *minbars* (pulpits) within the Arab Socialist Union; its center *minbar* was the Misr Party, which served as Sadat's faction. In February 1978 Fuad Sirag al-Din, an aging pre-1952 politician, revived the Wafd Party despite government obstructionism. The New Wafd surprisingly won support from upper- and middle-class Egyptians whose interests had suffered from the 1952 Revolution. They wanted to end state economic controls and to restore liberal capitalism. Sadat soon realized that the New Wafd posed too strong a challenge and shut it down. He also decided to replace the ASU with a "democratic socialist" party initially called the Arab Socialist Party of Egypt, then renamed the National Democratic Party (al-Hizb al-Watani al-Dimuqrati), a choice of names that invoked Egyptian patriotism.

Adding the Socialist Labor Party on the left and the Liberals on the right, Egypt had a full spectrum of political parties. Egypt was not fully democratic, though, for peace with Israel, superpower relations, economic policies, and Sadat's person were all excluded from political debate. The Islamic revolution was taking place in Iran at this time, but Egypt's 1971 constitution forbade the creation of a Muslim political party. Sadat underscored this lingering authoritarianism by holding another plebiscite to approve legislation to curb political dissent. Called the "Law of Shame," it prohibited advocating atheism or class war, setting a bad example to young people, publishing or broadcasting false and inflammatory news, forming an illegal organization, or attacking the government. Penalties included deprivation of civil rights, withdrawal of passports, house arrest, and sequestration of property. Sadat put himself forward as the national equivalent of a village headman or family patriarch. It was a disgrace, according to village mores, to oppose such a worthy man in public. Lawyers and civil libertarians objected to the Law of Shame, but it handed Sadat a new muzzle for his political opponents. It has remained in effect ever since it was promulgated.

Sadat's peace initiative raised hopes for a quick resolution of the Arab-Israeli conflict. The Carter administration resorted to heroic measures to bring peace to the Middle East, leading to the two-week marathon negotiating summit hosted by Carter at the presidential retreat at Camp David. Sadat called for a comprehensive settlement that included some provision for a Palestinian "homeland." Israel and its backers did not want to hand the occupied West Bank and Gaza over to the Palestinians lest these lands come to be ruled by the PLO, and Begin had also expanded Jewish settlements in these areas. If Carter, Sadat, and Begin wanted peace, they would have to devise a mutually acceptable plan for the Palestinians.

The result was a draft treaty between Egypt and Israel that constituted, in all but name, a separate peace and a vaguely worded framework providing autonomy for the inhabitants of the Gaza Strip and the West Bank, under the aegis of a transitional self-governing authority during a five-year period. King Hussein was to be invited to enter the negotiations. He declined. The apparent friendship among the leaders was impressive but misleading. Published accounts of the summit agree that Begin's personality and persistence irritated Sadat—and indeed Carter—but he protected his own country's interests better than the others (Quandt 1993, 277–283). Israel would evacuate the Sinai in stages and Egypt would be required to establish full diplomatic relations with Israel, no matter how much that harmed its ties with other Arab states. The two sides would continue to

Sadat with Carter and Begin. The signing of the Egyptian-Israel Peace Treaty in 1979, ending the state of war between the two countries, raised high hopes for an Arab-Israeli peace settlement. These hopes have not been realized. (Library of Congress)

negotiate to achieve autonomy for the Palestinians under Israeli administration. Begin's cabinet soon showed that these Palestinians would gain no effective control over their own lives. Israel would go on creating new Jewish settlements on the West Bank and enlarging existing ones.

It is not surprising, therefore, that other Arab states condemned the Camp David accords. Although U.S. secretary of state Cyrus Vance visited Amman, Riyadh, and Damascus seeking Arab support for the peace agreement, Jordan and Saudi Arabia joined the rejectionists, led by Iraq and Syria. The other Arab states held a "Rejectionist Summit" in Baghdad to condemn the Camp David accords and sent a delegation to Cairo with a $2 billion aid offer to dissuade Sadat from signing a peace treaty with Israel. Sadat refused to receive the delegates, and the Baghdad Summit voted to boycott Egypt.

Sadat's signature on a treaty with Israel was not yet assured, however. He demanded a detailed Israeli timetable for relinquishing the Gaza Strip and West Bank. The best that Vance could extract from Israel's cabinet was a vague commitment to talk about it. This was too little for Egypt. A U.S. team of international lawyers and Middle East experts could not devise a formula to bridge the gap between Jerusalem and Cairo. Carter had to go in person to the two capitals before Israel's cabinet and Sadat agreed on a compromise wording. The treaty's price, for the U.S. taxpayer, included $3 billion to help Israel pay the cost of evacuating the Sinai and $2 billion in planes, tanks, and antiaircraft weapons for Egypt. Both sides expected (and got) additional economic aid. The Israeli Knesset approved the treaty after a bitter debate. On March 26, 1979, Begin and Sadat signed it on the White House lawn, formally ending the state of war between their countries.

The Egyptian-Israeli Peace Treaty was a significant step toward resolving the Arab-Israeli conflict. It helped Egypt to stop serving as a "blood bank" for Palestinians and other Arabs opposed to recognizing Israel; now it could devote more of its slender resources to internal economic development. But the treaty won no autonomy for the inhabitants of the Gaza Strip and the West Bank, nor did any Arab state hasten to follow Egypt's example. Rather, the other Arab states, except for Sudan and Oman, broke diplomatic ties with Sadat's government, ended all economic aid, ousted Egypt from the Arab League, and moved the league's headquarters out of Cairo. Sadat and the other Arab leaders exchanged angry recriminations. Some Arab investors withdrew their money from Egypt. But if the Arabs had really wanted to ruin Sadat, they could have expelled all Egyptians working in their countries, thus depriving Egypt of $2–3 billion annually in emigrant remittances. The Arabs could not forgo their skills and relatively cheap labor.

Sadat's Last Years

Now that Egypt was at peace with Israel, the Egyptians hoped to reduce military expenditures, leaving more money for industrialization, education, social reforms, and general improvements in their standard of living. They also hoped Begin's government would make a good faith effort to negotiate toward Palestinian autonomy in the West Bank and Gaza. Backers of the peace process hoped that other Arab governments would change their minds and support Sadat. They expected improved U.S. ties to lead to more investment and tourism from the Western world, to make up for the loss of income from the Communist countries and the recalcitrant Arabs. Once Egypt was at peace, economic conditions did improve markedly, but those hopes were realized only in part. Instead, Egypt's government started buying new, more expensive arms from the United States, presumably for defense against Libya, but really to ensure that the Egyptian officers would go on backing Sadat and his policies. The Israeli government feared that turning over the occupied territories to a self-governing entity might lead to a terrorist regime that would endanger its security, so it blocked any progress toward Palestinian autonomy.

The other Arab governments, therefore, did not follow Sadat's example. The revolution in Iran stirred the hope of Muslims everywhere that they could affirm their own social and cultural values and free themselves from unwanted Western influences. Iraq's 1980 invasion of Iran, however, split the Arabs. Most backed Iraq, materially and morally, but Syria and Libya broke ranks to support Iran. When Egypt, too, offered to help Iraq, the Baathist regime in Baghdad wondered whether it could accept aid from a government it was condemning for having made peace with Israel. It did. As a result Egypt regained support from some Arab leaders, including King Hussein and even Yasir Arafat, without renouncing peace with Israel. Iraq, Jordan, and Saudi Arabia resumed investing in Egypt.

The number of tourists from Arab countries dropped briefly after the peace treaty but surpassed its previous level by 1981, whereas the number of visitors from Western Europe and North America skyrocketed in the last years of Sadat's presidency. Direct investment fluctuated but rose markedly from 1978 to 1981. Large-scale U.S. investment followed slowly. Egypt benefited from renouncing the Arab boycott of Israel and of firms doing business there, but it became more economically dependent on the United States.

Egyptians often ask themselves whether their leader should have chosen the Arabs over the Americans. On balance, Egypt serves its own best interests by pursuing policies that win the economic and political support of more than one bloc of states. Egypt eventually restored ties with Jordan, Iraq, Saudi Arabia, several smaller Gulf states, and Morocco. Soon other Arab governments took tentative steps toward peace with Israel; by contrast, Syria, a rejectionist state, failed to stop Israel's invasion of Lebanon in 1982 or its repression of Palestinian Arabs in the West Bank and Gaza, leading to the Intifada of 1987–93.

During the last years of Sadat's presidency, his close rapport with the Egyptian people dissipated. Economic and social conditions may have improved on paper, but most Egyptians did not feel the improvement. Rising income from investment, tourism, Suez Canal tolls, oil sales, and emigrant remittances widened the gap between haves and have-nots. Especially menacing was the rising tide of young men and women who graduated from the universities only to find that the jobs guaranteed to them by the government would not be available for several years, that the pay was too low, or that they had to work in areas lacking the comforts of Cairo or the amenities of Alexandria. Although they were now free to vote for opposition parties in elections for the People's Assembly, this freedom did not ease their plight.

Many young Egyptians sought more radical cures. In Nasser's time the prevalent mood of university students and recent graduates had been pro-government. During the student uprisings of 1972–73 they remained Nasserite or Marxist in their views. Hoping to channel the opposition into movements less threatening to his regime, Sadat had freed most of the Muslim Brothers still in jail and let them resume their propaganda. The released Society members tended to be cautious, older men, but their example led young Muslims to form more radical groups, thus attracting most of the student activists. One of these groups, Shabab Muhammad (Youth of Muhammad), tried to take control of the Technical Military Academy in 1974. Its coup was thwarted after many casualties. Three of its leaders were executed and dozens imprisoned. The best-known radical group was al-Takfir wa al-Hijra, a name inelegantly translated as "Exposing Unbelief and Fleeing Evil." Like Shabab Muhammad, these radicals sought to oust Sadat's regime and to set up a new government based on Muslim principles. It signaled its existence in 1977 by kidnapping the waqfs minister and "executing" him when the government refused to negotiate for his release. Its leaders, too, were captured and executed or imprisoned. It would later draw encouragement from Khomeini's Iranian revolution, but its inspiration came from the fiery agitation of 19th-century activist Jamal al-Din al-Afghani; the organizational skills of Hasan al-Banna, who had founded the Society of Muslim Brothers and been executed by Farouk's secret police in 1949; and the writings of Sayyid Qutb, whom Nasser had hanged. Other Islamist groups arose in Cairo and Alexandria, and in such provincial centers as Minya and Asyut. Especially prominent on the campuses were the *jamaat*, student groups that evolved into al-Jamaa al-Islamiyya, and an Upper Egyptian movement called Islamic Jihad.

Western journalists assumed that Islamist organizations appeal mainly to poor and uneducated city dwellers, especially newcomers from the countryside unsettled by the loss of rural family ties and traditional values or angered by the glaring disparities between wealth and poverty. The Egyptian sociologist Saad Eddin Ibrahim showed in a 1980 article reprinted in his book of essays, *Egypt, Islam, and Democracy*, that members of Shabab Muhammad and Takfir wa al-Hijra are typically well-educated young people from middle-class, rural or small-town families, many of them enrolled in colleges of medicine, pharmacy, and engineering, for which admission standards are the highest in Egypt's universities. Ibrahim showed that they believe God created humanity to build on earth an ideal community, as described in the Quran and Muhammad's words, that the Egyptian government forsook this ideal model under Western influence, and that good Muslims must work to overthrow the impious regime and replace it with one that will reestablish God's community. They model their private lives and relationships on Quranic principles. An outward sign of this observance is adoption of Islamic dress for both sexes: loose robes, sandals, and full beards for men; enveloping dresses, head scarves, and sometimes face veils and even gloves for women (Ibrahim 1996, 1–33).

Reacting to the universities' overcrowding, some students demanded segregated classrooms and staircases for men and women. They discouraged and even disrupted social gatherings that permitted interaction between the sexes. In Sadat's Egypt, once Marxist and Nasserite movements had been banned, joining Islamic groups became a way to oppose the regime. Most Egyptians, having been raised as Muslims, could more easily accept a movement that upholds their cultural norms than one introducing alien ideas.

Egypt's Muslim movements gained support as their coreligionists in Iran ousted the shah and took the American hostages in 1979, not because they hated U.S. citizens but because they resented American political and cultural sway over the Muslim world. They were angry when Sadat spoke out for the shah, condemned the taking of hostages, and finally invited the shah and his family to take refuge in Egypt (where he died and was given a state funeral in July 1980). Egypt's 4–6 million Copts were also growing more militant. Clashes had begun in 1972. The worst one broke out in the mixed Cairo quarter Zawiya al-Hamra in June 1981. Disparities between rich and poor, Westernized and traditional Egyptians, and Sadat's promises and social reality fueled the militancy of the Muslim movements. The Muslims condemned Egypt's peace with Israel not out of hatred for Jews but because it freed Begin's government to bomb civilian neighborhoods of Beirut, destroy Iraq's nuclear reactor, increase Jewish settlements on the West Bank, and oppress the Palestinians. Egypt, isolated from other Arab states, could not stop him.

Sadat knew that revolutionary societies were plotting to kill him and his wife. He took precautions to protect himself, often changing his travel plans, using his private helicopter, and wearing a bulletproof vest. In a televised address on September 5, 1981, he announced that he was jailing more than 1,500 of his opponents, including many of Egypt's top religious, political, and intellectual leaders. This infuriated many citizens and made the political atmosphere as oppressive as it had been in the last months of the monarchy or during the darkest days of Nasser's regime. Sadat no longer heeded his ministers or his other advisers. He was isolated from his own people.

On October 6, the eighth anniversary of the Egyptian crossing of the Suez Canal, Sadat's government staged a victory parade near the tomb of Egypt's unknown soldier in Nasr City. It was an impressive demonstration of Egypt's military hardware: long lines of tanks and personnel carriers, as fighter planes roared overhead in formation, televised and broadcast to impress Egyptians and their neighbors. Sadat sat in a reviewing stand with his cabinet ministers, foreign ambassadors, religious dignitaries, and journalists. Just before 1:00 P.M. one of the trucks in the parade stopped. A lieutenant bearing a Kalashnikov jumped out. Sadat rose to return what he thought was young officer's salute, and the man began firing at the reviewing stand, aided by three other uniformed officers holding rifles and hand grenades. The broadcast was cut off; the parade ended. Sadat was rushed to a military hospital, but it was too late to save his life.

The Egyptian cabinet met at once and proclaimed a state of emergency, for no one could be sure whether the assassination was part of a wider plot to seize the government. The next day the People's Assembly met and, following the constitution, named Vice President Hosni Mubarak (1928–) to succeed the slain leader, subject to a nationwide plebiscite. A state funeral was attended by many distinguished foreigners, including Israeli Prime Minister Begin, but almost no Arab leaders and few Egyptians other than high government officials. There were no scenes of public grief, as there had been for Nasser in 1970. The streets of Cairo were almost deserted except for soldiers on guard everywhere.

People stayed home for fear of being arrested or getting caught in a riot. Foreign broadcasting stations reported some fighting in Cairo's poorer neighborhoods. A major uprising in Asyut was put down by the army, and hundreds were killed or wounded. The government acted swiftly to stop any signs of revolution.

Sadat had not suppressed the Muslim militants, nor had he solved the political, economic, and social problems that made their message appeal to the Egyptian people. Sadat died wearing his Pierre Cardin uniform covered with ribbons and medals and viewing a parade, as if he were acting on a political stage. He bequeathed to Mubarak a country at peace with Israel, but not with its Arab neighbors, and certainly not with itself.

12

CONTEMPORARY EGYPT
(1981-2007)

When Hosni Mubarak succeeded the slain leader, he pledged to address Egypt's domestic and foreign problems, using a less flamboyant leadership style than either Nasser or Sadat but making few basic policy changes. At the time of this writing, he has ruled for more than a quarter century, making him Egypt's longest-serving head of state since Mehmet Ali. He has no vice president. If he were to resign his office or die suddenly, he seems increasingly likely to be followed by his son, Gamal.

Mubarak's succession was orderly in a dangerous time, a sign of Egypt's political maturity and stability. His leadership style has not been charismatic and at times has become downright dictatorial. Many Egyptians now endorse political Islam and want to base their country's laws on the sharia. Some wish to reestablish the Islamic caliphate. In a prolonged political or economic crisis, the advocates of political Islam would have enough supporters and the financial means to seize control of the government.

In international relations Egypt remains formally nonaligned. In practical terms the government's weapons and support come mainly from the United States. Although it is still committed to reaching a comprehensive peace with Israel, under Mubarak it resumed ties with the other Arab countries that had been ruptured under Sadat. Egyptians feel that their 1979 peace treaty freed Israel to annex the Golan Heights in 1981, invade Lebanon in 1982, crush the Palestinian Intifada in 1987–93, and prevent U.S. President Bill Clinton from brokering a peace settlement between 1995 and 2001. Although Egypt's government still sides with the United States in its war against terrorism, the public strongly opposed the American attacks, sanctions, and invasion of Iraq and U.S. support for Israel against the Palestinians. Four of the 19 Arab men who hijacked the U.S. passenger planes and flew them into the World Trade Center or the Pentagon on September 11, 2001, were Egyptians.

Mubarak's Early Years

Hosni Mubarak, like his predecessor, hails from Minufiyya Province. Egyptians say that Minufis claim to be brighter than those who come from the other governorates. Unlike Sadat, Mubarak rarely speaks or writes about his early life. Originally destined for the Higher Teachers College in Cairo, Mubarak chose instead to enter the Military Academy in 1947. After graduation he trained to be a fighter pilot at the Air Force Academy, where he taught for seven years. He received advanced military training in the USSR in the 1960s, then served as commandant of the Air Force Academy in 1967–69, Air Force chief of staff in 1969–72, and commander in chief of Egypt's Air Force before and during the October War. Because of the Air Force's stellar wartime performance, Mubarak received Egypt's three highest military medals and was promoted to air marshal in 1974. Although he lacked political experience, Sadat named him vice president in 1975. Mubarak served him loyally in that capacity and chaired the National Democratic Party board from 1979. His succession was never in doubt.

Less flamboyant than Sadat, Mubarak was unknown when he became president. He was popularly called *"La vache qui rit"* because of his alleged resemblance to the smiling cow pictured on a brand of processed French cheese sold in Egypt. His earliest acts were to refocus the assembly's attention on Egypt's socioeconomic problems and to free most of the leaders whom Sadat had jailed in September 1981. Some were bused directly from their prison cells to the Presidential Palace for an official reception. Most Egyptians were relieved that Sadat's assassination did not lead to a prolonged rebellion against the government, but many Islamists were imprisoned or put under house arrest, their publications banned, and their assets impounded. Students were especially suspect: males were forbidden to grow beards or to wear galabias (loose-fitting gowns) and women had to remove their head scarves to enter university campuses. Some of the shady economic deals made by Sadat's friends and relatives, notably his brother, were exposed to public scrutiny. One dramatic episode in the year following Sadat's death was the public destruction of several privately owned villas (including Sadat's rest house) on land close to the Giza Pyramids. Sadat's widow, Jihan, was occasionally accused of corruption, but this was never proved. She has lived mainly outside Egypt since her husband's death.

213

Egypt's Relations with Israel

A sensitive issue for Mubarak was dealing with Israel, which in December 1981 annexed the Golan Heights. Israel's transfer of the remaining areas of the Sinai to Egypt on April 25, 1982, seemed to remove that constraint on the Egyptian government, but the Israeli invasion of southern Lebanon infuriated almost all Egyptians. In fact, though, Egypt's inability to fight Israel was matched by the weakness of the other Arab governments. Syria and the Palestine Liberation Organization did intervene but could not halt the Israeli advance. Egypt did withdraw its ambassador from Tel Aviv and suspended the Palestinian autonomy talks mandated by its peace treaty with Israel; it never ruptured diplomatic relations with the Jewish state. Mubarak mended Egypt's fences with PLO chairman Arafat, who had denounced that treaty, but only after Arafat had been driven from Lebanon by a dissident Palestinian faction. A dispute arose between Egypt and Israel over possession of Taba, which the Israelis did not hand back with the rest of the Sinai Peninsula; the issue was referred to arbitration in 1986 and eventually restored Taba to Egypt in 1989.

A sign that many Arabs acquiesced in peace with Israel came when their governments restored diplomatic relations with Egypt, even though Mubarak never renounced Sadat's peace policy and even sent back his envoy to Tel Aviv in 1986. Jordan, Saudi Arabia, some of the Persian Gulf and North African states, and even Iraq resumed ties and trade with Egypt, implicitly validating its peace policies. The Arab League, which had removed its headquarters from Cairo in 1979, returned in 1990. Mubarak has played an important facilitating role between Israel and the Palestinians, notably in 1995 and following the failed Clinton-Barak-Arafat summit in 2000, when the negotiators held meetings in Sharm al-Sheikh and Taba. Israelis who read the Cairo press maintain that Egypt has reverted to its old posture of opposition to Jews, Zionism, and Israel.

Egypt and the Superpowers

Sadat's assassination opened the way for Cairo's reconciliation with Moscow, which agreed to reschedule Egypt's massive debt to the USSR, and the two countries resumed exchanging ambassadors in 1984. The United States remained Egypt's main benefactor, however, providing $1 to $3 billion annually in military and economic aid. Essentially, this is the price Washington has paid for ensuring Egyptian-Israeli peace. Most of this money paid for the importation of American arms, capital goods, and food, but projects in the 1980s included expanding the water and sewer system of greater Cairo, upgrading the telephone network, building new schools, introducing better varieties of wheat and rice, and extending family planning services. As the Agency for International Development took over several tall office buildings in central Cairo for its burgeoning staff, Egyptians came to view it as Egypt's second government. During the 1990s its focus shifted to education and promoting foreign trade. Its current projects include financing small business firms, lending to women entrepreneurs, building a garage for Cairo's growing fleet of buses powered by natural gas and several parking garages for private cars, and providing teaching materials about environmental education. Military aid involved training and the provision of fighter jet planes, modern artillery, tanks (now assembled in Egypt) and armored personnel vehicles. Its showpiece was Operation Bright Star, joint Egyptian-American military operations begun in 1981 and repeated in odd-numbered years. They have continued quietly with more involvement by other countries' armies.

Due in part to these close ties between Cairo and Washington, the United States managed to enlist the help of Egypt and most of the other Arab states in the campaign against Iraq's occupation of Kuwait. Mubarak had tried during July 1990 to mediate the two countries' quarrels, which centered on Iraq's repayment to Kuwait of debts incurred during the Iran-Iraq War, claims to an oilfield that lay athwart their territorial border, and Iraq's desire for greater access to the Persian Gulf. The surprise attack on August 2 violated commitments that Mubarak had received from Iraqi President Saddam Hussein (1937–2006), and Egypt spearheaded efforts by the other Arab heads of state to persuade him to pull his troops out of Kuwait. When Arab diplomacy failed, Mubarak joined the allied coalition to protect Saudi Arabia and eventually to liberate Kuwait; 40,000 Egyptian troops took part in Operation Desert Storm. Although Egypt and Syria hoped to set up a security force after the 1991 Gulf War to secure the smaller countries of the region against future Iraqi attack, the Gulf states decided not to accept such an Arab protectorate. But Egyptian workers continued to flood Saudi Arabia, Kuwait, and other Gulf states at a time when Palestinians and Yemenis (who had supported Iraq) were no longer welcome. The West also forgave $14 billion of Egypt's mounting debts, as part of an economic reform package described later.

Egyptian-U.S. relations nosedived in 1985 when four Palestinians hijacked an Italian cruise ship, the *Achille Lauro,* and murdered a disabled American tourist. The ship was allowed to dock in Port Said, after the Egyptian government had offered immunity to the hijackers. While they were being flown in an Egyptair 737 jet to Tunis, U.S. fighter planes buzzed the Egyptian airliner and ordered its pilot to land at a NATO airbase in Sicily. When the planes landed, Italian troops immediately surrounded the Americans and Egyptians and took the Palestinians into custody. Mubarak later decorated the Egyptair pilot and demanded an apology from U.S. president Reagan, who refused. The Palestinians were eventually tried in Italy and imprisoned. Both Americans and Egyptians were angered by the incident, but only briefly.

Lurching toward and away from Democracy

On the domestic scene Egypt edged hesitantly toward parliamentary democracy. The New Wafd Party, which Sadat had banned, was allowed to reorganize and compete in parliamentary elections under its flamboyant leader, Fuad Siraj al-Din, a quintessential pre-1952 pasha politician who sat on many corporate boards of directors and was called "Abu Sigar" because he was so often depicted with a cigar in his mouth. The revived Wafd gained in the 1984 and 1987 parliamentary elections. They enjoyed some support among middle-class and even landowning Egyptians. The parties Sadat had authorized also remained in existence, with Ibrahim Shukri (of Young Egypt) heading the right-wing Socialist Labor Party and Khalid Muhyi al-Din (once close to the Communists but never a party member) in charge of the National Progressive Unionist Party. Even the Muslim Brothers competed in coalition with the Wafd in the 1987 elections, and some of the independent deputies chosen in 1995, 2000, and 2005 were supporters of the Society, which was never really a party.

Since 1977 Egypt has had a multiparty system, but in practice the National Democratic Party remains the dominant legal participatory movement with Mubarak as its leader, even if his methods have been less dramatic than those of his predecessor. Regrettably, Mubarak's security forces have interfered in recent elections. Although a 1983 law requires a political party to receive 8 percent of the popular vote to have representation in the People's Assembly, and the 1971 constitution bans religious parties, candidates may run as "independents." In the 2005 election, which was marred by voter apathy, intimidation of would-be voters, and large-scale fraud, 72 of the deputies elected as independents turned out to be Muslim Brothers. The National Democratic Party retains a large majority of parliamentary seats, but it increasingly serves as a stepping-stone for ambitious power seekers, including Gamal

Mubarak, one of Hosni's sons, who many Egyptians think is preparing to succeed his father. In 2005 Egypt's parliament amended the 1971 constitution to permit direct popular election of the president and voted to allow an open electoral contest, but the main challenger to Hosni Mubarak, Ayman Nur, was later arrested, tried, and imprisoned. Nur was leader of the Ghad (Tomorrow) Party, which advocated liberal democracy and expressed concern about the state of human rights in Egypt. He was charged with forging signatures on petitions that he had submitted to form the Ghad Party.

Although regime politicians rarely speak critically of earlier leaders, Sadat's passing was no cause for public grieving, as noted. Egyptians often criticize him in private and may express nostalgia for the now rather hazy Nasser era. A popular film in recent years, *Nasser 1956,* recalls this heroic year of Egypt's history. The People's Assembly proved to be less active than Sadat may have envisioned early in his presidency, and on many foreign and defense policy issues it still has no role at all. Mubarak is more likely to initiate new laws than the parliamentarians, and even their committees are little more than sounding boards for the ministers. The assembly does serve as a stage for political actions that the government hopes will show its commitment to democracy, as in the 2005 decisions to allow public election contests for the presidency.

Egypt has a large and complicated court system, with an independent judiciary that has criticized and even nullified the acts of Mubarak's administration. It supervised the 2000 and 2005 elections, but it is vulnerable to pressure from the justice and interior ministries. In recent years many high-profile criminal cases, notably that of the prominent intellectual Saad Eddin Ibrahim, have been tried in the military courts (although a civilian appeals court finally acquitted him in 2003). In May 2006 the government stirred up mass protest demonstrations by arresting two senior judges and reprimanding one of them. The police violently suppressed the demonstrators, and many now languish in prison.

Human rights constitute a major issue for Egypt. Although close American ties may seem to foster more respect for individual liberties than was evident during the period of the monarchy or the Nasser dictatorship, this is illusory. Foreign visitors notice the proliferation of Benetton shops, Hilton and Sheraton Hotels, cola beverages, and Kentucky Fried Chicken and McDonald's fast food restaurants, and assume they are seeing freedom of choice. State-run television stations offer a variety of foreign sitcoms, and there are competing satellite and private channels. The spread of videocassette recorders in the 1980s and of satellite dishes in the

Egyptian couple eating beneath the golden arches. As Egypt's economy has moved from the Arab socialism of the 1960s toward capitalism, it has welcomed multinational corporations, including the ubiquitous fast-food chain McDonald's. (Dick Doughty/Saudi Aramco World/PADIA)

1990s enabled viewers to choose programs not prescribed by any ministry of national guidance. Newsstands display a variety of papers and magazines. Although state censorship of books, periodicals, and films continues, the intrusive habits of Nasser's censors, who routinely opened letters and taped telephone calls, have not been resumed. On the other hand, al-Azhar and the Islamist groups screen books and even professors. Individuals and groups often censor themselves to avert future trouble, knowing that they can be pressured by Islamists as well as by the government. Access to the Internet provides new opportunities for self-expression, but its use is carefully monitored by the police. A 2007 estimate is that 5 million Egyptians have Internet access.

Government censorship and repression are applied against Communists, obstreperous groups and individuals, and Islamists, usually in the name of "fighting terrorism." Using its emergency laws, the Mubarak regime has banned newspapers and magazines, placed its foes under house arrest or preventive detention without charges or trial, tortured suspects in police stations and prisons, broken up meetings, and restricted political rallies and demonstrations. In fact, when demonstrations do occur, as in March 2003 against the U.S. attack on Iraq, outside observers know that they convey a message from Mubarak's government, which like its citizens opposed Bush's policies.

Economic Development

In economic matters the government still tries to combine state planning and ownership of basic industries with private enterprise, both domestic and foreign. The trend, however, has been toward privatization of most businesses. Mubarak seems more dedicated to solving Egypt's economic problems than Sadat ever was, but it is not clear whether some of them can ever be solved. The country's population, 80 million in 2007, increases by another million every 10 months, but Egypt's arable land has declined from 10 million *feddans* in 1971 to slightly fewer than 8 million (10.38 to 8.1 million acres) in 2006. This decline has been due partly to the demand for housing but also to a legacy of ill-planned agricultural policies that made it more profitable for some farmers to turn their soil into bricks than to raise three crops per year, as facilitated by perennial irrigation. Although the Aswan High Dam initially increased the amount of cropland and now generates enough electricity for Egypt to export some, it has deprived the land of the silt that formerly came down with the annual flood and hence has increased Egypt's need for artificial fertilizers. The dam also raised the water table, making it harder to flush away salt accumulations that reduce soil productivity. By 1980 Egypt imported more than half the grain its inhabitants consumed, an ironic fate for a land that was the

Aswan High Dam. Highly controversial when governments argued in the 1950s over its financing and construction, it was built by Soviet engineers between 1964 and 1971 and has become the linchpin in Egypt's irrigation and electrical power generation. (Tor Eigeland/Saudi Aramco World/PADIA)

breadbasket of ancient and medieval empires, but higher grain production has reduced this dependency in the last two decades.

There have been other hopeful agricultural trends. The percentage of Egyptians who actually work as farmers has steadily declined, while their use of farm machinery, modern techniques of cultivation and irrigation, and their technical knowledge have all increased. Egyptian cotton remains an important export crop, but it uses a decreasing share of the country's agricultural land, while wheat, corn, rice, and sugar have taken up the slack. The diversion of some of the waters that have backed up behind the Aswan High Dam for the Toshka Project, inaugurated in January 1997, is designed to create a second Nile Valley eventually in Egypt's Western Desert. This could increase the amount of cultivated land from 5 to 20 percent. Much of the new land will be used for cash crops. It is widely understood that the future success of Egyptian agriculture generally will depend on the development of products that can be sold to Europeans and to other Arabs, such as fruit, vegetables, beet and cane sugar, honey, poultry, eggs, cut flowers, and decorative plants. No one can predict how many Egyptians will agree to move to this remote new region. There is also concern lest the second Nile draw away water still needed by the original River Nile.

Egypt's gross domestic product has risen from $25.5 billion in 1980 to $84.5 billion in 2006, and its human development index score, which measures progress in longevity, knowledge, and standard of living, has increased from 0.430 in 1975 to 0.635 in 1999. Indonesia is the only country that has recorded a higher increase.

Egypt has industrialized more slowly than most Asian countries. Nasser's showcase heavy industries all lost money. Sadat retained most of them in order not to antagonize public-sector factory workers. Mubarak's government has sold them off or entered into partnerships that allow the government and private investors to share in their ownership and management. Unemployment has become rampant among secondary school and university graduates, running to between 15 and 20 percent, causing many to put off marriage and child bearing; by contrast, in many skilled trades, even some agricultural ones, the labor supply has been inadequate. The main reason for this scarcity was that 3 million Egyptians were lured to the oil-exporting Arab countries by wages 10 times the amount they could earn at home.

But the decline in oil prices in the 1980s and 1990s severely reduced employment opportunities abroad. Because of the 1991 Gulf War, many expatriate Egyptians lost their jobs in Iraq and returned home. Oil-exporting countries like Saudi Arabia, the United Arab Emirates, and Kuwait are now trying to replace their foreign workers with their own nationals. The earnings sent home by expatriate workers have been a major source of hard currency. As large numbers of Egyptian professionals, managers, and laborers get laid off in the oil-exporting countries and return to Egypt, they become frustrated by local wages and working conditions, even if they find jobs. It is hard for their families to adjust to lower living standards and the presence of disgruntled breadwinners who had long lived far away and sent money home.

Falling oil revenues in the 1980s and 1990s reduced the flow of Arab tourists to Egypt and slowed Arab investment in its economy. Egypt's own petroleum production peaked in 1996, but natural gas output has risen. Prices parallel those received by the major oil exporters, even though Egypt never joined the Organization of Petroleum Exporting Countries. Egypt has made less income than it hoped from the Suez Canal, which since its reopening in 1975 has been used by more oil tankers than freighters or passenger liners. Since 1977, however, this has been offset by earnings from the Suez-to-Mediterranean (Sumed) Pipeline.

Income disparities are nearly as large as they were before the 1952 Revolution, but the egalitarian propaganda of the Nasser era has made Egyptians less willing to accept vast differences between rich and poor, and of course they now know far better how the other half lives. Radios have been ubiquitous since the 1950s, and television sets have proliferated since 1960, when TV broadcasting began. In the 1980s VCRs and personal stereos swept through the land. Since the late 1990s computers and Internet cafés have been spreading in Cairo and Alexandria. These media have made the Egyptian people more conscious of others and how they live. Near universal primary education may get higher marks for quantity than quality, but it certainly has added to the public's awareness of the difference between the reality with which they are contending and the ideals of either capitalism or socialism. One interesting change has been the degree to which technicians and skilled workers have managed to increase their wages; by contrast, public servants and those dependent on disability or retirement pensions have suffered. The value of the Egyptian pound has dropped from $2.80 in 1952 to 17 cents in 2006. A weak currency helps to promote exports but makes it harder for businesses to import capital equipment and for individuals to buy foreign-made consumer goods. Annual double-digit price inflation has usually ensued, and morale has suffered.

The government narrowly avoided a crisis in repaying its foreign debts in 1987 when it opened extensive negotiations with the World Bank, the International Monetary Fund, and Western governments to reschedule its payments. In May 1991 the negotiating parties signed the Economic Reform and Structural Adjustment Program (ERSAP), which called for macroeconomic policy adjustments (higher taxes relative to state expenditures), removal of government subsidies on consumer goods, elimination of price controls, reduction of quotas and protective tariffs, reform of labor legislation, and privatization of state-owned enterprises. Mubarak did implement these reforms during the 1990s, strengthening the Egyptian pound yet reducing the trade deficit. Egypt suffered another financial crisis in 2000–01, and a conference of 34 donor nations and groups met in February 2002 to address the issue. Egypt decided to stop pegging its currency to the dollar in 2003, but the pound has actually increased slightly in value since then. Overall national income has risen, but some economists say that the rich have benefited at the expense of the poor.

Ownership of land and real estate is still the safest way to get rich, but rewards have risen for entrepreneurial skill. Under Sadat this often meant milking the public-sector companies, one common form of corruption; but Mubarak's government has demanded stricter standards of honesty. The Sadat era spawned at least a thousand new millionaires, the so-called fat cats (*munfatihin*); since then it has been harder to climb the economic ladder through graft or corruption (but some succeed). Many Egyptians welcome the new rules, but they are resented, of course, by those whose ambitions for wealth and power are unfulfilled. Not surprisingly, they are prime recruits for the Society of Muslim Brothers; younger malcontents often find their way to Egypt's leading terrorist organizations: Islamic Jihad and al-Jamaa al-Islamiyya.

The Search for an Ideology

The issue of legitimacy remains. The president of Egypt needs some kind of ideological glue that will bind the people to his government. He is neither a pharaoh who can rely on belief in divine kingship nor a caliph drawing on the political principles of Islam to ensure that his orders will be obeyed. Egypt is now both a nation (an object of loyalty) and a state (a political and legal system). The concept of the nation-state arose in early modern times in Western Europe and North America. It is related neither to the traditional loyalties of most Middle Eastern peoples nor to the policies of their rulers. Faith and family remained the foci of popular identification. French and British imperialism (and schooling) spread the spirit of nationalism, but mainly among a narrow stratum of the educated elite. Unless identified with popular resistance to non-Muslim rulers, nationalism was slow to appear and spread in the Middle East. It grew in both intensity and extent in Egypt during the 20th century, especially under Nasser, Sadat, and Mubarak, because of expanding public education, radio and television broadcasting, and almost universal male military service. Nationalism is supposed to be the main reason why Egyptians obey their government; in reality, it is the government's ability to force their compliance.

Comparisons with other Middle Eastern states are hard to make, but Egyptians have probably developed a clearer sense of nationality than any other Arabic-speaking people, except maybe Moroccans. Egyptians do tend to meander among their Egyptian, Arab, and Muslim identities, responding to current political conditions. Egypt's Arab identity went into eclipse after 1973, but it is now reviving, for the ties of language and culture with other Arabs are strong, as is resentment against Israel for what Egyptians view as its repression of the Palestinians and its manipulation of U.S. foreign policy.

Egyptian attachment to the land and its history, deep-seated though it may be, does not exclude other loyalties. Islamic sentiment has increased ever since the June 1967 War and the 1979 Iranian Revolution. Sadat's assassins, or those whom the government managed to capture, belonged to a relatively new secret society, al-Jihad (Struggle). Their feat has actually increased the appeal to the Egyptian people of Islamic revolutionary groups, although they are strictly outlawed. Allied with the Jihadists in killing Sadat was al-Jamaa al-Islamiyya, which grew out of the student Muslim groups Sadat had encouraged in Egypt's universities. The two groups set up a consultative council led by Sheikh Umar Abd al-Rahman, who later escaped to Afghanistan, Sudan, and finally the United States, where he was arrested, tried, and convicted for the 1993 bombing of the World Trade Center in New York City. Egyptians of both groups went to Afghanistan and aided the Muslim rebels against the Soviet military occupation of that country. Those who returned home in the early 1990s, often called "Afghans," became leading assassins of government ministers, secularist writers, foreign tourists, and Copts between 1992 and 1997. One of the Egyptian "Afghans" was Dr. Ayman al-Zawahiri, a physician who allied himself with Osama Bin Laden and helped to form the terrorist network, based in Afghanistan and elsewhere, known as al-Qaeda (The Base), now the target for the "War on Terrorism."

Although most educated Egyptians do not want their country to become an Iranian-style Islamic republic, they have rejected Sadat's liberalism. Some, however, are drawn to the extremist groups. More will join them if economic and social conditions deteriorate. The

Egyptian Muslims praying during feast day. Public piety is ever more evident in Egyptian life: Women increasingly cover their hair, and voters incline toward "independent" candidates who in fact support the Society of the Muslim Brothers. (Dick Doughty/Saudi Aramco World/PADIA)

Muslim extremists do not accord any legitimacy to the present regime and look to Libya and other radical states to help them deliver Egypt from its state of *jahiliyya* (pre-Islamic ignorance). This term, applied by the Islamist writer Sayyid Qutb to secularized governments and Westernized societies, has strong resonance for religious Muslims, who condemn consumerism and immorality. These are evident not only in films and television shows imported from the West, but also in the behavior of Gulf Arabs escaping from their governments' restrictions on extramarital sex, gambling, and alcohol, all available to foreigners but not Egyptians in their country's luxury hotels.

It was easy for extremists to exploit the resentment among the thousands of young men who served in the Security Police for six Egyptian pounds a month—so easy that they exploded into mass demonstrations that destroyed three tourist hotels near the Giza Pyramids in February 1986. The Islamists organized campus demonstrations against Egypt's participation in the 1991 Gulf War. They also provided textbooks, lecture notes, Islamic clothing, and transportation to campus for Muslim students. After the severe Egyptian earthquake of October 1992, Islamist organizations provided faster and more effective health services and

224

SAYYID QUTB

Sayyid Qutb was a seminal Islamist thinker and writer. Born in a village near Asyut in 1906, he was educated at his village primary school, a Cairo secondary school, and Dar al-Ulum (the training school for Arabic teachers), where he became interested in English literature. After graduating in 1934, he worked for *al-Ahram,* wrote articles for several respected literary magazines, taught Arabic, and served as an education inspector of the Egyptian government. Sent to study educational administration in the United States from 1948 to 1951, he grew disenchanted with the West as he observed what he considered the moral corruption of American society, its racial prejudice, and its strong anti-Arab bias caused by the Palestine War.

Upon returning, Qutb criticized Egypt's educational programs as British-influenced and called for a more Islamic curriculum. He developed close ties to some of the Free Officers, was considered for the post of education minister after the 1952 Revolution, and served as the first secretary-general of the Liberation Rally. He resigned from the government in 1953 and joined the Muslim Brothers, taking charge of their instructional program and editing their newspaper. Imprisoned with other Brothers after their failed attempt to assassinate Nasser, he began writing books that were smuggled out of Egypt and published abroad, notably *al-Adala al-ijtimaiyya fi al-Islam* (translated into English as *Social Justice in Islam*), *Fi zalal al-Quran* (translated as *In the Shade of the Quran*), and *Maalim fi al-tariq* (Signposts along the Way).

During his incarceration Qutb became bitterly disillusioned with the Nasser government and argued that every person is an arena in the battle between godly and satanic forces. He called for a small community of good people to expel evil and establish righteousness in the world. Drawing on Quranic passages, he taught that Jews and Christians will always be implacably opposed to Islam and that Muslims must be prepared to combat Zionism, "Crusaderism," and communism to protect their community and its values. His 30-volume interpretation of the Quran has become a standard reference work in mosques and homes throughout the Muslim world. Released in 1964, he was imprisoned again in 1965 and vilified by the press before being hanged for treason in August 1966. Since his death his ideas have inspired many Muslim individuals and groups, notably *al-Takfir wa al-*Hijra and al-*Jamaa al-Islamiyya* in Egypt, and the Iranian revolution and various groups linked to al-Qaeda abroad.

reconstruction aid to injured and homeless victims than did Egyptian government agencies. Their protests against American missile attacks on Iraq in 1993 and 1998 expressed the sentiments of most of the Egyptian people and presaged their popularly supported opposition to the American war on Iraq since 2003. More ominously, many Muslims (in Egypt and elsewhere) cheered when Egyptian and Saudi terrorists hijacked American passenger jets on September 11, 2001, and flew them into the World Trade Center towers and the Pentagon. Egypt's government was appalled, but the reaction of the Arab street was that the United States deserved what it got. The succession in 2006 of an expatriate Egyptian, Abu Ayyub al-Masri, to the leadership of al-Qaeda in Iraq is another ominous sign.

The Islamists' slogan, "Islam is the solution," expresses the basic loyalty of many Egyptians. Islamist groups resorted to violence to weaken the hold of the government over its citizens during the 1990s, but their terrorism antagonized the people as it threatened Egypt's economy, with its dependence on tourism and foreign trade. Proud of the traditional coexistence between Muslims and Copts, Egyptians fault the Islamist groups for stirring up intercommunal tensions. Egypt's traditional subordination of women to men, often ascribed to Islam even by Muslims, serves no purpose in a society where women's earnings outside the home are needed to support most families, urban or rural. Both sexes need all the training and education they can get to ensure their ability to make a living and to live a better life. Gender discrimination still exists in the Egyptian workplace, but it will probably diminish. As long as Islamic values counteract tendencies toward consumerism and hedonism, they do Egypt a great service. When they prescribe politics, economics, society, and cultural life, they become harmful. Mubarak and his successors must act carefully for the sake of Egypt's future.

CONCLUSION

This book has related Egypt's history from its beginnings to the present, and it is time to think about its future. Historians as a group shy away from making predictions, which often turn out to be wrong, but of course both Egyptians and foreigners must think about how the country's direction will affect them.

We can be reasonably certain that Egypt's population will grow and that rising numbers will move abroad to seek their fortune. The decline in child mortality from 100 per 1,000 live births in 1990 to 29.5 in 2006 has meant that larger numbers of children will grow to maturity and marry. We cannot know for certain at what age they will marry or how many children they will have. The marriage age has been rising, girls and women are more apt to get educated, married women increasingly use contraceptives and Egyptians are becoming urbanized. All these trends will probably depress the birth rate. Some young adults will move abroad, mainly men but increasingly women as well, but emigration rarely solves a country's economic problems. Fewer Egyptians are likely to be absorbed by other Arab states, which are filling up, but more will go to European countries whose populations are already declining. Some of these émigrés—or their children—will later come home.

Egypt will remain a hot, dry country that gets its water from the Nile. There is no short-term prospect of increasing the water supply, unless the cost of removing salt from seawater goes down. Moreover, Sudan and other countries through which the Nile flows before it gets to Egypt will need more of its waters for their own agriculture, industry, and burgeoning populations. This has ominous implications for Egypt's economic security. Some experts predict that the Middle East wars of the 21st century will be fought over water rights rather than oil or land.

Relations between Middle Eastern countries are especially hard to predict, but Egypt's central location almost guarantees that it will remain a key player. It and Jordan are natural intermediaries between Israel, with which it continues to have diplomatic and trade relations, and the other Arabs, even the Palestinians. Because Egypt has a well-developed economic and educational infrastructure, it is increasingly likely to provide financial services and advanced schooling to neighboring

Arab countries. As Egypt has become hooked to the Internet, it should try to develop computer services comparable to those now offered by India's version of Silicon Valley, but especially for other Arab countries. If Islamists ever take power, Egypt's foreign relations, educational policies, and culture will certainly change, but the economy and society will remain competitive in areas where the infrastructure is sound.

Mubarak's regime will survive only as long as it succeeds in alleviating (though perhaps not solving) Egypt's economic problems. Relations with other Arab and Muslim peoples, while certainly better than they were in Sadat's time, matter less. When will Egypt have its next revolution? Sadat's regime showed ominous parallels with that of Khedive Ismail, whose deposition preceded the abortive Urabi Revolution, and with that of King Farouk, whose personal and political ineptitude contributed to the 1952 Revolution. In all three cases Western cultural and political influences impinged heavily on Egypt, fueling a reactive Muslim resistance. Egyptians rebel less often than other Arabic-speaking peoples; their patience is legendary. They defer to autocratic rulers and bureaucrats to a degree that astonishes Syrians and Palestinians. Centuries of dependence on a strong ruler to ensure equitable distribution of Nile waters and protection from foreign invasion have created a political culture that glorifies order, tranquility, and forbearance. Modernization has sapped this ethos, however, and the danger of a new popular uprising is never remote. It cannot be predicted. A chance encounter or an exceptional incident could set it off.

The United States since 1979 has spent on average $2 billion a year to support the Egyptian government, more than what it gives to any other country except Israel. U.S. aid policy in 2007 is geared more to politics than to need. In the case of Egypt, U.S. economic aid helps to pay for the subsidies that hold down the price of bread, rice, cooking oil, and butane gas, thus staving off a popular uprising and the spread of terrorism.

Egyptians comprehend this reasoning behind Washington's policy, and the degree of their gratitude depends on how much they want the present regime to last. Some complain that U.S. aid is hard to see amid the continuing problems of congestion, unemployment, and low wages. This raises some interesting questions about American aid policy. Would it be better if the Americans built showcase projects, such as the sports stadium and the concert hall erected by the USSR during the Nasser era? Or should they stand in the streets handing out one-hundred-dollar bills to individual Egyptians? The best projects are the ones that enable Egyptians to solve their own problems, but U.S. aid is flawed in its administration: Washington demands a degree of supervision far stricter than that imposed on Israel. Egyptians view this as an aspersion against their competence. On the personal level, U.S. diplomats and AID workers could do more to befriend Egyptians, who tend to be cordial, hospitable, and eager to learn more about American culture. But the growing coerciveness of U.S. policy in Iraq and elsewhere has made Egyptians resent Americans. Any speculation about the future of the Middle East may depend on what happens in Washington. Readers of this book should act circumspectly in a difficult time.

Foreign governments and foundations could do more to promote Egyptian scientific, technological, and intellectual development by supporting existing libraries, laboratories, universities, and higher institutes. Rebuilding the Alexandria Library put Egypt back in the limelight, but more help is needed for Dar al-Kutub and the national universities' libraries. Scientific laboratories need modern equipment and especially computers to keep their engineers, scientists, and technicians from going abroad and never returning. The brain drain is a serious threat to Egyptian society and culture. It has already cost Egypt much of its leading role within the Arab world. Many Egyptian professionals and entrepreneurs have gone to Europe or the United States, where they have made their fortunes or found fame; it is time for these citizens to repay some of the benefits that they brought with them from Mother Egypt. Already, some of their sons and daughters are returning to do just that.

Egypt is a great and enduring country with a civilization that has lasted for 60 centuries. It has one of the world's largest and most beneficent rivers, heavily modified by the hand of humanity but capable of further improvement. Its people are diligent and resourceful. They have a long tradition of patience under adverse conditions. The storms of Middle East politics may rumble around and disturb their equanimity. But Egypt has weathered such storms before, and it will do so again.

APPENDIX 1

GLOSSARY OF TERMS AND ORGANIZATIONS

Abdin (ab-DEEN)   Official residence of Egypt's ruler up to 1952, located in central Cairo. Also the site and sometimes the name of the 1942 incident in which the British ambassador ordered King Farouk to appoint a Wafdist cabinet.

Abu Qir (ah-boo-KEER)   Village near Alexandria, site of British victory over Napoléon (1798)

Al-Ahram (el-ah-RAHM)   Influential Cairo daily newspaper, founded in 1876

amir (ah-MEER)   Muslim ruler or prince

Anglo-Egyptian Treaty   1936 pact defining Britain's military position in Egypt, denounced by Egypt in 1951

Arab League   Political association of Arab states, founded in 1945

Arab Nationalism   Movement seeking unification of all Arabic-speaking countries and their independence from non-Arab control

Arab Socialist Union   Egypt's popular mobilization movement (1962–77)

Arian   Pertaining to the belief of some early Christians that Jesus was human, not of the same substance as God the Father

Al-Arish (el-a-REESH)   (1) Abortive 1800 treaty between France and Britain, providing for evacuation of French forces from Egypt; (2) site of alleged abuse by Israel of Egyptian POWs in 1967

Aswan High Dam   Large earthen dam mainly financed and built for Egypt by the USSR (1958–70)

Attrition, War of   Artillery and air struggle between Egypt and Israel (1969–70), which ended when both sides accepted the Rogers Peace Plan

Al-Azhar (el-OZ-har) Muslim mosque-university in Cairo, founded in 971

Baath Party Arab nationalist and socialist party ruling Syria since 1963 and Iraq (1968–2003)

Baghdad Pact Anticommunist military alliance formed in 1955

Bahri (BAH-ree) Turkish Mamluks who ruled Egypt from 1250 to 1384

Bank Misr Egyptian bank and holding company founded by Talaat Harb in 1920

Barrage, Delta Dam built by French and repaired by British to regulate Delta irrigation

Black Saturday Burning and looting of European buildings in central Cairo by Egyptian mob on January 26, 1952, widely seen as a precursor of the July 23 revolution

caliph (KAY-lif) Successor to Muhammad as head of the Muslim community

Camp David (1) US president's vacation home in Maryland; (2) site of intensive talks by Begin, Carter, and Sadat in 1978; (3) adjective applied to the Egyptian-Israeli accords or to the 1979 peace treaty

Capitulations System by which Muslim states granted extraterritorial immunity from local laws and taxes to subjects of Western countries, applied to foreigners in Egypt up to 1949

Centers of Power Cabal of Egyptian leaders at end of Nasser era and political foes of Sadat

Charter, National 1962 Egyptian document describing the goals of Arab socialism

Circassian Native of the Caucasus region or descendant; term for Mamluk rulers after 1382

Constitution, 1923 Egypt's most liberal constitution, flouted by the king and many politicians

Constitution, 1956 Post-revolutionary Egyptian governmental principles, enhancing Nasser's power

Constitution, 1964 Interim constitution, basing power within the Arab Socialist Union

Constitution, 1971 Authoritative basis for Egypt's current government, amended in 1977 to allow opposing political parties and in 1980 to create the Consultative Council

Coptic Pertaining to Egyptian (or Ethiopian) Christians, constituting about 10 percent of Egypt's population, or to their liturgical language, a derivative of ancient Egyptian

Corrective Revolution Sadat's purge of his political foes to liberalize Egypt's government

Debt Commission, Public Council representing Egypt's major European creditor nations between 1876 and 1914

Delta Triangular area of the Nile north of Cairo to the Mediterranean Sea

demotic Simplified form of the hieratic script, adopted during the Twenty-sixth Dynasty

Dinshaway (den-sha-WYE) **Incident** British atrocity against Egyptian peasants in 1906

divine kingship Idea that ascribed superhuman powers to ancient Egypt's rulers by virtue of their office

Dual (Financial) Control Joint Anglo-French financial administration in Egypt (1876–82)

Dufferin Commission Group sent by the British government to study Egypt's government (and to recommend improvements) just after the 1882 occupation

Economic Reform and Structural Adjustment Program (ERSAP) Financial reform scheme accepted by Egypt in 1991 in return for rescheduling its foreign debt

Egyptian-Israeli Peace Treaty Formal document ending state of war between Egypt and Israel

emir See AMIR

emmer Species of wheat grown in ancient Egypt

Ezbekia (ez-beh-KEE-ya) **Gardens** Public park in Cairo, often the site of political rallies

Fatah (FET-ah) Palestinian guerrilla group founded by Yasir Arafat

Fedayeen (fe-dah-YEEN) Muslims who sacrifice themselves for a cause; Palestinians fighting against Israel, militant Shiis, or Iraqi insurgents, formerly also Egyptians fighting British in the Suez Canal zone

feddan (fed-DAN) Egyptian unit of land measure, about 1.038 acres

Four Reserved Points Britain's limitations on its unilateral declaration of Egypt's independence (1922) and a sticking point in later negotiations

Free Officers Secret Egyptian army group led by Nasser that conspired to overthrow King Farouk

galabia (gal-la-BEE-ya) Gownlike garment worn by male Egyptian peasants and workers

Gaza Strip small part of southwestern Palestine held by Egyptian forces in 1948 and inhabited wholly by Arabs, administered by Egypt (1948–56 and 1957–67), captured by Israel in 1956 and 1967, administered by Israel from 1967 to 1994, then by the Palestinian Authority

hajj (HODGE) Muslim rite of pilgrimage to Mecca

hieratic Ancient Egyptian writing system using simplified symbols for persons, things, or concepts

hieroglyphic Original ancient Egyptian writing system using pictures to represent objects or actions

imam (ee-MAHM) (1) Muslim religious or political leader; (2) one of the succession of leaders, beginning with Ali, viewed by Shiites as legitimate; (3) leader of Muslim congregational prayer

infitah (in-fi-TAH) Sadat's free-enterprise policy, a reaction against Nasser's Arab socialism

Islamic Jihad Egyptian Islamist group behind assassination of Sadat, now linked to al-Qaeda

Islamic Socialist Party Name assumed by Young Egypt after World War II

Jahiliyya (ja-he-LEE-ya) Pre-Islamic period of ignorance; also a term applied by Islamists to secular governments in Muslim countries

Al-Jamaa al-Islamiyya (el-ja-MAA-a el-iss-la-MEE-ya) Egyptian Islamist movement

Al-Jarida (el-ja-REE-da) Liberal paper (1907–15) attached to the Umma Party

janissary (JAN-i-se-ree) Christian conscript foot soldier in the Ottoman army, converted to Islam and trained to use firearms

Jarring Mission (YAR-ring) Abortive UN mediation effort between Israel and the Arab states (1967–71)

jihad (jee-HAD) (1) Defense of Islam against attackers; (2) Muslim struggle against evil; (3) name of several militant Islamist groups

jizya (JIZ-ya) Per capita tax paid by non-Muslim males living under Muslim rule

Joint Note Anglo-French letter backing Egyptian government against Urabi, sent January 1882

July Laws Nasser's decrees instituting Arab socialism in the United Arab Republic (1961)

June War 1967 conflict between Israel and Egypt, Jordan, and Syria, also called the Six Day's War

kharaj (kha-RODGE) Land tax paid by peasants in early Islamic history

Khartoum (khar-TOOM) (1) Capital of Sudan; (2) site of 1967 Arab summit opposing peace negotiations with Israel

khedive (khe-DEEV) Title of Egypt's viceroy (1867–1914)

Land Law, Ottoman Ottoman reform (1858) of land ownership system, enforced in Egypt

Land Reform RCC decree (1952) limiting land ownership to 200 *feddans* (208 acres) per individual

Law of Shame Regulations proposed by Sadat and passed by plebiscite in 1980 limiting individual freedom to criticize the Egyptian government

Legislative Assembly Representative body, established under the 1913 Organic Law, with limited legislative power and Saad Zaghlul as its elected vice president

Liberal Constitutional Party Largest parliamentary rival of the Wafd Party from 1922 to 1952

Liberation Rally Nasser's first organization to mobilize popular support (1953–58)

Al-Liwa (el-lee-WA) Nationalist daily newspaper (1900–1914)

London, Treaty of 1840 treaty among the European powers affirming Egypt's autonomy from the Ottoman Empire under the rule of Mehmet Ali and his heirs

maat Principle or rule of order, truth, balance, and justice maintained by ruler of ancient Egypt

madrasa (MA-dres-sa) Muslim school, especially for law

Mahdi (MEH-dee) (1) Right-guided one, precursor of the Judgment Day; (2) title claimed by leader of Sudanese rebellion against Egyptian rule (1881–85)

Mamluk (mem-LOOK) (1) Turkish or Circassian slave soldier; (2) member of military oligarchy that ruled Egypt and Syria (1250–1517) and retained power until destroyed by Mehmet Ali in 1811 *mawali* (ma-WA-lee) (1) Client member of Arab tribe, entitled to protection but not all membership privileges; (2) non-Arab convert to Islam during the early Arab conquests

Milner Mission Official British commission sent in 1919 to ascertain Egyptian political aspirations; its report indicated strong support for independence

minbar (MIM-bar) (1) Pulpit of a mosque; (2) Sadat's term for faction of Arab Socialist Union

Misr Party Sadat's center party in 1977–78, during the breakup of the Arab Socialist Union

Mixed Courts Egyptian tribunals (1876–1949) for civil cases involving foreign nationals protected by the Capitulations

Montreux Convention 1937 agreement to phase out Capitulations and the Mixed Courts in Egypt

Al-Muayyad Khedivist daily newspaper published from 1889 to 1914

Muslim Brothers, Society of Islamist political group that flourished from 1928 to 1954, then banned by Nasser but allowed to revive (but not formally legalized) under Sadat

National Committee of Workers and Students ephemeral anti-British alliance formed in 1946

National Democratic Party Egypt's governing party since 1978

National Progressive Unionist Party Leftist party led since 1978 by Khalid Muhyi al-Din

National Union Nasser's second organization intended to mobilize popular support (1958–62)

New Wafd Party Middle-class political party, revived in 1978 by Fuad Sirag al-Din

Nubia Upper Egyptian region south of the First Cataract, largely flooded by the Aswan High Dam

October Paper Sadat's 1974 policy statement proposing liberalized economy for Egypt

October War Conflict started by Egypt and Syria in 1973 to regain lands occupied by Israel since 1967, also called the Yom Kippur War or Ramadan War

Organic Law Quasi-constitution prepared for Egypt by the British in 1883 and amended in 1913

Palestine Liberation Organization Umbrella group for Palestinian military, political, economic, and social organizations, originally created by Arab heads of state in 1964

Palestine War 1948 conflict between Israel and the Arab countries opposing partition of Palestine and creation of the Jewish state, also called Israel's War for Independence

Palestinian Autonomy Talks Egyptian-Israeli negotiations mandated by 1979 Peace Treaty, aimed at creating an autonomous region for Palestinians under Israeli rule, but terminated by Egypt after Israel invaded Lebanon in 1982

pan-Islam Idea or movement calling for unity of all Muslims, promoted by some Ottoman sultans and some popular leaders

Paris Peace Conference (1919) Meeting of the victorious World War I Allies to restore peace in Europe and the Middle East; Egypt's delegation, formed to attend it, was excluded

pasha High rank in the Ottoman (and hence Egyptian) administration or army

People's Assembly Official name of the lower house of Egypt's parliament since 1971

pharaoh From the Eighteenth Dynasty, the title held by the ruler of ancient Egypt

pharaonic Pertaining to the government or culture of ancient Egypt

pharaonism Nationalist movement that distinguishes Egypt from all other Arab countries

Positive Neutrality Nasser's policy of not siding with either the former Soviet bloc or the West

Al-Qaeda (el-KAH-e-da) Network of Islamist organizations, including Egypt's Islamic Jihad

Quran (koor-AWN) Collection of revelations that Muslims believe God vouchsafed to Muhammad via Gabriel between 610 and 632, and one of the main sources of Islamic law, literature, and culture

Ramadan (ra-ma-DAWN) Month of the Arabic calendar during which Muslims refrain from eating, drinking, and sexual activity from daybreak to sunset, commemorating first Quranic revelation

Resolution 242 Principles, adopted in 1967 by the UN Security Council, for achieving peace between the Arabs and Israel, accepted by both sides but with differing interpretations

Revolutionary Command Council (RCC) Governing board established by the 1952 junta

Rogers Peace Plan U.S. proposal (1969–70), calling on Israel to withdraw from lands occupied since 1967, endorsed by both Egypt and Israel but not implemented

Russo-Turkish War Conflict (1877–78) between Russia and the Ottoman Empire, in which the latter lost land in Anatolia and the Balkans

Saadist (SAH-dist) **Party** Breakaway faction from the Wafd in 1937, led by Ahmad Mahir and Mahmud Fahmi al-Nuqrashi, and often included in anti-Wafdist coalition

Satrap (SAT-rap) Title of provincial governor in Achaemenid Persia, hence of Egypt (525–404 and 343–332 B.C.E.)

Secret Apparatus Terrorist division of the Muslim Brothers during the 1940s

Shabab (sha-BAB) **Muhammad** Islamist group formed about 1974

sharia (sha-REE-a) The elaborate code of approved Muslim behavior, based primarily on the Quran and Muhammad's *sunna* (sayings and actions) and secondarily on analogy, consensus, and judicial opinion

Shepheard's Cairo hotel, destroyed by fire on Black Saturday 1952 and later rebuilt

Shiite Muslim who believes that Muhammad's leadership of the *umma* was bequeathed to Ali and his descendants, to whom special legislative powers and spiritual knowledge were vouchsafed

Sinai Peninsula Egyptian territory between the Suez Canal and the Israeli border, invaded by Israel in 1949, 1956, and 1967, then occupied by Israel up to 1982

Socialist Labor Party Right-wing party formed in 1978

Soviet-Egyptian Treaty Pact signed by Sadat with Moscow in 1971 and renounced in 1976

Sufi (SOO-fee) Pertaining to Muslim mystics, or to their beliefs, practices, or organizations

sultan (sool-TAWN) Title for ruler of various Muslim states, including the Mamluk and Ottoman Empires, and for Egypt's nominal ruler from 1914 to 1922

Sumed Pipeline Oil conduit from the Gulf of Suez to the Mediterranean, built in 1974–77

Sunni Muslim who believes that the caliphs were the legitimate successors of Muhammad

Taba (TAW-ba) **Affair** 1906 Anglo-Ottoman dispute over possession of the Sinai, notable because Egypt's nationalists supported Ottoman against Egyptian claims

Takfir wa al-Hijra (et-tak-FEER wal-HIJ-ra) Islamist group formed in late 1970s

tax farming System of collecting government imposts that authorizes the collector to keep a share of the proceeds, common in Egypt up to the 19th century

Tel-el-Kebir (tel el-ka-BEER) Site of 1882 battle in which a British expeditionary force decisively defeated the Egyptian army, leading to Britain's occupation of Egypt

ulama (OO-le-ma) Muslim scholars and jurists, often the intermediaries between rulers and Egyptians

Umma (1) Egyptian moderate party (1907–14). (2) Sudanese party opposing union with Egypt. (3) Community of Muslim believers

United Arab Republic Union of Egypt and Syria (1958–61) under Nasser

United Nations Emergency Force (UNEF) International army stationed between Egypt and Israel (1957–67 and 1974–   )

Vanguard Organization Elite section of the Arab Socialist Union in late 1960s

vizier (ve-ZEER) Government minister, especially in ancient Egypt or in any Muslim state

Voice of the Arabs Egyptian radio program broadcast to Arabs, popular from 1856 to 1978

Wafd (WAHFT) (1) Egypt's unofficial delegation to the Paris Peace Conference in 1919; (2) Egypt's main nationalist party up to 1952, revived in 1978 as the "New Wafd"

waqf (WAHKF) Muslim endowment of land or other property, usually set up for a beneficent purpose

West Bank Area of Arab Palestine annexed by Jordan in 1948 and captured by Israel in 1967; partly governed by the Palestine Authority since 1996

Yemen Civil War Struggle (1962–67) in northern Yemen between Saudi-backed royalists and Egyptian supported republican revolutionaries

Young Egypt   Popular Egyptian nationalist movement (1933–52)

zakat (za-KAT)   fixed share of income or property that all Muslims must pay as tax or charity for the welfare of the needy

Zionism   (1) nationalist ideology stressing solidarity of the Jewish people; (2) movement to create or maintain a Jewish state, especially in Palestine/Israel.

APPENDIX 2

BASIC FACTS ABOUT EGYPT

Official Name
Arab Republic of Egypt (Jumhuriyat Misr al-Arabiyah)

Geography

Location	22°–32°N, 20°–35°E, in the NE corner of the African continent.
Land area	385,210 square miles (997,690 sq. km)
Land borders	Libya, Sudan, Israel, Gaza Strip
Coastal borders	Mediterranean Sea, Red Sea
Elevations	Highest: Jabal Katarina, 8,650 ft. (2,637 m); Jabal Musa, 7,495 ft. (2,285 m), also called Mount Sinai. Lowest: Qattara Depression, -436 ft. (-133 m)

Government
Republic with a president elected by the people for a six-year term and allowed to run for additional terms, and a bicameral parliament: Majlis al-Shaab (People's Assembly, composed of 444 elected and 10 appointed members) and Majlis al-Shura (Consultative Assembly, having 176 popularly chosen and 88 appointed members). The Council of Ministers, presided over by a Prime Minister, is appointed and dismissed by the President. The judicial system includes the Court of Cassation with five judges, the highest court of appeal in both civil and criminal cases; Court of Appeals with three judges dealing with all cases of serious crime; Central Tribunals with three judges dealing with ordinary civil and commercial cases; and summary tribunals presided over by a single judge to hear minor civil disputes and criminal offenses. Judges are appointed and promoted

by the president. The public prosecutor's office (*niyaba*) investigates cases before trial.

Political Divisions

Capital	Cairo (estimated 2007 population of metropolitan area: 16 million)
Other cities	Alexandria (4 million), Giza (2.6 million, part of Cairo metropolitan area), Shubra al-Khayma (1 million, part of Cairo metropolitan area), Port Said (538,000), al-Mahalla al-Kubra (462,000)
Subdivisions	26 governorates

People

Population	80,335,036 (2007 est.)
Annual growth rate	1.72% (2007 est.)
Ethnic groups	Egyptians (98%), Bedouins, Berbers, Nubians, Greeks
Language	Arabic, English and French understood by educated people
Religions	Islam, 90%; Coptic or other Christian, 10%
Literacy rate	58% (2003 est.)
Age structure	0–14 years 32.6% 15–64 62.9% 65 and over 4.5%
Birth rate	22.53/1,000 (2007 est.)
Death rate	5.11/1,000 (2007 est.)
Sex ratio	1.017 males/1 female (2007 est.)
Net migration	-0.21 migrants/1,000 (2007 est.)
Infant mortality rate	29.5/1,000 live births (2007 est.)
Life expectancy at birth	71.57 years (males 69.04 years, females 74.22 years)
Total fertility rate	2.77 children/woman (2006 est.)

Economy

Although for most of its recorded history Egypt has been an agricultural country, most of its people are now employed in the services sector, and its largest single exports are petroleum and natural gas. The government exercises control over most major economic activities but during the past 30 years has slowly enhanced the private sector to increase efficiency and employment. The economy depends heavily on income from emigrant remittances, revenues from tourism (mainly from Europe and nearby Arab countries), Suez Canal tolls, and Sumed pipeline fees. About 3 million Egyptians are working abroad at any given time. The country has 70,000 Palestinian refugees and has admitted 13,700 new refugees from Sudan and 100,000 from Iraq as of 2007.

GDP	$84.5 billion (2006 est.); purchasing power parity $328.1 billion
GDP growth rate	5.7% (2006 est.)
GDP per capita	$4,200 (2006 est.)
Natural resources	petroleum, natural gas, iron ore, phosphates, manganese, limestone
Petroleum reserves	2.6 billion barrels (2006 est.)
Natural gas reserves	1.657 trillion cu m (2006 est.)
Arable land	2.92% of total land area
Permanent crops	0.5%
Irrigated land	33,000 sq. km (1998 est.)

Proportion of GDP by economic sectors

Agriculture	14.7%
Industry	35.5%
Services	49.8%

Agricultural products	cotton, rice, corn, sugar, wheat, beans, fruit, vegetables; cattle, water buffalo, sheep, goats
Industries	textiles, food processing, chemicals, pharmaceuticals, hydrocarbons, construction, cement, metals, light manufacturing
Services	tourism, banking, insurance, education
Major exports	crude oil, petroleum products, natural gas, raw cotton, textiles, metal products, chemicals
Labor force	21.8 million (2006)

Distribution of labor force by sector (2001 est.)

Agriculture	32%
Industry	17%
Services	51%

Environmental Issues

Loss of land to urban sprawl and windblown sands; soil salination downstream from the Aswan High Dam; oil pollution in Red Sea, Gulf of Suez, Gulf of Aqaba; Nile pollution from agricultural pesticides, raw sewage, and industrial waste; very limited supply of fresh water; rapid population growth.

Transnational Issues

Water use issues with all other countries in Nile River basin; border dispute over Halaib triangle with Sudan; international terrorism in Sinai Peninsula; issue with Israel over Gaza Strip administration.

Appendix 3

CHRONOLOGY

Ancient Egypt

to 3100 B.C.E.	Predynastic Period
3100–2686	Early Dynastic Period
2686–2181	Old Kingdom
2181–2040	First Intermediate Period
2040–1750	Middle Kingdom
1750–1550	Second Intermediate Period; Hyksos occupation
1550–1069	New Kingdom
1069–715	Third Intermediate Period
747–332	Late Period
728–656	Nubian rule (25th Dynasty)
671, 663	Assyrian Invasions
664–525	Saite Pharaohs (26th Dynasty)

Persian, Greek, Roman, and Arab Rule

525–404 and 343–332	Persian rule (27th Dynasty)
332–323	Reign of Alexander III "the Great"
323–305	Interregnum
305–30	Ptolemaic Period
30 B.C.E.–639 C.E.	Egypt under Roman/Byzantine administration
639–642	Arab conquest of Egypt
642–661	Egypt ruled by right-guided caliphs from Medina
661–750	Umayyad caliphs, ruling from Damascus
750–868	Abbasid caliphs, ruling from Baghdad
868–905	Tulunid dynasty in Egypt and Syria
905–935	Abbasid caliphs restored in Egypt
935–969	Ikhshidid dynasty in Egypt and Syria

969–1171	Fatimid caliphs in Egypt, Syria, and the Hejaz
1171–1250	Ayyubid dynasty in Egypt and Syria

Mamluk and Ottoman Rule

1250–1382	Bahri Mamluks in Egypt and Syria
1382–1517	Circassian Mamluks in Egypt and Syria
1517–1798	Ottoman sultans, ruling from Istanbul
1760–1772	Ali Bey, governor of Egypt
1772–1775	Muhammad Bey "Abu al-Dhahab," governor

Early Westernizing Reform (1798–1882)

1798	Napoléon Bonaparte's forces land in Alexandria, defeat Mamluks at Imbaba. Nelson defeats French fleet at Abu-Qir
1798–1801	French occupation of Egypt
1801–1802	First British occupation of Egypt
1801–1914	Restored Ottoman suzerainty (nominal)
1805–1848	Mehmet Ali, governor
1807	British briefly occupy Alexandria
1811	Mamluks massacred in Cairo
1811–1818	Egyptian campaign against the Wahhabis in Arabia
1820–1822	Egyptian conquest of the Sudan
1822	Long-staple cotton introduced in the Delta
1831–1840	Egyptian conquest and occupation of Syria
1833	Convention of Kütahya
1839	Egypt defeats Ottoman army; Ottoman fleet surrenders to Egypt
1840	London Convention makes Egypt autonomous Ottoman province
1841	Sultan's decree recognizes Mehmet Ali and heirs as governors of Egypt
July–November 1848	Ibrahim, acting governor
1848–1854	Abbas Hilmi I, governor
1851	Beginning of Alexandria–Cairo railway
1854–1863	Said, governor
1854	Said and Ferdinand de Lesseps sign Suez Canal concession
1859–1869	Construction of Suez Canal

1863–1879	Ismail, governor and khedive
1875	Most powers approve Mixed Courts (opened formally 1876)
1875	Britain buys Egyptian government's Suez Canal Company shares
1876	Public Debt Commission established
1876–1878, 1879–1882	Egypt under Dual Financial Control

British Occupation and Nationalist Resistance

1879–1892	Tawfiq, khedive
1881	Egyptian officers rebel against war minister, confront Khedive Tawfiq at Abdin Palace
1882	Anglo-French Joint Note threatens Nationalists; Tawfiq appoints Nationalist cabinet led by Mahmud Sami al-Barudi, with Ahmad Urabi as minister of war and marine; Egyptians riot in Alexandria against Europeans; British fleet bombards harbor fortifications, fire breaks out in Alexandria, and British troops invade; British defeat Egyptians at Tel-el-Kabir and occupy Cairo; Urabi surrenders
1882–1956	British occupation of Egypt
1883	Dufferin Report on Egypt's government; Organic Law and National Court system established
1883–1907	Sir Evelyn Baring, Earl of Cromer, British agent in Cairo
1885	Mahdi of the Sudan defeats Gordon and takes Khartoum
1887	Drummond Wolff Convention (later rejected by the sultan)
1888	Constantinople Treaty (Suez Canal Convention)
1892–1914	Abbas Hilmi II, khedive
1893	Ministerial crisis between Abbas and Cromer
1894	Frontiers Incident between Abbas and Kitchener
1896–1898	Anglo–Egyptian forces reconquer Sudan
1899	Anglo–Egyptian Sudan Convention
1904	Britain and France sign Entente Cordiale
1906	Taba Affair; Dinshaway Incident

1907–1911	Sir Eldon Gorst, British agent
1907	National Party formed in Cairo
1908	National Party leader Mustafa Kamil dies, succeeded by Muhammad Farid
1909	Press Law revived.
1910	Prime minister assassinated; General Assembly blocks extension of Suez Canal Company concession; Cabinet enacts Exceptional Laws to curb Nationalist agitation
1911–1914	Lord Kitchener, British agent
1913	New Organic Law creates Legislative Assembly
1914	British declare protectorate over Egypt, end its nominal ties to the Ottoman Empire, and depose Khedive Abbas Hilmi II
1914–1917	Hussein Kamil, sultan
1915–1916	Sir Henry McMahon, high commissioner
1916–1919	Sir Reginald Wingate, high commissioner

Ambiguous Independence (1918–1936)

1917–1936	Fuad I, sultan and king (from 1923)
1918	Saad Zaghlul asks to lead delegation (*wafd*) to London, later to Paris Peace Conference, to seek Egypt's independence
1919	British exile Zaghlul, causing riots throughout Egypt
1919–1922	1919 Revolution against British occupation
1919–1925	Sir Edmund, later Viscount, Allenby, high commissioner
1919–1920	Egyptians boycott Milner Mission; Milner meets with Zaghlul
1921	Adli-Curzon negotiations in London
1922	British declare Egypt independent, subject to four points reserved for later negotiation
1923	Liberal constitution promulgated; Wafd Party wins first elections
1924	Zaghlul, prime minister; Lee Stack, Sudan governor, assassinated
1925–1929	Baron George Lloyd, high commissioner
1929–1934	Sir Percy Loraine, high commissioner

1930	Wafd Party wins election; abortive negotiations follow; Royalist constitution replaces 1923 document
1934–1946	Sir Miles Lampson, later Baron Killearn, high commissioner and later British ambassador to Egypt
1935	Nationalist demonstrations against royalist government
1936–1952	Farouk, king
1936	Wafd wins election and forms cabinet; Anglo-Egyptian Treaty signed
1939	Egypt declares neutrality as World War II begins
1942	British force Farouk to appoint Wafdist cabinet, later stop German advance at El Alamein
1945	Arab League formed under Egyptian leadership
1946	Widespread student and worker demonstrations against British; Bevin-Sidqi negotiations on the Sudan held in London
1947	UN General Assembly votes to partition Palestine, despite Arab opposition
1948–1949	Israel defeats Egypt in Palestine War
1950	Wafd wins elections; Mustafa al-Nahhas becomes prime minister; Arab League Collective Security Pact signed by Egypt, Jordan, Lebanon, Saudi Arabia, and Syria
1951	Nahhas abrogates 1936 Treaty; mass demonstrations against British occupation of Suez Canal
January 1952	Central Cairo burned by angry demonstrators

Military Rule and Arab Nationalism (1952–1961)

July 1952	Free Officers seize government; Farouk abdicates and leaves Egypt
1952–1953	Fuad II, king (nominal)
September 1952	Muhammad Naguib named prime minister, proposes land reforms
1953–1954	Naguib, president
1953	British and Egyptian negotiators reach accord on the Sudan.

February–April 1954	Power struggle between Naguib and Gamal Abdel Nasser
October 1954	Anglo–Egyptian Suez agreement signed; Muslim Brothers attempt to assassinate Nasser
1954–1970	Nasser, president
1955	Israeli raid on Gaza; Nasser attends Bandung Conference; Czech arms deal; United States and Britain offer to finance Aswan High Dam construction
June 1956	Egyptians accept constitution and elect Nasser president
July 1956	John Foster Dulles withdraws U.S. High Dam offer; Nasser nationalizes Suez Canal Company
October 1956	Israel invades Sinai; Britain and France attack Suez Canal
November 1956	USSR threatens to intervene in Suez War; UN presses Britain and France to halt advance and forms United Nations Emergency Force (UNEF)
December 1956	Britain and France evacuate Suez Canal zone; Egyptian government nationalizes British and French businesses and properties in Egypt
February 1957	Israel agrees to leave Sinai and Gaza
February 1958	Egypt and Syria form United Arab Republic (UAR)

Arab Socialism

July 1961	July Laws proclaimed, many firms nationalized
September 1961	Syria secedes from UAR
May 1962	Nasser offers Charter draft to National Congress of Popular Forces
October 1962– September 1967	Egypt involved in Yemen civil war
April 1963	Egypt, Syria, and Iraq discuss federation in Cairo, sign charter
July 1963	Nasser rejects ties with Baath Party, which rules Syria and Iraq
January 1964	Egypt hosts summit of Arab heads of state regarding Israel
March 1964	Nasser releases draft of 1964 constitution

May 1964	Nasser and Soviet premier Nikita Khrushchev inaugurate first stage of High Dam
August 1965	Muslim Brothers' plot discovered, 4,000 arrested
August 1966	Three Muslim Brothers, including Sayyid Qutb, hanged
November 1966	Egypt and Syria sign joint defense pact
May 1967	Egypt places its armed forces on alert, orders UNEF to leave Sinai posts, and declares blockade of Aqaba Gulf; Egypt and Jordan form military alliance
June 1967	Israel attacks Egypt by air, invades Gaza Strip and Sinai Peninsula; Suez Canal closed; Egypt accepts cease-fire; Nasser resigns his presidency; war ends; Nasser withdraws his resignation
August– September 1967	Arab leaders meet in Khartoum, bar direct talks with Israel
November 1967	UN Security Council passes Resolution 242
February 1968	Widespread student demonstrations
March 1968	Nasser announces political reforms
1969–1970	Egyptian-Israeli War of Attrition
December 1969	U.S. secretary of state William Rogers proposes peace settlement, at first spurned by Egypt; Anwar Sadat named vice president
July 1970	Nasser accepts revised Rogers Plan, leading to indirect peace talks with Israel
September 1970	Nasser dies, widespread mourning ensues

Anwar Sadat

1970–1981	Anwar Sadat, president
November 1970	Egypt agrees to federate with Libya and Sudan; Syria to join later
March 1971	Cease-fire with Israel ends as peace negotiations fail
May 1971	Corrective Revolution ousts Sadat's foes from power; Egypt and USSR sign 15-year friendship and cooperation treaty
August 1971	Federation of Arab Republics formally announced
September 1971	New constitution announced following referendum
July 1972	Sadat expels Soviet advisers and troops from Egypt

October 1973	Egyptians cross Suez Canal; Israelis launch Sinai counterattack, troops cross Suez Canal; UN Security Council passes Resolution 338, calling for cease-fire in place; Resolution 340 sets up emergency force
October–November 1973	Inconclusive Kilometer 101 talks between Egypt and Israel
November 1973	U.S. secretary of state Henry Kissinger meets with Sadat
December 1973	Geneva Peace Conference
January 1974	Kissinger's shuttle diplomacy; Egyptian-Israeli Separation of Forces agreement
May 1974	Plebiscite approves Sadat's *Infitah* policies
June 1974	U.S. president Richard Nixon visits Egypt
June 1975	Suez Canal reopened
June–September 1975	Kissinger brokers negotiations; Egypt and Israel sign agreement in Geneva, renouncing war and creating new buffer zone in the Sinai Peninsula
March 1976	Egypt abrogates Soviet Friendship Treaty
August 1976	Gulf Organization for Development of Egypt (GODE) begins
October 1976	Arab Socialist Union *minbar*s vie in People's Assembly elections
November 1976	Sadat permits formal political parties
January 1977	Widespread protest riots against food price hikes
July 1977	Egyptian-Libyan border war
November 1977	Sadat flies to Jerusalem and proposes peace in Israeli Knesset
December 1977	Peace conference of Egypt, Israel, United States, and United Nations in Cairo; Begin meets Sadat in Ismailia
September 1978	Camp David talks and accord among United States, Egypt, and Israel
November 1978	Rejectionist Arab leaders meet in Baghdad to boycott Egypt
January–March 1979	U.S. mediation efforts lead to Egypt-Israel formal peace treaty
March 1979	New rejectionist meeting in Baghdad; Arab League expels Egypt; Arab states break diplomatic ties with Egypt; Gulf Organization for Development of Egypt suspends all aid projects
1979–1982	Phased Israeli withdrawals from Sinai

May 1980	Plebiscite approves amendments to 1971 constitution, creating Consultative Council
1980–1988	Iran-Iraq War; Egypt aids Iraq
June 1981	Strife between Muslims and Copts in Zawiya al-Hamra
September 1981	Sadat orders arrest of more than 1,500 political opponents
October 1981	Sadat assassinated during military parade; national plebiscite approves succession of Hosni Mubarak

Contemporary Egypt

1981–present	Hosni Mubarak, president
December 1981– March 1982	Trial of Islamists accused of killing Sadat
April 1982	Israel's forces leave Sinai, except Taba
June 1982	Israel invades Lebanon; Egypt suspends Palestinian Autonomy Talks
October 1985	*Achille Lauro* Incident harms Egypt-U.S. ties
February 1986	Central Security Force riots in Cairo
September 1986	Egypt and Israel submit Taba dispute to arbitration
November 1987	Amman summit allows other Arab states to resume diplomatic ties with Egypt
August 1988	Arbiters award Taba to Egypt (ceded March 1989)
October 1988	Naguib Mahfouz wins Nobel Prize in literature
May 1989	Egypt readmitted to Arab League
September 1990	Arab League Headquarters moved back to Cairo
August 1990– March 1991	First Gulf War; Egypt aids allied coalition against Iraq; Western countries forgive $14 billion of Egypt's debt
May 1991	Economic Reform and Structural Adjustment Program inaugurated in Egypt, as Paris Club promises further debt forgiveness
1992–1997	Islamists attack Egyptian writers, foreign tourists, others
October 1992	Earthquake destroys large areas around Cairo
February 1995	Mubarak meets successively in Cairo with King Hussein, PLO Chairman Yasir Arafat, and Israeli Premier Yitzhak Rabin

June 1995	Al-Jama'a al-Islamiyya tries to kill Mubarak in Addis Ababa
October 1995	U.S. Federal court convicts Umar Abd al-Rahman and nine other Egyptians for 1993 World Trade Center bombing
January 1997	Mubarak inaugurates Toshka Project
April 1998	Egypt launches Nilesat
October 2000	Mubarak and Bill Clinton assist Arafat's meeting with Israeli Prime Minister Ehud Barak in Sharm al-Sheikh after July 2000 Camp David summit fails
January 2001	Egypt hosts renewed Israel-PLO talks in Taba; no accord reached
May 2001	Military court convicts Saad Eddin Ibrahim of defaming Egypt and issues seven-year prison sentence.
September 2001	Egyptian government backs U.S. antiterrorism campaign, following attacks against New York's World Trade Center and the Pentagon by al-Qaeda, which includes members of Egypt's Jihad group
February 2002	Thirty-four donor nations and groups, meeting at Sharm al-Sheikh, offer Egypt $10.4 billion to resolve its liquidity crisis
October 2002	Bibliotheca Alexandrina inaugurated
January 2003	Egyptian government decides to float its currency
March 2003	Ibrahim acquitted by High Court of Cassation; large-scale protest demonstrations in Cairo against U.S. war in Iraq
July 2004	Ahmad Nazif appointed prime minister
October 2004	Palestinian plots bombing of Taba hotel and Sinai tourist camp, killing at least 34 people
March 2005	Parliament amends 1971 constitution to allow direct election of president
April 2005	Mass student demonstrations led by Muslim Brothers against government
May 2005	Parliament approves constitutional amendment, allowing opposition candidates to run in presidential elections
July 2005	Bombings in Sharm al-Sheikh kill 88, wound 200

September 2005	Egypt's first contested presidential election draws only 23 percent of registered voters; Mubarak wins 86.6 percent; Ayman Nur, who finishes second, tried for bribery and forging signatures
October 2005	Opposition groups form united front for parliamentary elections
November–December 2005	Parliamentary elections, marked by violence, mass arrests, and 25% voter turnout, give majority of seats to NDP candidates, but Muslim Brothers, running as independents, win 72 seats
April 2006	50 pro-reform judges protest rigging of parliamentary elections; police break up sit-in demonstration, arresting 15 and injuring one judge severely; Parliament extends for two more years the Emergency Laws enacted after Sadat's assassination in 1981
July 2006	Parliament enacts new restrictions on press freedom after two journalists were jailed for insulting President Mubarak
September 2006	Egyptian officials announce resumption of Egypt's civil nuclear program after a 20-year freeze
November 2006	Mubarak calls on parliament to enact laws making it easier for opposition parties (but not the Muslim Brothers) to run candidates in future presidential elections
December 2006	Arrests of several leading Muslim Brothers are followed by a government raid on bookstores and other businesses owned by them
March 2007	Parliament approves changes to the 1971 constitution, including a ban on religious parties, greater powers to the police to fight terrorism, and an end to judicial supervision of ballot boxes. These changes were approved in a popular referendum in which only 27 percent of eligible voters actually voted.

APPENDIX 4

BIBLIOGRAPHY

Adès, Harry. *A Traveller's History of Egypt*. Northampton, Mass.: Interlink Books, 2007.

Bell, C. F. Moberly. *Khedives and Pashas*. London: Sampson Low, 1884.

Blunt, Wilfrid Scawen. *Secret History of the English Occupation of Egypt*. London: Fifield, 1907.

The Cambridge History of Egypt. Vol. 1. Edited by Carl Petry; Vol. 2. Edited by M. W. Daly. Cambridge: Cambridge University Press, 1998.

Copeland, Miles. *The Game of Nations: The Amorality of Power Politics*. New York: Simon & Schuster, 1970.

Crabitès, Pierre. *Ismail, the Maligned Khedive*. London: George Routledge & Sons, 1933.

Cromer, Earl of (Sir Evelyn Baring). *Modern Egypt*. London and New York: Macmillan, 1908.

Eveland, Wilbur. *Ropes of Sand: America's Failure in the Middle East*. New York: Norton, 1980.

Flower, Raymond. *Napoleon to Nasser: The Story of Modern Egypt*. London: London Editions, 1976.

Ghorbal, Shafik. *Beginnings of the Egyptian Question and the Rise of Mehemet-Ali*. London: George Routledge & Sons, 1928.

Goldschmidt, Arthur, Jr. *Modern Egypt: The Formation of a Nation State*. 2d ed. Boulder, Colo.: Westview Press, 2004.

Goldschmidt, Arthur, and Robert C. Johnston. *Historical Dictionary of Egypt*. 3rd ed. Lanham, Md.: Scarecrow Press, 2003.

Herold, J. Christopher. *Bonaparte in Egypt*. New York: Harper & Row, 1962.

Hunter, F. Robert. *Egypt under the Khedives, 1805–1879*. Pittsburgh: University of Pittsburgh Press, 1984.

Hurewitz, J. C. *Diplomacy in the Near and Middle East,* Princeton, N.J.: D. Van Nostrand, 1956.

Ibrahim, Saad Eddin. *Egypt, Islam, and Democracy.* Cairo: American University in Cairo Press, 1996.

Jankowski, James. *Egypt: A Short History.* Oxford: OneWorld Publications, 2000.

Karabell, Zachary. *Parting the Desert: The Creation of the Suez Canal.* New York: Knopf, 2003.

Kerisel, Jean. *The Nile and Its Masters: Past, Present, Future.* Rotterdam: A.A. Balkema, 2001.

Kinross, Lord (Sir Patrick Balfour). *Between Two Seas: The Creation of the Suez Canal.* New York: William Morrow, 1969.

Landes, David S. *Bankers and Pashas: International Finance and Economic Imperialism in Egypt.* Cambridge, Mass.: Harvard University Press, 1958.

Lane, Edward. *An Account of the Manners and Customs of the Modern Egyptians.* London: Society for the Promotion of Useful Knowledge, 1936; introduction by Jason Thompson. Cairo: American University in Cairo Press, 2003.

Little, Tom. *Modern Egypt.* London: Ernest Benn, 1967.

Lloyd, George A., Lord. *Egypt since Cromer.* 2 vols. London: Macmillan, 1933.

Marlowe, John. *The Making of the Suez Canal.* London: The Cresset Press, 1964.

———. *Spoiling the Egyptians.* New York: St. Martin's Press, 1975.

McCarthy, Justin, "Nineteenth Century Egyptian Population." In *The Middle Eastern Economy: Studies in Economics and Economic History,* edited by Elie Kedourie. London: Cass, 1976.

Metz, Helen Chapin, ed. *Egypt: A Country Study.* Washington, D.C.: Library of Congress, 1990.

Meyer, Gail E. *Egypt and the United States.* Rutherford, N.J.: Fairleigh Dickinson University Press, 1980.

Morris, Benny. *The Birth of the Palestinian Refugee Problem, 1947–1949.* Cambridge: Cambridge University Press, 1987.

Nasser, Gamal Abdel. *The Philosophy of the Revolution.* Cairo: Egyptian State Printing Office, 1955.

Perry, Glenn E. *The History of Egypt.* Westport, Conn.: Greenwood Press, 2004.

Quandt, William. *Peace Process: American Diplomacy and the Arab-Israeli Conflict since 1967.* Washington, D.C.: Brookings Institution, 1993.

Richmond, John C. B. *Egypt, 1798–1952: Her Advance toward a Modern Identity.* New York: Columbia University Press, 1977.

Sadat, Anwar. *In Search of Identity.* New York: Harper & Row, 1978.

Al-Sayyid, Afaf Lutfi. *Egypt and Cromer.* London: John Murray, 1968.

Al-Sayyid-Marsot, Afaf Lutfi. *Short History of Modern Egypt.* Cambridge: Cambridge University Pres, 1985.

Schechtman, Joseph. *The Arab Refugee Problem.* New York: Philosophical Library, 1952.

Springborg, Robert. *Family, Power, and Politics in Egypt.* Philadelphia: University of Pennsylvania Press, 1982.

Stadiem, William. *Too Rich: The Life and High Times of King Farouk.* New York: Carroll & Graf, 1991.

Storrs, Sir Ronald. *Orientations.* London: Ivor Nicholson & Watson, 1937.

Vatikiotis, P. J. *The History of Modern Egypt from Muhammad Ali to Mubarak.* 4th ed. Baltimore: Johns Hopkins University Press, 1991.

Waterfield, Gordon. *Egypt.* New York: Walker and Company, 1967.

Young, George. *Egypt.* New York: Charles Scribner's Sons, 1927.

Appendix 5

Suggested Reading

The Land and Its People

Bernstein, Burton. *Sinai: The Great and Terrible Wilderness.* New York: Viking, 1979.

Coleman, Robert Griffin. *Geologic Evolution of the Red Sea.* Oxford: Oxford University Press, 1993.

Collins, Robert O. *The Nile.* New Haven, Conn., London: Yale University Press, 2002.

Erlich, Haggai, and Israel Gershoni, eds. *The Nile: History, Cultures, Myths.* Boulder, Colo.: Lynne Rienner, 2000.

Fakhry, Ahmed. *The Oases of Egypt.* 2 vols. Cairo: American University in Cairo Press, 1973–74.

Held, Colbert C. *Middle East Patterns: Places, Peoples, and Politics.* 4th ed. Boulder, Colo.: Westview Press, 2006.

Howell, Paul Philip. *The Nile: Sharing a Scarce Resource.* Cambridge: Cambridge University Press, 1994.

Hurst, H. E. *The Nile.* London: Constable, 1952.

Said, Rushdi, ed. *The Geology of Egypt.* Rotterdam, Netherlands: A.A. Balkema, 1990.

Said, Rushdi. *The River Nile: Geology, Hydrology and Utilization.* Oxford: Pergamon Press, 1993.

Tawadros, E. Edward. *Geology of Egypt and Libya.* Rotterdam, Netherlands: A.A. Balkema, 2001.

Tregenza, L. *The Red Sea Mountains of Egypt.* Oxford: Oxford University Press, 1955.

Waterbury, John. *Hydropolitics of the Nile Valley.* Syracuse, N.Y.: Syracuse University Press, 1979.

Ancient Egypt

Aldred, Cyril. *The Egyptians.* 3d ed. Revised and updated by Aidan Dodson. New York and London: Thames & Hudson, 1998.

Arnold, Dieter. *Encyclopedia of Ancient Egyptian Architecture.* Translated by Sabine H. Gardiner and Helen Strudwick. Princeton, N.J.: Princeton University Press, 2003.

Baines, John, and Jaromir Malek. *Cultural Atlas of Ancient Egypt.* Rev. ed. New York: Checkmark Books, 2000.

Bierbrier, Morris L. *Historical Dictionary of Ancient Egypt.* Lanham, Md.: Scarecrow Press, 1999.

Bohn, Dorothy. *Egypt.* London: Thames & Hudson, 1989.

Bothmer, Bernard V. *Egyptian Art: Selected Writings of Bernard V. Bothmer.* Edited by Madeleine E. Cody. Oxford: Oxford University Press, 2004

Brier, Bob, and Hoyt Hobbs. *Daily Life of the Ancient Egyptians.* Westport, Conn., and London: Greenwood Press, 1999.

Bunson, Margaret. *Encyclopedia of Ancient Egypt.* Rev. ed. New York: Facts On File, 2002.

Casson, Lionel. *Everyday Life in Ancient Egypt.* Baltimore: Johns Hopkins University Press, 2001.

David, A. Rosalie. *Handbook to Life in Ancient Egypt.* Rev. ed. New York: Facts On File, 2003.

Davies, W. V. *Egypt.* London: British Museum Press, 1998.

Dunand, Françoise, and Christine Zivie-Coche. *Gods and Men in Egypt 3000 BCE to 395 CE.* Translated by David Lorton. Ithaca, N.Y.: Cornell University Press, 2004.

Emery, Walter B. *Archaic Egypt.* Harmondsworth, U.K.: Penguin Books, 1961.

Fagan, Brian. *Egypt of the Pharaohs.* Washington, D.C.: National Geographic, 2001.

Grimal, Nicolas. *A History of Ancient Egypt.* New York: Barnes & Noble, 1997.

Hawass, Zahi. *Hidden Treasures of Ancient Egypt: Unearthing the Masterpieces of Egyptian History.* Washington, D.C.: National Geographic, 2004.

———. *Tutankhamun and the Golden Age of the Pharaohs.* Washington, D.C.: National Geographic, 2005.

Hobson, Christine. *The World of the Pharaohs: A Complete Guide to Ancient Egypt.* New York: Thames & Hudson, 2000.

James, T. G. H. *The British Museum Concise Introduction to Ancient Egypt.* Ann Arbor: University of Michigan Press, 2005.

Kemp, Barry J. *Ancient Egypt: Anatomy of a Civilization.* 2d ed. London: Routledge, 2006.

Malek, Jaromir. *Egypt: 4000 Years of Art.* London: Phaidon, 2003.

Morkot, Robert G. *The Egyptians: An Introduction.* London: Routledge, 2005.

———. *Historical Dictionary of Ancient Egyptian Warfare.* Lanham, Md.: Scarecrow Press, 2003.

Redford, Donald B. *The Ancient Gods Speak: A Guide to Egyptian Religion.* Oxford: Oxford University Press, 2002.

Reeves, Nicholas. *Ancient Egypt: The Great Discoveries.* London: Thames & Hudson, 2000.

Rice, Michael. *Egypt's Legacy: The Archetypes of Western Civilization, 3000–30 BC.* London: Routledge, 1997.

———. *Egypt's Making: The Origins of Ancient Egypt 5000–2000 BC.* 2d ed. London and New York: Routledge, 2003.

Rogan, Eugene, ed. *Agriculture in Egypt from Pharaonic to Modern Times.* Oxford: Oxford University Press, 1999.

Shaw, Ian. *Ancient Egypt: A Very Short Introduction.* Oxford: Oxford University Press, 2004.

———. *Exploring Ancient Egypt.* Oxford: Oxford University Press, 2003.

———, ed. *The Oxford History of Ancient Egypt.* Oxford and New York: Oxford University Press, 2000.

Silverman, David P., ed. *Ancient Egypt.* Oxford: Oxford University Press, 2003.

Spencer, Jeffrey, ed. *Aspects of Early Egypt.* London: British Museum Press, 1996.

Teeter, Emily. *Ancient Egypt: Treasures from the Collection of the Oriental Institute.* Chicago: University of Chicago, 2003.

Tiradritti, Francesco. *Ancient Egypt: Art, Architecture, and History.* London: British Museum, 2002.

Watterson, Barbara. *The Egyptians.* Oxford, UK: Blackwell, 1997.

Wilkinson, Toby. *The Thames & Hudson Dictionary of Ancient Egypt.* London: Thames & Hudson, 2005.

Persian, Greek, Roman, and Arab Rule

Bagnall, Roger S., and Domenic W. Rathbone, eds. *Egypt from Alexander to the Early Christians.* Los Angeles: J. Paul Getty Museum, 2004.

Bianchi, Robert, ed. *Cleopatra's Egypt: The Age of the Ptolemies.* New York: Brooklyn Museum, 1988.

Bowman, Alan K. *Egypt after the Pharaohs, 332 BC–AD 642.* 2d ed. Berkeley: University of California Press, 1996.

Brett, Michael. *The Rise of the Fatimids.* Leiden, Netherlands, Boston, Cologne: Brill, 2001.

Butler, Albert Joshua. *The Arab Conquest of Egypt and the Last Thirty Years of Roman Dominion.* 2d ed. Oxford: Clarendon Press, 1978.

Cannuyer, Christian. *Coptic Egypt: The Christians of the Nile.* New York: Harry N. Abrams, 2001.

Chauveau, Michel. *Egypt in the Age of Cleopatra.* Translated by David Lorton. Ithaca, N.Y.: Cornell University Press, 2000.

Cohen, Amnon, and Gabriel Baer, eds., *Egypt and Palestine: A Millennium of Association* (868–1948) New York: St. Martin's Press, 1984.

Dodge, Bayard. *Al-Azhar: A Millennium of Muslim Learning.* Washington, D.C.: Middle East Institute, 1974.

Fahmy, Aly Mohamed. *Muslim Naval Organization in the Eastern Mediterranean from the Seventh to the Tenth Century A.D.* 2d ed. Cairo: National Publishing and Printing, 1963.

————. *Muslim Sea-Power in the Eastern Mediterranean from the Seventh to the Tenth Century A.D.* Cairo: National Publishing and Printing, 1966.

Goitein, S. D. *A Mediterranean Society: Jewish Communities of the Arab World as Portrayed in the Documents of the Cairo Geniza.* 6 vols. Berkeley: University of California Press, 1967–1994.

Hamdani, Abbas. *The Fatimids.* Karachi: Pakistan Publishing House, 1962.

Hövlbl, Günther. *A History of the Ptolemaic Empire.* Translated by Tina Saavedia. London: Routledge, 2001.

Hughes-Hallett, Lucy. *Cleopatra: Histories, Dreams, and Distortions.* New York: Harper & Row, 1990.

Humphreys, R. Stephen. *From Saladin to the Mongols: The Ayyubids of Damascus, 1193–1260.* Albany: State University of New York Press, 1977.

Kennedy, Hugh. *The Historiography of Islamic Egypt, c. 950–1800.* Leiden, Netherlands: Brill, 2001.

————. *The Prophet and the Age of the Caliphates: The Islamic Near East from the Sixth to the Eleventh Century.* London: Longman, 1986.

Lane-Poole, Stanley. *A History of Egypt in the Middle Ages.* Reprint, London: Methuen, 1901 New York: Haskell House, 1969.

Lev, Yaacov. *Saladin in Egypt.* Leiden, Netherlands: Brill, 1999.

————. *State and Society in Fatimid Egypt.* Leiden, Netherlands: E.J. Brill, 1991.

Petry, Carl F., ed. *The Cambridge History of Egypt, Volume One, Islamic Egypt, 640–1517.* Cambridge: Cambridge University Press, 1998.

Raymond, André. *Cairo.* Cambridge, Mass.: Harvard University Press, 2000.

————. *Cairo: An Illustrated History.* New York: Rizzoli, 2002.

Russell, Dorothea. *Medieval Cairo and the Monasteries of Wadi Natrun: A Historical Guide.* London: Weidenfeld & Nicolson, 1962.

Shaban, M. A. *Islamic History, A.D. 600–750 (A.H. 132): A New Interpretation.* Cambridge: Cambridge University Press, 1970.

————. *Islamic History: A New Interpretation, A.D. 750–1055 (A.H. 132–448).* Cambridge: Cambridge University Press, 1976.

Walker, Paul E. *Exploring an Islamic Empire: Fatimid History and Its Sources.* London: I.B. Tauris, 2002.

Walker, Susan, and Peter Higgs, eds. *Cleopatra of Egypt: From History to Myth.* Princeton, N.J.: Princeton University Press, 2001.

Mamluk and Ottoman Rule

Amitai-Preiss, Reuven. *Mongols and Mamluks: The Mamluk-Ilkhanid War, 1260–1281.* Cambridge: Cambridge University Press, 1995.

Ayalon, David. *The Mamluk Military Society.* London: Variorum Reprints, 1979.

Behrens-Abouseif, Doris. *Egypt's Adjustment to Ottoman Rule: Institutions, Waqf and Architecture in Cairo (16th and 17th centuries).* Leiden, Netherlands: E.J. Brill, 1994.

Crecelius, Daniel. *The Roots of Modern Egypt: A Study of the Regimes of Ali Bey al-Kabir and Muhammad Bey Abu al-Dhahab, 1760–1775.* Minneapolis: Bibliotheca Islamica, 1981.

Crecelius, Daniel, ed. *Eighteenth Century Egypt: The Arabic Manuscript Sources.* Claremont, Calif.: Regina Books, 1990.

Cuno, Kenneth M. *The Pasha's Peasants: Land, Society, and Economy in Lower Egypt, 1740–1858.* Cambridge: Cambridge University Press, 1992.

Glubb, Sir John. *Soldiers of Fortune: The Story of the Mamlukes.* New York: Stein and Day, 1973.

Gran, Peter. *Islamic Roots of Capitalism: Egypt, 1760–1840.* 2d ed. Syracuse, N.Y.: Syracuse University Press, 1998.

Hanna, Nelly. *Making Big Money in 1600: The Life and Times of Isma'il Abu Taqiyya, Egyptian Merchant.* Syracuse, N.Y.: Syracuse University Press, 1998.

————. *In Praise of Books: A Cultural History of Cairo's Middle Class, Sixteenth to the Eighteenth Century.* Syracuse, N.Y.: Syracuse University Press, 2003.

————. *An Urban History of Bulaq in the Mamluk and Ottoman Periods.* Cairo: Institut Français d'Archéologie Orientale, 1983.

Hanna, Nelly, ed. *The State and Its Servants: Administration in Egypt from Ottoman Times to the Present.* Cairo: American University in Cairo Press, 1995.

Hathaway, Jane. *The Politics of Households in Ottoman Egypt: The Rise of the Qazdaghlis.* Cambridge: Cambridge University Press, 1997.

———. *A Tale of Two Factions: Myth, Memory and Identity in Ottoman Egypt and Yemen.* Albany: State University of New York Press, 2003.

Holt, P. M. *Egypt and the Fertile Crescent, 1516–1922.* Ithaca, N.Y.: Cornell University Press, 1966.

Holt, P. M., ed. *Political and Social Change in Modern Egypt.* London: Oxford University Press, 1968.

Irwin, Robert. *The Middle East in the Middle Ages: The Early Mamluk Sultanate, 1250–1382.* Carbondale: Southern Illinois University Press, 1986.

Marsot, Afaf Lutfi al-Sayyid. *Women and Men in Late Eighteenth-Century Egypt.* Austin: University of Texas Press, 1995.

Al-Nahel, Gamal H. *The Judicial Administration of Ottoman Egypt in the Seventeenth Century.* Minneapolis: Bibliotheca Islamica, 1979.

Petry, Carl F. *The Civilian Elite of Cairo in the Later Middle Ages.* Princeton, N.J.: Princeton University Press, 1981.

——— *Protectors or Praetorians: The Last Mamluk Sultans and Egypt's Waning as a Great Power.* Albany: State University of New York Press, 1994.

———. *Twilight of Majesty. The Reigns of the Mamluk Sultans al-Ashraf Qaitbay and Qansuh al-Ghawri in Egypt.* Seattle: University of Washington Press, 1993.

Phillip, Thomas, and Ulrich Haarmann, eds. *The Mamluks in Egyptian Politics and Society.* Cambridge: Cambridge University Press, 1998.

Pipes, Daniel. *Slave Soldiers and Islam: The Genesis of a Military System.* New Haven, Conn.: Yale University Press, 1981.

———. *Arab Cities in the Ottoman Period: Cairo, Syria, and the Maghreb.* London: Ashgate, 2002.

Sabra, Adam. *Poverty and Charity in Medieval Islam: Mamluk Egypt, 1250–1517.* Cambridge: Cambridge University Press, 2000.

Shaw, Stanford J. *The Financial and Administrative Organization and Development of Ottoman Egypt, 1517–1798.* Princeton, N.J.: Princeton University Press, 1962.

Thorau, Peter. *The Lion of Egypt: Sultan Baybars I and the Near East in the Thirteenth Century.* London: Longman, 1987.

Walz, Terence. *Trade between Egypt and Bilad as-Sudan: 1700–1820.* Cairo: Institut Français d'Archéologie Orientale, 1978.

Wasserstein, David J., and Ami Ayalon. *Mamluks and Ottomans: Studies in Honour of Michael Winter.* London: Routledge, 2006.

Winter, Michael. *Egyptian Society under Ottoman Rule, 1517–1798.* London: Routledge, 1992.

Early Westernizing Reform

Aroian, Lois. *The Nationalization of Arabic and Islamic Education in Egypt: Dar al-'Ulum and al-Azhar.* Cairo: American University in Cairo Press, 1983.

Baer, Gabriel. *Egyptian Guilds in Modern Times.* Jerusalem: Israel Oriental Society, 1964.

———. *Fellah and Townsman in the Middle East: Studies in Social History.* London: Frank Cass, 1982.

———. *History of Landownership in Modern Egypt, 1800–1950.* London: Oxford University Press, 1962.

———. *Studies in the Social History of Modern Egypt.* Chicago: University of Chicago Press, 1969.

Bierman, Irene, ed. *Napoleon in Egypt.* Reading, England: Ithaca Press, 2003.

Cannon, Byron. *Politics of Law and the Courts in Nineteenth-Century Egypt.* Salt Lake City: University of Utah Press, 1988.

Crabbs, Jack A., Jr. *The Writing of History in Nineteenth-Century Egypt.* Detroit: Wayne State University Press, 1984.

De Jong, Fred. *Turuq and Turuq-Linked Institutions in Nineteenth Century Egypt.* Leiden, Netherlands: E.J. Brill, 1978.

Dodwell, Henry. *The Founder of Modern Egypt.* Cambridge: Cambridge University Press, 1931.

Dunn, John P. *Khedive Ismail's Army.* London and New York: Routledge, 2005.

Ener, Mine. *Managing Egypt's Poor and the Politics of Benevolence, 1800–1952.* Princeton, N.J.: Princeton University Press, 2003.

Fahmy, Khaled. *All the Pasha's Men: Mehmed Ali, His Army, and the Making of Modern Egypt.* Cairo: American University in Cairo Press, 2002.

Farnie, D. A. *East and West of Suez: The Suez Canal in History.* Oxford: Clarendon Press, 1969.

Ghorbal, Shafik. *Beginnings of the Egyptian Question and the Rise of Mehemet-Ali.* London: G. Routledge, 1928.

Herold, J. Christopher. *Bonaparte in Egypt.* New York: Harper & Row, 1962.

Heyworth-Dunne, J. *An Introduction to the History of Education in Modern Egypt* London: Luzac, 1938.

Hunter, F. Robert. *Egypt under the Khedives, 1805–1879.* Pittsburgh: University of Pittsburgh Press, 1984.

Karabell, Zachary. *Parting the Desert: The Creation of the Suez Canal.* New York: Knopf, 2003.

Kuhnke, LaVerne. *Lives at Risk: Public Health in Nineteenth-Century Egypt.* Berkeley: University of California Press, 1990.

Landau, Jacob M. *Jews in Nineteenth-Century Egypt.* New York: New York University Press, 1969.

———. *Parliaments and Parties in Egypt.* Tel Aviv: Israel Oriental Society, 1953.

Landes, David S. *Bankers and Pashas: International Finance and Economic Imperialism in Egypt.* Cambridge, Mass.: Harvard University Press, 1958.

Lane, Edward. *An Account of the Manners and Customs of the Modern Egyptians.* Introduction by Jason Thompson. Cairo: American University in Cairo Press, 2003.

Lawson, Fred H. *The Social Origins of Egyptian Expansionism During the Muhammad 'Ali Period.* New York: Columbia University Press, 1992.

Marlowe, John (pseud.). *Anglo-Egyptian Relations, 1800–1953.* London: Cresset Press, 1954.

———. *Perfidious Albion: The Origins of Anglo-French Rivalry in the Levant.* London: Elek, 1971.

———. *Spoiling the Egyptians.* New York: St. Martin's Press, 1975.

Marsot, Afaf Lutfi al-Sayyid. *Egypt in the Reign of Muhammad Ali.* Cambridge: Cambridge University Press, 1984.

Mitchell, Timothy. *Colonizing Egypt.* Cambridge: Cambridge University Press, 1988.

Owen, Roger. *Cotton and the Egyptian Economy, 1820–1914.* Oxford: Clarendon Press, 1969.

Philipp, Thomas, and Moshe Perlmann, eds., *Abd al-Rahman al-Jabarti's History of Egypt.* Stuttgart: Franz Steiner Verlag, 1994.

Polk, William R., and Richard L. Chambers, eds. *Beginnings of Modernization in the Middle East: The Nineteenth Century.* Chicago: University of Chicago Press, 1966.

Reid, Donald Malcolm. *Whose Pharaohs? Archaeology, Museums, and Egyptian National Identity from Napoleon to World War I.* Berkeley: University of California Press, 2002.

Reimer, Michael. *Colonial Bridgehead: Government and Society in Alexandria, 1807–1882.* Cairo: American University in Cairo Press, 1997.

Richards, Alan. *Egypt's Agricultural Development, 1800–1950*. Boulder, Colo.: Westview Press, 1982.

Rivlin, Helen A. B. *The Agricultural Policy of Muhammad Ali in Egypt.* Cambridge, Mass.: Harvard University Press, 1961.

Sabini, John A. P. *Armies in the Sand: The Struggle for Mecca and Medina.* New York: Thames & Hudson, 1981.

Safran, Nadav. *Egypt in Search of Political Community, 1805–1952*. Cambridge, Mass.: Harvard University Press, 1961.

Shamir, Shimon, ed. *The Jews of Egypt: A Mediterranean Society in Modern Times.* Boulder, Colo.: Westview Press, 1987.

Sonbol, Amira el-Azhary. *The Creation of a Medical Profession in Egypt.* Syracuse, N.Y.: Syracuse University Press, 1991.

Toledano, Ehud. *State and Society in Mid-Nineteenth-Century Egypt.* Cambridge: Cambridge University Press, 1990.

Tucker, Judith. *Women in Nineteenth Century Egypt.* Cambridge: Cambridge University Press, 1985.

The British Occupation and Nationalist Resistance

Abbas Hilmi II. *The Last Khedive of Egypt: Memoirs of Abbas Hilmi II.* Translated by Amira El Azhary Sonbol. Reading, U.K.: Ithaca Press, 1998.

Adams, C. C. *Islam and Modernism in Egypt.* Reprint, New York: Russell & Russell, 1968.

Adelson, Roger. *London and the Invention of the Middle East: Money, Power, and War, 1902–1922.* New Haven, Conn.: Yale University Press, 1995.

Ahmed, Jamal M. *The Intellectual Origins of Egyptian Nationalism.* London: Oxford University Press, 1960.

Badawi, Zaki. *The Reformers of Egypt: A Critique of al-Afghani, Abduh, and Rida.* Slough: Open Press, 1976.

Badran, Margot. *Feminists, Islam, and the Nation: Gender and the Making of Modern Egypt.* Princeton, N.J.: Princeton University Press, 1995.

Badran, Margot, and Miriam Cooke, eds. *Opening the Gates: An Anthology of Arab Feminist Writing.* 2d ed. Bloomington: Indiana University Press, 2004.

Badrawi, Malak. *Political Violence in Egypt, 1910–1924.* Richmond, U.K.: Curzon, 2000.

Baron, Beth. *Egypt as a Woman: Nationalism, Gender, and Politics.* Berkeley: University of California Press, 2005.

———. *The Women's Awakening in Egypt: Culture, Society, and the Press.* New Haven, Conn.: Yale University Press, 1994.

Beinin, Joel, and Zachary Lockman. *Workers on the Nile: National-ism, Communism, Islam, and the Egyptian Working Class, 1882–1954*. Princeton, N.J.: Princeton University Press, 1987.

Berque, Jacques *Egypt: Imperialism and Revolution*. Translated by Jean Stewart. London: Faber & Faber 1972.

Booth, Marilyn. *May Her Likes Be Multiplied: Biography and Gender Poli-tics in Egypt*. Berkeley: University of California Press, 2001.

Botman, Selma. *Engendering Citizenship in Egypt*. New York: Columbia University Press, 1999.

Chalcraft, John T. *The Striking Cabbies of Cairo and Other Stories: Crafts and Guilds in Egypt, 1863–1914*. Albany: State University of New York Press, 2004.

Cole, Juan R.I. *Colonialism and Revolution in the Middle East: Social and Cultural Origins of Egypt's 'Urabi Movement*. Princeton, N.J.: Princeton University Press, 1993.

Coury, Ralph M. *The Making of an Egyptian Arab Nationalist: The Early Years of Azzam Pasha*. Reading, U.K.: Ithaca Press, 1998.

Collins, Jeffrey G. *The Egyptian Elite under Cromer, 1882–1907*. Berlin: Klaus Schwarz Verlag, 1984.

Elgood, P. G. *Egypt and the Army*. London: Oxford University Press, 1924.

Empereur, Jean-Yves. *Alexandria Rediscovered*. New York: George Bra-ziller, 1998.

Gershoni, Israel, and James P. Jankowski. *Egypt, Islam, and the Arabs: The Search for Egyptian Nationhood, 1900–1930*. Oxford: Oxford Uni-versity Press, 1986.

———. *Commemorating the Nation: Collective Memory, Public Commem-orating, and National Identity in Twentieth-Century Egypt*. Chicago: Middle East Documentation Center, 2004.

Hourani, Albert. *Arabic Thought in the Liberal Age, 1789–1939*. 3d ed. Cambridge: Cambridge University Press, 1983.

Keddie, Nikki R. *Sayyid Jamal al- Din "al-Afghani."* Berkeley: University of California Press, 1972.

Kerr, Malcolm H. *Islamic Reform: The Political and Legal Theories of Muhammad Abduh and Rashid Rida*. Berkeley: University of California Press, 1966.

Khouri, Mounah A. *Poetry and the Making of Modern Egypt*. Leiden, Netherlands: E.J. Brill, 1971.

Long, C. W. P. *British Pro-Consuls in Egypt, 1914–1929: The Challenge of Nationalism*. London: RoutledgeCurzon, 2005.

Lloyd, George A., Lord. *Egypt since Cromer.* 2 vols. London: Macmillan, 1933.

Mansfield, Peter. *The British in Egypt.* New York: Holt, Rinehart & Winston, 1971.

Marlowe, John. *Cromer in Egypt.* London: Elek, 1971.

Marsot, Afaf Lutfi al-Sayyid. *Egypt and Cromer: A Study in Anglo-Egyptian Relations.* New York: Praeger, 1968.

Mayer, Thomas. *The Changing Past: Egyptian Historiography of the Urabi Revolt.* Gainesville: Florida Universities Press, 1988.

Mellini, Peter. *Sir Eldon Gorst: The Overshadowed Proconsul.* Stanford, Calif.: Hoover Institution, 1977.

Owen, Roger. *Lord Cromer: Victorian Imperialist, Edwardian Proconsul.* Oxford: Oxford University Press, 2004.

Pollard, Lisa. *Nurturing the Nation: The Family Politics of Modernizing, Colonizing, and Liberating Egypt (1805–1923).* Berkeley: University of California Press, 2005.

Pollock, John Charles. *Kitchener: Architect of Victory, Artisan of Peace.* London: Carroll & Graf, 2001.

Reid, Donald Malcolm. *Cairo University and the Making of Modern Egypt.* Cambridge: Cambridge University Press, 1990.

———. *Lawyers and Politics in the Arab World, 1880–1960.* Minneapolis: Bibliotheca Islamica, 1981.

Robinson, Ronald, and John Gallagher, *Africa and the Victorians.* New York: St. Martin's Press, 1961.

Schölch, Alexander. *Egypt for the Egyptians! The Socio-Political Crisis in Egypt, 1878–1882.* London: Ithaca Press, 1981.

Tignor, Robert L. *Modernization and British Colonial Rule in Egypt, 1882–1914.* Princeton, N.J.: Princeton University Press, 1966.

Tripp, Charles, ed. *Contemporary Egypt Through Egyptian Eyes: Essays in Honour of P.J. Vatikiotis.* London: Routledge, 1993.

Warburg, Gabriel. *Egypt and the Sudan.* London: Frank Cass, 1985.

Wendell, Charles. *The Evolution of the Egyptian National Image from its Origins to Ahmad Lutfi al-Sayyid.* Berkeley: University of California Press, 1972.

Ambiguous Independence

Abdalla, Ahmed. *The Student Movement and National Politics in Egypt, 1923–1973.* London: Al Saqi Books, 1985.

Badrawi, Malak. *Isma'il Sidqi (1875–1950): Pragmatism and Vision in Twentieth Century Egypt.* London: Curzon, 1996.

Baraka, Magda. *The Egyptian Upper Class between Revolutions, 1919–1952*. Reading, U.K.: Ithaca Press, 1998.

Botman, Selma. *Egypt from Independence to Revolution, 1919–1952*. Syracuse, N.Y.: Syracuse University Press, 1991.

Charmley, John. *Lord Lloyd and the Decline of the British Empire*. London: Weidenfeld & Nicolson, 1987.

Crouchley, A. E. *The Economic Development of Modern Egypt*. London: Longmans, Green, 1938.

Daly, Martin. *The Sirdar: Sir Reginald Wingate and the British Empire in the Middle East*. Philadelphia: American Philosophical Society, 1997.

Danielson, Virginia. *The Voice of Egypt: Umm Kulthum, Arabic Song, and Egyptian Society in the Twentieth Century*. Chicago: University of Chicago Press, 1997.

Darwin, John. *Britain, Egypt, and the Middle East*. New York: St. Martin's, 1981.

Davis, Eric. *Challenging Colonialism: Bank Misr and Egyptian Industrialization, 1920–1941*. Princeton, N.J.: Princeton University Press, 1983.

Deeb, Marius. *Party Politics in Egypt: The Wafd and Its Rivals*. London: Ithaca Press, 1979.

Egger, Vernon. *A Fabian in Egypt: Salamah Musa and the Rise of the Professional Classes in Egypt, 1909–1939*. Lanham, Md.: University Press of America, 1986.

Erlich, Haggai. *Students and University in 20th Century Egyptian Politics*. London: Frank Cass, 1989.

Gershoni, Israel, and James Jankowski, *Redefining the Egyptian Nation, 1930–1945*. Cambridge: Cambridge University Press, 1995.

Goldberg, Ellis. *Tinker, Tailor, and Textile Worker: Class and Politics in Egypt, 1930–1952*. Berkeley and Los Angeles: University of California Press, 1986.

Goldschmidt, Arthur, Amy J. Johnson, and Barak Salmoni, eds. *Re-Envisioning Egypt, 1919–1952*. Cairo: American University in Cairo Press, 2005.

Gorman, Anthony. *Historians, State, and Politics in Twentieth Century Egypt: Contesting the Nation*. London: RoutledgeCurzon, 2003.

Hill, Enid. *Mahkama! Studies in the Egyptian Legal System*. London: Ithaca Press, 1979.

Ismael, Tareq, and Rifa'at el-Sa'id. *The Communist Movement in Egypt, 1920–1988*. Syracuse, N.Y.: Syracuse University Press, 1990.

James, Lawrence. *Imperial Warrior: The Life and Times of Field Marshal Viscount Allenby, 1861–1936*. London: Weidenfeld & Nicolson, 1993.

Kedourie, Elie. *The Chatham House Version and Other Middle-Eastern Studies.* Reprint, Hanover, N.H.: University Press of New England, 1984.

Krämer, Gudrun. *The Jews in Modern Egypt, 1914–1952.* Seattle: University of Washington Press, 1989.

Laskier, Michael M. *The Jews of Egypt, 1920–1970: In the Midst of Zionism, Anti-Semitism, and the Middle East Conflict.* New York: New York University Press, 1992.

Lia, Brynjar. *The Society of the Muslim Brothers in Egypt: The Rise of an Islamic Mass Movement, 1928–1942.* London: Ithaca Press, 1998.

Maghraoui, Abdeslam M. *Liberalism without Democracy: Nationhood and Citizenship in Egypt, 1992–1936.* Durham, N.C.: Duke University Press, 2006.

Marsot, Afaf Lutfi al-Sayyid. *Egypt's Liberal Experiment: 1922–1936.* Berkeley: University of California Press, 1977.

McIntyre, John D., Jr. *The Boycott of the Milner Mission: A Study in Egyptian Nationalism.* New York: Peter Lang, 1985.

Monroe, Elizabeth. *Britain's Moment in the Middle East, 1914–1971.* 2d ed. Baltimore: Johns Hopkins University Press, 1981.

Morewood, Steven. *The British Defence of Egypt, 1935–1940: Conflict and Crisis in the Eastern Mediterranean.* London: Frank Cass, 2005.

Musa, Salama. *The Education of Salama Musa.* Translated by L. O. Schuman. Leiden, Netherlands: E.J. Brill, 1961.

Nordeen, Lon O., and David Nicolle. *Phoenix over the Nile: A History of Egyptian Air Power, 1932–1994.* Washington, D.C.: Smithsonian Institution Press, 1996.

Porath, Yehoshua. *In Search of Arab Unity, 1930–1945.* London: Frank Cass, 1986.

Powell, Eve Troutt. *A Different Shade of Colonialism: Egypt, Great Britain and the Mastery of the Sudan, 1865–1925.* Berkeley: University of California Press, 2003.

Smith, Charles D. *Islam and the Search for Social Order in Modern Egypt: A Biography of Muhammad Husayn Haykal.* Albany: SUNY Press, 1983.

Terry, Janice Joles. *Cornerstone of Egyptian Political Power: The Wafd, 1919–1952.* London: Third World Center, 1979.

Tignor, Robert L. *State, Private Enterprise, and Economic Change in Egypt, 1918–1952.* Princeton, N.J.: Princeton University Press, 1984.

Zayid, Mahmud. *Egypt's Struggle for Independence.* Beirut: Khayat's, 1965.

Ziadeh, Farhat J. *Lawyers, the Rule of Law, and Liberalism in Modern Egypt.* Stanford, Calif.: Hoover Institution, 1968.

The Palestine Question and World War II

Amin, Galal. *Whatever Happened to the Egyptians?* Cairo: American University in Cairo Press, 2000.

El-Awaisi, Abd al-Fattah Muhammad. *The Muslim Brothers and the Palestine Question, 1928–1947.* London: Tauris Academic Studies, 1998.

Botman, Selma. *The Rise of Egyptian Communism, 1939–1970.* Syracuse, N.Y.: Syracuse University Press, 1991.

Carter, B. L. *The Copts in Egyptian Politics.* London: Croom Helm, 1986.

Cooper, Artemis. *Cairo in the War.* London: Penguin, 1995.

Doran, Michael. *Pan-Arabism before Nasser: Egyptian Power Politics and the Palestine Question.* New York and Oxford: Oxford University Press, 1999.

Gallagher, Nancy Elizabeth. *Egypt's Other Wars: Epidemics and the Politics of Public Health.* Syracuse, N.Y.: Syracuse University Press, 1991.

Gershoni, Israel, and James Jankowski, eds., *Rethinking Nationalism in the Arab Middle East.* New York: Columbia University Press, 1997.

Hopwood, Derek. *Egypt: Politics and Society 1945–1990.* 3d ed. London: Routledge, 1991.

Jankowski, James P. *Egypt's Young Rebels.* Stanford, Calif.: Hoover Institution, 1975.

Johnson, Amy J. *Reconstructing Rural Egypt: Ahmed Hussein and the History of Egyptian Development.* Syracuse, N.J.: Syracuse University Press, 2004.

Kirk, George. *Great Britain and Egypt, 1914–1951.* London: Royal Institute of International Affairs, 1951.

———. *The Middle East in the War.* London: Oxford University Press, 1952.

Lampson, Sir Miles. *The Killearn Diaries, 1934–1946: The Diplomatic and Personal Record of Lord Killearn.* Edited by Trefor Evans. London: Sidgwick & Jackson, 1972.

———. *Politics and Diplomacy in Egypt: The Diaries of Sir Miles Lampson, 1935–1937.* Edited by Malcolm Yapp. Oxford: Oxford University Press, 1997.

Louis, W. Roger. *The British Empire in the Middle East, 1945–1951.* New York: Oxford University Press, 1984.

Mabro, Robert, and Samir Radwan. *The Industrialization of Egypt 1939–1973: Policy and Performance.* Oxford: Clarendon Press, 1976.

Mayer, Thomas. *Egypt and the Palestine Question, 1936–1945.* Berlin: Schwarz, 1983.

Meijer, Roel. *The Quest for Modernity: Secular Liberal and Left-Wing Political Thought in Egypt, 1945–1958.* London: RoutledgeCurzon, 2002.

Mitchell, Richard. *The Society of the Muslim Brothers.* Princeton, N.J.: Princeton University Press, 1969.

Nasser, Hoda Gamal Abdel. *Britain and the Egyptian Nationalist Movement 1936–1952.* Reading, U.K.: Ithaca Press, 1994.

Radwan, Abu al-Futouh. *Old and New Forces in Egyptian Education.* New York: Columbia University Teachers College, 1951.

Sachar, Howard M. *Europe Leaves the Middle East, 1936–1954.* New York: Knopf, 1972.

Stadiem, William. *Too Rich: The High Life and Tragic Death of King Farouk.* New York: Carroll & Graf, 1991.

Talhami, Ghada Hashem. *Palestine and Egyptian National Identity.* New York: Praeger, 1992.

Vitalis, Robert. *When Capitalists Collide: Business Enterprise and the End of Empire in Egypt.* Berkeley: University of California Press, 1995.

Wilmington, Martin W. *The Middle East Supply Centre.* Albany: State University of New York Press, 1971.

Military Rule and Arab Socialism

Abdel-Malek, Anouar. *Egypt: Military Society.* Translated by Charles Lam Markmann. New York: Random House, 1968.

Aburish, Saïd K. *Nasser, the Last Arab: A Biography.* New York: St. Martin's Press, 2004.

Alterman, Jon. *Egypt and American Foreign Assistance, 1952–1956.* New York: Palgrave Macmillan, 2002.

Ansari, Hamied. *Egypt: The Stalled Society.* Albany: State University of New York Press, 1986.

Aronson, Geoffrey. *U.S. Policy toward Egypt, 1946–1956.* Boulder, Colo.: Lynne Rienner, 1986.

Ashton, Nigel John. *Eisenhower, Macmillan, and the Problem of Nasser: Anglo-American Relations and Arab Nationalism, 1955–59.* New York: St. Martin's Press, 1996.

Beattie, Kirk J. *Egypt during the Nasser Years: Ideology, Politics, and Civil Society.* Boulder, Colo.: Westview Press, 1994.

Binder, Leonard. *In a Moment of Enthusiasm: Political Power and the Second Stratum in Egypt.* Chicago: University of Chicago Press, 1987.

Burns, William J. *Economic Aid and American Policy toward Egypt, 1955–1981.* Albany: State University of New York Press, 1985.

Childers, Erskine B. *The Road to Suez.* London: Macgibbon & Kee, 1962.

Copeland, Miles (pseud.). *The Game of Nations.* New York: Simon & Schuster, 1969.

Cremeans, Charles. *The Arabs and the World: Nasser's Arab Nationalist Policy.* New York: Frederick A. Praeger, 1963.

Dawisha, A. I. *Egypt in the Arab World: The Elements of Foreign Policy.* New York: Wiley, 1976.

Dekmejian, R. Hrair. *Egypt Under Nasir: A Study in Political Dynamics.* Albany: State University of New York Press, 1971.

DuBois, Shirley Graham. *Gamal Abdel Nasser, Son of the Nile: A Biography.* Chicago Third Press, 1972.

Eccel, A. Chris. *Egypt, Islam, and Social Change: al-Azhar in Conflict and Accommodation.* Berlin: Schwarz, 1984.

Eden, Anthony. *The Suez Crisis of 1956.* Boston: Beacon Press, 1968.

Eveland, Wilbur. *Ropes of Sand: America's Failure in the Middle East.* New York: Norton, 1980.

Fawzi, Mahmoud. *Suez 1956: An Egyptian Perspective.* London: Shorouk, 1986.

Gordon, Joel. *Nasser: Hero of the Arab Nation.* Oxford, England: One-World Publications, 2006.

———. *Nasser's Blessed Movement: Egypt's Free Officers and the July Revolution.* New York: Oxford University Press, 1992.

———. *Revolutionary Melodrama: Popular Film and Civic Identity in Nasser's Egypt.* Chicago: Middle East Documentation Center, 2002

Hahn, Peter L. *The United States, Great Britain, and Egypt, 1945–1956.* Chapel Hill: University of North Carolina Press, 1991.

Hasou, Tawfig Y. *The Struggle for the Arab World: Egypt's Nasser and the Arab League.* London: Routledge, Kegan Paul, 1985.

Heikal, Mohamed. *The Cairo Documents.* Garden City, N.Y.: Doubleday, 1973.

———. *Cutting the Lion's Tail: Suez through Egyptian Eyes.* London: André Deutsch, 1986.

———. *Secret Channels: The Inside Story of Arab-Israeli Peace Negotiations.* London: HarperCollins, 1996.

Hussein, Mahmoud. *Class Conflict in Egypt.* New York: Monthly Review Press, 1973.

Ismael, Tareq Y. *The U.A.R. in Africa: Egypt's Policy under Nasser.* Evanston, Il.: Northwestern University Press, 1971.

Issawi, Charles. *Egypt at Mid-Century: An Economic Survey.* London: Oxford University Press, 1954.

———. *Egypt in Revolution: An Economic Analysis.* London: Oxford University Press, 1963.

Izzeddin, Nejla Mustapha. *Nasser of the Arabs: An Arab Assessment.* Third World Center for Research and Publishing, 1981.

Jankowski, James. *Nasser's Egypt, Arab Nationalism, and the United Arab Republic.* Boulder, Colo.: Lynne Rienner, 2002.

Kenney, Jeffrey T. *Muslim Rebels: Kharijites and the Politics of Extremism in Egypt.* Oxford and New York: Oxford University Press, 2006.

Kerr, Malcolm H. *The Arab Cold War: Gamal Abdel Nasser and his Rivals, 1958–1970.* 3d ed. London: Oxford University Press, 1971.

Kyle, Keith. *Suez: Britain's End of Empire in the Middle East.* 2d ed. London: I.B. Tauris, 2002.

Lacouture, Jean and Simonne Lacouture. *Egypt in Transition.* Translated by Francis Scarfe. New York: Criterion, 1958.

Lacouture, Jean. *Nasser: A Biography.* New York: Knopf, 1973.

Louis, William Roger, and Roger Owen, eds. *Suez 1956: The Crisis and Its Consequences.* Oxford: Clarendon Press, 1989.

Mayfield, James B. *Rural Politics in Nasser's Egypt: A Quest for Legitimacy.* Austin: University of Texas Press, 1971.

Meyer, Gail E. *Egypt and the United States: The Formative Years.* Rutherford, N.J.: Fairleigh Dickinson University Press, 1980.

Naguib, Mohammed. *Egypt's Destiny: A Personal Statement.* Garden City, NY: Doubleday, 1955.

Nasser, Gamal Abdul. *Egypt's Liberation: The Philosophy of the Revolution.* Washington, D.C.: Public Affairs Press, 1955.

Nasser, Munir K. *Press, Politics, and Power: Egypt's Heikal and Al-Ahram.* Ames: Iowa State University Press, 1979.

Nutting, Anthony. *Nasser.* New York: E. P. Dutton, 1972.

O'Brien, Patrick. *The Revolution in Egypt's Economic System: From Private Enterprise to Socialism, 1952–1965.* London: Oxford University Press, 1966.

Podeh, Elie. *The Decline of Arab Unity: The Rise and Fall of the United Arab Republic.* Brighton, U.K.: Sussex Academic Press, 1999.

Podeh, Elie, and Onn Winckler, eds. *Rethinking Nasserism: Revolution and Historical Memory in Modern Egypt.* Gainesville: University Press of Florida, 2004.

Posusney, Marcia Pripstein. *Labor and the State in Egypt, 1952–1994.* New York: Columbia University Press, 1997.

Saab, Gabriel. *The Egyptian Agrarian Reform, 1952–1962*. London: Oxford University Press, 1967.

Sadat, Anwar El, *Revolt on the Nile*. London: Allan Wingate, 1957.

St. John, Robert. *The Boss: The Story of Gamal Abdel Nasser.* New York: McGraw-Hill, 1960.

Sayed-Ahmed, Muhammad A. Wahab. *Nasser and American Foreign Policy, 1952–1956*. London: LAAM Ltd., 1989.

Shamir, Shimon, ed. *Egypt from Monarchy to Republic*. Boulder, Colo.: Westview Press, 1995.

Shuckburgh, Evelyn. *Descent to Suez: Foreign Office Diaries, 1951–1956*. New York: Norton, 1986.

Springborg, Robert. *Family, Power, and Politics in Egypt*. Philadelphia: University of Pennsylvania Press, 1982.

Troen, Selwyn Ilan, and Moshe Shemesh, eds. *The Sinai-Suez Crisis, 1956: Retrospective and Reappraisal.* London: Frank Cass, 1990.

Vatikiotis, P. J. *The Egyptian Army in Politics: Pattern for New Nations?* Bloomington: Indiana University Press, 1961.

———. *Nasser and His Generation*. New York: St. Martin's Press, 1978.

Vatikiotis, P. J., ed. *Egypt since the Revolution*. London: George Allen and Unwin Ltd., 1968.

Wheelock, Keith. *Nasser's New Egypt. A Critical Analysis.* New York: Frederick A. Praeger, 1960.

Woodward, Peter. *Nasser.* London: Longman, 1992.

Wynn, Wilton. *Nasser of Egypt: The Search for Dignity.* Cambridge, Mass.: Arlington Books, 1959.

Arab Socialism in Egypt

Ajami, Fouad. *The Arab Predicament: Arabic Political Thought and Practice since 1967*. 2d ed. Cambridge: Cambridge University Press, 1992.

Ayubi, Shaheen. *Nasser and Sadat: Decision Making and Foreign Policy (1970–1972)*. Lanham, Md.: University Press of America, 1994.

Baker, Raymond William. *Egypt's Uncertain Revolution under Nasser and Sadat*. Cambridge, Mass.: Harvard University Press, 1978.

Bulloch, John. *The Making of a War: The Middle East from 1967 to 1973*. London: Longman, 1974.

Dawisha, Karen. *Soviet Foreign Policy towards Egypt*. New York: St. Martin's Press, 1978.

Fahmi, Ismail. *Negotiating for Peace in the Middle East*. Baltimore: Johns Hopkins University Press, 1983.

Farid, Abdel Majid. *Nasser: The Final Years*. Reading, U.K.: Ithaca Press, 1994.

Green, Stephen. *Taking Sides: America's Secret Relations with a Militant Israel*. New York: William Morrow, 1984.

al-Hakim, Tawfiq. *The Return of Consciousness*. Translated by R. Bayly Winder. New York: New York University Press, 1985.

El-Hussini, Mohrez Mahmoud. *Soviet-Egyptian Relations, 1945–85*. New York: St. Martin's Press, 1987.

Korn, David A. *Stalemate: The War of Attrition and Great Power Diplomacy in the Middle East, 1967–1970*. Boulder, Colo.: Westview Press, 1992.

Meital, Yoram. *Egypt's Struggle for Peace: Continuity and Change, 1967–1977*. Gainesville: University Press of Florida, 1997.

Oren, Michael B. *Six Days of War: June 1967 and the Making of the Modern Middle East* Oxford: Oxford University Press, 2002.

Perlmutter, Amos. *Egypt: The Praetorian State*. New Brunswick, N.J.: Transaction Books, 1974.

Waterbury, John. *The Egypt of Nasser and Sadat: The Political Economy of Two Regimes*. Princeton, N.J.: Princeton University Press, 1983.

Anwar Sadat

Alterman, Jon, ed. *Sadat and His Legacy: Egypt and the World, 1977–1997: A Special Conference on the Twentieth Anniversary of President Sadat's Journey to Jerusalem*. Washington, D.C.: Washington Institute for Near East Policy, 1997.

Atiya, Nayra. *Khul-Khaal: Five Egyptian Women Tell Their Stories*. Syracuse, N.Y.: Syracuse University Press, 1982.

Beattie, Kirk J. *Egypt during the Sadat Years*. New York: Palgrave, 2000.

Boutros-Ghali, Boutros. *Egypt's Road to Jerusalem: A Diplomat's Story of the Struggle for Peace in the Middle East*. New York: Random House, 1997.

Cooper, Mark N. *The Transformation of Egypt*. Baltimore: Johns Hopkins University Press, 1982.

Fernandez-Ernesto, Felipe. *Sadat and his Statecraft*. London: Kensal Press; Salem, N.H.: Merrimack, 1983.

Friedlander, Melvin A. *Sadat and Begin: The Domestic Politics of Peacemaking*. Boulder, Colo.: Westview Press, 1983.

Heikal, Mohamed. *Autumn of Fury: The Assassination of Sadat*. New York: Random House, 1983.

————. *The Sphinx and the Commissar.* New York: Harper & Row, 1978.

Hinnebusch, Raymond. *Egyptian Politics under Sadat.* 2d ed. Boulder, Colo.: Lynne Rienner, 1988.

Hirst, David, and Irene Beeson. *Sadat.* London: Faber and Faber, 1982.

Israeli, Raphael. *"I, Egypt": Aspects of President Anwar al-Sadat's Political Thought* Jerusalem: Magnes Press, 1981.

————. *Man of Defiance: A Political Biography of Anwar al-Sadat.* Totowa, N.J.: Barnes and Noble Books, 1985.

Kays, Doreen. *Frogs and Scorpions: Egypt, Sadat, and the Media.* London: Muller, 1984.

Lippman, Thomas W. *Egypt after Nasser: Sadat, Peace, and the Mirage of Prosperity.* New York: Paragon House, 1989.

Sadat, Anwar El. *In Search of Identity.* New York: Harper & Row, 1978.

Shazly, Saad El. *The Crossing of the Suez.* San Francisco: American Mideast Research, 1980.

Telhami, Shibley. *Power and Leadership in International Bargaining: The Path to the Camp David Accords.* New York: Columbia University Press, 1990.

Waterbury, John. *Egypt: Burdens of the Past, Options for the Future.* Bloomington: Indiana University Press, 1978.

Contemporary Egypt

Adams, Richard H., Jr., *Development and Social Change in Rural Egypt.* Syracuse, N.Y.: Syracuse University Press, 1986.

Aftandilian, Gregory L. *Egypt's Bid for Arab Leadership: Implications for U.S. Policy.* New York: Council on Foreign Relations, 1993.

Ayyubi, Nazih. *Bureaucracy and Politics in Contemporary Egypt.* London: Ithaca Press, 1980.

————. *The State and Public Policy in Egypt since Sadat.* Reading, U.K.: Ithaca Press, 1991.

Baker, Raymond William. *Islam without Fear: Egypt and the New Islamists.* Cambridge, Mass.: Harvard University Press, 2003.

————. *Sadat and After: Struggles for Egypt's Political Soul.* Cambridge, Mass.: Harvard University Press, 1990.

Clark, Janine A. *Islam, Charity, and Activism: Middle Class Networks and Social Welfare in Egypt, Jordan, and Yemen.* Bloomington: Indiana University Press, 2004.

Cohen, Raymond. *Culture and Conflict in Egyptian-Israeli Relations: A Dialogue of the Deaf.* Bloomington: Indiana University Press, 1990.

Dunne, Michele Durocher. *Democracy in Contemporary Egyptian Political Discourse.* Philadelphia: John Benjamins, 2003.

Fahmy, Ninette. *The Politics of Egypt: State-Society Relationship.* Richmond, U.K.: Curzon Press, 2001.

Ibrahim, Saad Eddin. *Egypt, Islam, and Democracy.* Cairo: American University in Cairo Press, 1996.

Kassem, Maye. *Egyptian Politics: The Dynamics of Authoritarian Rule.* Boulder, Colo.: Lynne Rienner, 2004.

Kepel, Giles. *The Prophet and Pharaoh: Muslim Extremism in Egypt.* Translated by Jan Rothschild. London: Al Saqi Books, 1985.

Kienle, Eberhard. *A Grand Delusion: Democracy and Economic Reform in Egypt.* London: I. B. Tauris, 2001.

MacLeod, Arlene Elowe. *Accommodating Protest: Working Women, the New Veiling, and Change in Cairo.* New York: Columbia University Press, 1993.

Marr, Phebe, ed. *Egypt at the Crossroads: Domestic Stability and Regional Role.* Washington, D.C.: National Defense University Press, 1999.

El-Mikawy, Noha. *The Building of Consensus in Egypt's Transition Process.* Cairo: American University in Cairo Press, 1999.

Mitchell, Timothy. *The Rule of Experts; Egypt, Technopolitics, and the Military.* Berkeley: University of California Press, 2002.

Murphy, Caryle. *Passion for Islam, Shaping the Middle East: The Egyptian Experience.* New York: Scribner, 2002.

Nagi, Saad Z. *Poverty in Egypt: Human Needs and Institutional Capacities.* Lanham, Md.: Lexington Books, 2001.

Palmer, Monte, Ali Leila, and El Sayed Yassin. *The Egyptian Bureaucracy.* Syracuse, N.Y.: Syracuse University Press, 1988.

Radwan, Hanan Hamdy. *Democratization in Rural Egypt: A Study of the Village Popular Council.* Cairo: American University in Cairo Press, 1994.

Saadawi, Nawal El. *The Hidden Face of Eve.* Boston: Beacon Press, 1980.

Sadowski, Yahya M. *Political Vegetables? Businessman and Bureaucrat in the Development of Egyptian Agriculture.* Washington, D.C.: Brookings Institution, 1991.

Shoukri, Ghali. *Egypt: Portrait of a President, 1971–1981.* London: Zed Books, 1981.

Singer, Hanaa Fikri. *The Socialist Labor Party: A Case Study of a Contemporary Egyptian Opposition Party.* Cairo: American University in Cairo Press, 1993.

Singerman, Diane. *Avenues of Participation: Family, Politics, and Networks in Urban Quarters of Cairo.* Princeton, N.J.: Princeton University Press, 1995.

Singerman, Diane, and Homa Hoodfar, eds. *Development, Change, and Gender in Cairo: A View from the Household.* Bloomington: Indiana University Press, 1996.

Springborg, Robert. *Mubarak's Egypt: Fragmentation of the Political Order.* Boulder, Colo.: Westview Press, 1989.

Sullivan, Denis J. *Private Voluntary Organizations in Egypt: Islamic Development, Private Initiative, and State Control.* Gainesville: University Press of Florida, 1994.

Sullivan, Earl L. *Women in Egyptian Public Life.* Syracuse, N.J.: Syracuse University Press, 1986.

Talhami, Ghada Hashem. *The Mobilization of Muslim Women in Egypt.* Gainesville: University Press of Florida, 1996.

Tripp, Charles, and Roger Owen, eds. *Egypt under Mubarak.* London: Routledge, 1989.

Weaver, Mary Anne. *A Portrait of Egypt: A Journey through the World of Militant Islam.* New York: Farrar, Straus & Giroux, 1999.

Weinbaum, Marvin. *U.S. Aid to Egypt.* Boulder, Colo.: Westview Press, 1986.

Yohannes, Okbazghi. *Political Economy of an Authoritarian Modern State and Religious Nationalism in Egypt.* Lewiston, N.Y.: Edwin Mellen Press, 2001.

Zaalouk, Malak. *Power, Class, and Foreign Capital in Egypt: The Age of the New Bourgeoisie.* London: Zed Books, 1989.

Zaki, Moheb. *Civil Society & Democratization in Egypt, 1981–1994.* Cairo: Konrad-Adenauer-Stiftung and Ibn Khaldoun Center, 1994.

Zuhur, Sherifa. *Revealing Reveiling: Islamist Gender Ideology in Contemporary Egypt.* Albany: State University of New York Press, 1992.

INDEX

Page numbers in *italic* indicate illustrations. Pages numbers followed by *m* indicate maps, by *t* indicate tables, and by *c* indicate chronology.